PAUL THE APOSTLE
At the Edge by Faith

Paul the Apostle

At the Edge by Faith

Stuart H. Merriam, Ph.D.

I Cor. 6:12 b!

Fenestra Books

FE NE
ST RA ™

Paul the Apostle: At the Edge by Faith

Unless otherwise noted, Scripture quotations are taken from the New American Standard Bible®, Copyright © 1960, 1962, 1963, 1968, 1971, 1972, 1973, 1975, 1977, 1995 by The Lockman Foundation. Used by permission. (www.Lockman.org)

Scripture quotations marked (NIV) are taken from the HOLY BIBLE, NEW INTERNATIONAL VERSION®.

NIV®. Copyright © 1973, 1978, 1984 by International Bible Society. Used by permission of Zondervan. All rights reserved.

ISBN: 1-58736-176-0
LCCN: 2003112340

Published (2004) by Fenestra Books™

610 East Delano Street, Suite 104, Tucson, Arizona 85705, U.S.A.
www.fenestrabooks.com

Cover photo by the author

Cover and book design by Atilla Vékony

Printed in the United States of America

To my beloved wife, Carol,
who for thirty-five years
pioneered with me
on the edge by faith

Contents

List of Illustrations

All photographs were taken by the author unless otherwise noted.
* Photographs taken by Maurice S. Thompson, used by permission.

Preface

More than one half of the New Testament concerns the life and writings of the Apostle Paul. Though a detailed biography of Paul can never be written, since practically nothing is known of his first thirty-five years up to his conversion, and then very little of his next eight to ten years, this does not preclude Paul being known. What Luke has recorded of Paul's life in the book of Acts and what is found in Paul's thirteen epistles[1] are more than enough to give the essentials of his teaching and his ministry and to portray the warp and woof of his character.

Physical features of Paul

Nothing in Scripture indicates the physical features of Paul except the statement of his detractors that his "personal presence is unimpressive" (literally "bodily presence is weak") (2Cor. 10:10). Not until the third century, in a writing entitled *The Acts of Paul and Thecla* do we have a purported description of Paul. Here he is depicted as "small in size, bald-headed, bandy-legged, with meeting eyebrows, hook-nosed, full of grace."[2] But this description, based as it is on oral tradition, is not reliable. Indeed, if Paul looked as this writing portrays him, it is highly improbable that the Lystrians would have received him as one of the Greek gods, all of whom were notably handsome with impressive physiques. "Imagine worshipping a short, bald-headed, bow-legged god!"[3]

---

[1] Some add the book of Hebrews to Paul's epistles, but its polished Greek style, like that of a master rhetorician, along with its vocabulary, figures of speech, and method of argument, all differ greatly from that which is found in the acknowledged epistles of Paul.

Further, Paul's familiar phrases when referring to the Old Testament—"just as it has been written" (nineteen times), "it has been written" (ten times), and "the scripture says" (sixteen times)—never occur in Hebrews, although its author quotes extensively from the Old Testament. See introduction to Hebrews in the *New American Standard* Master Study Bible.

Apollos seems best to qualify as the author of Hebrews, having been a well-educated Alexandrian, trained in Philonic reasoning and known for his ability to expound the Scriptures.

[2] *Paul and His Epistles*, D. A. Hayes, p. 35.

[3] Ibid.

Keeping in mind that there is no portrait of Paul in sacred or secular history, it is therefore best to concentrate on what we know of Paul's life and thought and from these form our own opinion of his appearance.

Chief of the apostles

Paul was the most eminent of the apostles and the undisputed spokesman of the "Way." It was he who "lifted the Christian religion out of its Palestinian cradle, and tore away its swaddling clothes, and trained it to walk along the highways of the Roman Empire."[4] He more than any other clothed the gospel with credibility. Always his preaching stirred and motivated. It challenged the mind and warmed the heart. Always it was Christ-centered.

Paul's message demolished racism and religious bigotry and broke down the wall between Jew and Gentile. It eventually eliminated slavery and re-established the God-given equal rights of men and women. "There is neither Jew nor Greek," Paul exclaimed to the Galatians, "there is neither slave nor free man, there is neither male nor female; for you are all one in Christ Jesus" (Gal. 3:28; cf. Col. 3:11).

Unexcelled as a pioneer missionary of the Cross and unsurpassed as a Christian thinker, Paul preserved the moral and ethical teachings of Christianity and formulated its major doctrines. Though Jesus left no written creed or theology,[5] He clearly enunciated the seminal principles on which the Christian faith is based, and Paul, under divine inspiration, became the authoritative expounder of these principles. It was he who gave the gospel its systematic theology: "all of Paul's theology is latent in Christ's teaching, and all of Christ's teaching is patent in Paul's epistles."[6]

The gospel of Paul

The gospel of Jesus was unquestionably the gospel of Paul. He claimed he received it from the Lord: "For I would have you know brethren, that the gospel which was preached by me is not according to man. For I ... received it through a

---

[4] *The Character of Paul*, Charles Edward Jefferson, p. 19.

[5] Only thirty to thirty-five days of Jesus' life are known.

[6] *Paul and His Epistles*, D. A. Hayes, p. 129.

revelation of Jesus Christ" (Gal. 1:11, 12). All the leaders of the Christian church, down through the ages, have accepted the gospel of Paul as the gospel of Jesus.

It was Paul's piercing intellect and keen moral discernment which penetrated to the very heart of Jesus' teaching. It was Paul who

> saw in it a force to conquer the world and to rid men of all bondage and evil of every kind. It was he who applied to the whole range of human life and duty the inexhaustible ethical force which lay in Christ and thus lifted at one effort the heathen world to a new level of morality. He was the first to show the superiority of love to law, and to point out how God trusted to love, and to summon men to meet the trust God thus reposed in them.[7]

Though oriental religions were tolerant of other faiths,

> the religion of Paul, like the ancient religion of Israel, demanded an absolutely exclusive devotion. A man could become initiated into the mysteries of Isis or Mithras without at all giving up his former beliefs; but if he were to be received into the Church according to the preaching of Paul, he must forsake all other saviours for the Lord Jesus Christ.[8]

Christian discipleship was an eternal relationship and "No one, after putting his hand to the plow, and looking back is fit for the kingdom of God" (Lk. 9:62). This teaching of Jesus, seen clearly through the teaching of Paul, is the very essence of Christian discipleship.

In the footsteps of Paul

In preparation for this study I was privileged to journey extensively in the footsteps of Paul, visiting ancient Tarsus where he was born, living in Damascus where he was converted and traveling with him in all seasons. I climbed—where Paul may well have climbed—to the rock-crowned summit of Mt. Sinai, walked with him through desert sands and traveled with him over hill and dale.

Harbors known to Paul, such as Seleucia, Troas, Assos and Caesarea are now silted up and no longer navigable; and many of the great cities he visited in Cyprus, Asia Minor (Turkey) and Greece now lie in ruins.

---

[7] *The First Epistle to the Corinthians*, Marcus Dods, p. 68.
[8] *The Origin of Paul's Religion*, J. Gresham Machen, p. 9.

But the mountains and valleys and lakes and rivers familiar to Paul still remain. Mt. Olympus, snowcapped and aloof and once the "home of the gods," is still the towering backdrop of Thessalonica (Salonica); and the river Gangites, where Paul first baptized in Europe, still flows quietly not far from the heaped-up marble of deserted Philippi.

On my way to Puteoli I saw, as Paul must have seen, the smoking cone of Etna and the fiery displays of Stromboli; in Rome I peered into the Mamertine dungeon where he was last imprisoned. Finally, I passed through the Ostian Gate through which Paul may have walked on the way to his execution.

But exploring the byways and beachheads of Paul's ministry, while revealing the topography of his world, contributed but little to my knowledge of Paul. Who was this extraordinary individual whose writings still serve as the doctrinal foundation of the Christian church and which teach justification by faith—the watchword of the gospel? How to know the Apostle Paul?

The only way I could hope to achieve this was by studying his life and thought as revealed in Luke's book of Acts and in Paul's thirteen epistles. Though I had often read these writings as historical and devotional literature, I needed now to read them for their biographical insights.

Concerning Paul's letters

All of Paul's extant letters were personal letters and must always be viewed as such. Though much Christian teaching is found in most of them, especially Romans, Galatians, Philippians and Colossians, never must any of Paul's epistles be classed as theological dissertations or philosophical treatises. They were never intended as such; they were only meant to be personal letters, letters, not only teaching Christian theology and related doctrines, but also touching on a great variety of other subjects such as, how to live the Christian life, the basis of Christian giving, divisions in the church, spiritual gifts, Christians in litigation, marriage and divorce, masters and slaves, personal instructions, etc.

Paul's letters were often written impetuously to express gratitude for a gift or to address some urgent need or to answer hard to answer questions. Most often Paul's letters were warm and affectionate, but then there were times when Paul rightly became caustic and rigidly defensive when his name was slandered and his ministry maligned. Paul, in keeping with all great leaders, including Jesus Himself, had the capacity to be vehemently angry when encountering wrongdoing and sinful behavior. He was intensely human in this regard.

Inspiration of Paul's letters[9]

Paul wrote to Timothy, "All Scripture is God-breathed and is useful for teaching, rebuking, correcting and training in righteousness" (2Tim. 3:16 NIV). By *Scripture*, of course, Paul meant the Old Testament, the New Testament not yet having been formed. Though Paul believed that most of what he wrote was with God's approval and stated "in Christ we speak before God with sincerity, like men sent from God" (2Cor. 2:17 NIV),[10] Paul had no thought that his letters would ever be pronounced divinely inspired and would one day actually comprise nearly one half of the New Testament!

The doctrine of inspiration must never be seen as having the Scriptures dictated by God and the writers mechanically recording what was said. This erroneous view of inspiration is to reduce biblical writers to mere automatons deprived of their God-given right to express themselves in their own unique way. This is not to say that the writers of Scriptures, including Paul, were not divinely inspired when they wrote (even though not conscious of this). It only means that "God superintended these human authors so that, using their individual personalities, they composed and recorded without error God's word to man...."[11]

Paul dictated all his epistles to an amanuensis who tried to keep pace with his rapid dictation while Paul corrected and inserted and modified what he had said, sometimes logically, sometimes illogically. But Paul was not a politician, logician, or philosopher. He was primarily a fervent evangelist with the strong conviction that God had given him a message to give to the world, not just to the Jews, but also to the Gentiles—a message of salvation and hope for everyone with an open heart and a contrite spirit. Paul wanted to win all he met to the Savior's side. It was his passion in life.

---

[9] See Chapter 37, "Mamertine's Message" on p. 251.

[10] See also Paul's statement to the Thessalonians, "when you received the word of God, which you received from us, you accepted it not as the word of men, but as it actually is, the word of God ..." (1Thess. 2:13).

[11] Footnote to 2Tim. 3:16, *Ryrie Study Bible*.

Paul uses ideas which the Greek mind had never imagined, let alone expressed, and strives to tell men what righteousness is when no word represents his concept of righteousness. He re-clothes old words and puts new meaning into them. He even creates the Greek word, *agape*, to explain Christian love—the kind of outgoing and unconditional love totally unknown to Paul's world.

Without Paul's letters, we would know little of Paul's personality and very little regarding his character. It is his letters which reveal most clearly his heart and mind and how he viewed life and his missionary call. To read and study Paul's epistles is to make Paul come alive and see him in action. We can hear him preach and teach and sometimes burst into laughter; and also see him frown and break out in angry disapproval (and even weep) over the evil and abominable idolatry existing all around him.

Paul's letters, it must be remembered, are personal communications to his friends and brothers and sisters in Christ—not polished epistles, not grammatically always correct, not always refined and polite, but always straightforward, practical and intensely sincere. They come from a man with a highly sensitive nature and a keenly perceptive mind. But above all, they come from a man with a deeply compassionate heart.

What made this Pharisee of Pharisees, once the mortal enemy of Christians, turn champion of the gospel? Why did his preaching draw the crowds and bring men contrite to their knees when at other times it riled the masses until they clamored for his blood? Why, after years of tribulation, torture and six or seven imprisonments was Paul finally convicted of a capital offense? Who indeed was this man who called himself the "foremost of sinners" (1 Tim. 1:15), and yet through the centuries has been loudly acclaimed "the chief of saints"? What was the secret of his charisma and overwhelming drive? What was the all important principle which underlay his every endeavor?

Acknowledgements

This work owes much to the following friends:

Ed and Louise Hayward served as missionaries with Highland Christian Mission for two years (1978-79) and proved themselves every bit as helpful as "Aquila and Priscilla" of Paul's day. Ed with his keen analytical mind and Louise with years of teaching English, graciously accepted the challenge of critiquing my manuscript, for which I shall always be grateful.

Lois James, whom I first met as a missionary in the Territory of New Guinea, was trained at Eastern Baptist Theological Seminary and New York Theological Seminary. She holds a master's in Religious Education from Biblical Seminary, New York, and was kind enough to see that all I had written was doctrinally sound. Nothing escaped her well-trained eye—everything must be buttressed by Scripture.

Virgil Megill, of Toccoa Falls College, Georgia, spent long hours pouring over my manuscript and I found his sage counsel immensely helpful. His description of what transpires at the edge by faith is so perceptive that I have quoted it in full in my chapter on the edge-by-faith principle.

Frank Farrell, former associate editor of *Christianity Today* and editor of *World Vision Magazine,* and professor of church history and theology at Nyack Bible College, Nyack, N.Y., carefully examined my writing. I was constantly inspired by his advice to "keep keeping on"—the same advice he gave me years ago when we were studying for our doctorates in Edinburgh, Scotland.

Tom Murray, closer than a brother, has been an inspiration to me ever since I met him and his wife, Nancy, in Iran in 1963, where they had been serving as medical missionaries for twenty years. Tom's insights as a trained psychiatrist and his insistence on "sticking with the facts," rather than building on hearsay or theory, taught me to adhere to my goal—to know Paul as he really was.

Geoffrey Simpson, born in Australia and a naturalized citizen of Papua New Guinea, proved a veritable "walking encyclopedia." Always I was stimulated by his wide learning as I studied Paul. As a teacher, he taught many prominent parliamentarians, among them two prime ministers. He well deserves his BEM (British Empire Medal).

Peter Iyolasa, born in our home at Highland Christian Mission in the early sixties, was a constant encouragement to me as I wrote on Paul. Always I counted on his warm support which never failed regardless of where we found ourselves.

Kenny Merriam, a skilled cameraman and editor, and our much-loved "adopted" Papua New Guinea "son," often surprised me in ferreting out grammatical errors he found in my study of the Great Apostle. Though English was his second language, one would never have known it. Always I will miss Kenny who left this world in a head-on collision. He was only twenty-nine.

Ever will I be grateful to my former secretary, Miss Heather Chapman, for her willingness to spend countless hours typing and retyping my manuscript in its early stages. She did it all as a labor of love for Christ.

But the one to whom I owe most for this work is my much-beloved, talented wife, Carol. She above all encouraged me to live by the edge-by-faith principle. "[H]er worth [was] far above jewels ... she stretche[d] out her hands to the needy ... she smile[d] at the future. She open[ed] her mouth in wisdom, and the teaching of kindness [was] on her tongue ... many daughters have done nobly, but you [Carol] [excelled] them all" (Prov. 31:10, 20, 25, 26, 29).

Carol entered Glory on November 6, 2001, in Port Moresby General Hospital, Papua New Guinea.

Stuart H. Merriam
Papua New Guinea, 2004

The Edge-by-Faith Principle

Everyone consciously or subconsciously exercises pragmatic faith, that is, faith in tangible things: what we see, hear, smell, taste and touch. Every time we travel, exchange our money or sit down at a meal, we trust that our vehicle is sound, our money valid and our food safe. To live without such faith would of course be impossible, since no one can test everything before trusting it.

But to acknowledge the existence of God as Creator and Sustainer of the universe and the source of all life, and as being lovingly concerned with His creation, demands a distinctly different kind of faith, a faith in One who cannot be seen or proven to exist. Without such faith the author of Hebrews declares, "it is impossible to please God, for he who comes to God must believe that He is and that He is a rewarder of those who seek Him" (Heb. 11:6). Jeremiah agrees when he states, "you will seek Me and find Me, when you search for Me with all your heart" (Jer. 29:13).

Herein lies the edge-by-faith principle by which Christians are challenged to live. It calls for wholehearted belief in God and trust that He will reveal to His children their next step when they have gone as far as they can in faith. Whatever then He allows to come to them, they will know, is for their best (Rom. 8:28).

Such faith is radically different from Stoicism which taught that all are under inexorable laws laid down by an unloving, emotionless deity. Christian faith knows God as "Father" (Mk. 14:36; Rom. 8:15; Gal. 4:6), One of infinite love and justice who promises to provide for and lead His children as they trust and follow Him (Prov. 3:5, 6; Phil. 4:19).

The only definition of such faith in the Bible is found in Hebrews 11:1: "faith is the assurance of things hoped for, the conviction of things not seen." But after attempting to define such faith, the author becomes aware that it cannot be defined; it can only be experienced and exemplified. Therefore he lists eighteen examples of pilgrims of faith.

"The world says, 'seeing is believing'; the Gospel says, 'believing is seeing.'"[1] Though faith and hope both look forward to the future, they differ.

---

[1] *Master Study Bible, New American Standard*, p. 1821.

Faith looks over the horizon, sees the things of the future, makes them real, and brings them to one's feet; whereas, hope looks over the horizon, sees the things of the future, makes them real, and leaves them in the future ... faith takes a step toward them; while hope stands still. Faith is active; hope is passive. Faith lifts us into fellowship with the Unseen, while hope is the confident anticipation of a future regarded as future; faith appropriates that future as an experience of the present.[2]

At the edge by faith one faces possibilities no longer determined by one's previous, prejudiced perception. Here breakthroughs occur, insights are obtained, Herculean strength from God is revealed and decisive action ensues. Here God's intervening power reinforces His will against all odds.[3]

Throughout the Scriptures the edge-by-faith principle is clearly demonstrated. Abraham, by faith, on Mt. Moriah totally submits to God's hard command and raises his knife to slay his son, then he is shown the substitute sacrifice (Gen. 22:1-13). Moses, by faith, leads Israel all the way—to the very *edge* of the Red Sea—then miraculously the waters divide and Israel passes through (Ex. 14:10-30). Joshua by faith follows God's orders and marches his army once around Jericho for six days and on the seventh day, seven times around, then the walls collapse and the victory is won (Josh. 6:1-16, 20). And the widow of Zaraphath by faith, though destitute and hungry, shares all she has, then finds her flour and oil replenished (1 Ki. 17:8-16).

In the New Testament the same edge-by-faith principle pertains. The water at Cana is turned to wine when by faith Jesus' orders are followed and the stone jars are filled to the brim (Jn. 2:6-10). Peter's nets overflow when by faith he lets them down as far as they will go (Lk. 5:4-6). The man's withered hand is restored when by faith he obeys Jesus' command and fully extends it (Lk. 6:8-10); and the woman bent for eighteen years is healed when by faith she responds to the Savior's call and comes and stands at His feet (Lk. 13:10-13).

Paul, however, as a Pharisee, did not live by the edge-by-faith principle but strove to live by the Jewish law and obey all its 613 regulations. The law controlled his life. It was not until he was saved by Grace through faith (Eph. 2:8, 9) that he began to follow the edge-by-faith principle. Now as a committed servant of Christ

---

[2] Ibid.

[3] Virgil Megill, Professor of Communications (retired) at Toccoa Falls College (Georgia), provided this description to the author after numerous discussions about the edge-by-faith principle.

he believed that God would lead him as he trusted Him completely. No longer did he demand to know what lay ahead before he forged ahead. "Lead me on, Lord," was his constant prayer. "Keep thou my feet. I do not ask to see the distant scene—one step enough for me."[4]

---

[4] "Lead Kindly Light," John Henry Newman, stanza 1.

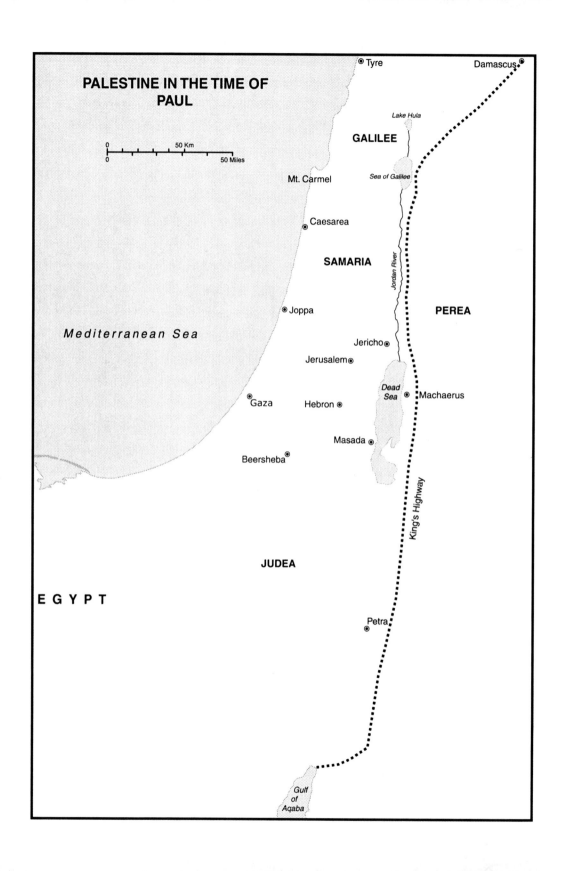

Chapter 1

Introducing Saul

About one year after the birth of Christ, Saul, whose Gentile name was Paul, was born in Tarsus, the capital of the province of Cilicia in Asia Minor (modern-day Turkey). The province was at the northeast corner of the Mediterranean.

Saul's family

Since Saul never mentions his mother and nothing is recorded of her, very possibly she died in his very early years. Perhaps this accounts for his sending greetings to the mother of Rufus whom evidently he held close to his heart and looked upon as his own mother. "Greet Rufus, a choice man in the Lord, also his mother and mine" (Rom. 16:13).[1]

Regarding Saul's father, it is certain he was a Pharisee of the tribe of Benjamin (Ac. 23:6; Rom. 11:1; Phil. 3:5) from which King Saul, Israel's first monarch, had come. Named after this king, Saul was thus nurtured in the strictest Hebraic traditions and later referred to himself as a "Hebrew of the Hebrews" (Phil. 3:5).

Saul's father, as a Pharisee, would doubtless have been a strict disciplinarian who believed in the proverb, "He who spares his rod hates his son, but he who loves him disciplines him diligently" (Prov. 13:24). He may, however, have found his alert, high-strung boy not easy to rear, judging from Saul's aggressive nature and stubborn will so apparent throughout his life (see 1Cor. 6:12b). Then too, if bereft of his wife at Saul's early age, Saul's father would sorely have missed her controlling influence and maternal wisdom in bringing up his child.

Saul's father thus may have used the rod too often and too severely on his son and failed to spend enough time with him and counsel him in love. Perhaps the memory of such whippings (if indeed his father was a tyrant) was that which prompted Saul to write to the fathers in Ephesus, "do not provoke your children to anger; but bring them up in the discipline and instruction of the Lord" (Eph. 6:4).

---

[1] Saul's mother would doubtless have been a pure-blooded Jewess.

And again, to the fathers in Colossae, "Fathers, do not exasperate your children, that they may not lose heart" (Col. 3:21).

Saul's paternal grandfather may have been a native of Galilee carried captive by Pompey to Rome and sold into slavery. Later it appears he was emancipated and vested with Roman citizenship and allowed to return to Palestine. Probably he remained there until persecution broke out after the death of Herod the Great, then settled in Tarsus, a city having the status of *civitus libera* granted by Augustus.[2] This would explain Saul's Roman citizenship by birth which exempted him from the dreaded tortures of flagellation, rods and crucifixion.

Of Saul's siblings all that is known is that Saul had one sister who lived in Jerusalem with her son (Ac. 23:16).[3] One wonders if they became Christians and if Saul resided with them when he visited the city.

Cleopatra

Tarsus had access to the sea via the Cydnus River,[4] which broadened into Lake Rhegma five miles inland and formed a natural harbor for the city. It was into this popular and well-protected port, about forty years before Saul was born, that Cleopatra sailed from Egypt to keep her first rendezvous with Mark Antony.

Mark Antony was in Tarsus, resting after his triumphant tour following his victory at Philippi. Knowing that Cleopatra had aided Cassius in the struggle against him, he sent for her with the intention of publicly punishing her, perhaps with a hefty fine. The queen, well aware of how vindictive Antony could be toward his enemies, decided to make a spectacular appearance. Among the thousands who witnessed the sensational pageant may well have been Saul's father who later on certainly would have described it for his son.

---

[2] *The Mind of St. Paul*, William Barclay, p. 18. The Romans divided their empire into two groups: citizens of Rome and citizens of the empire. Romans living outside Italy but who were born Italians were termed "citizens of the dispersion." Others, like Paul, who were foreigners but had been granted citizenship were called "political proselytes."

[3] In the list of twenty-six people to whom Paul sends greetings in his letter to the Romans (16:3-15) six of them are referred to as Paul's kinsmen" (vv. 7, 11 and 21). But this is not to mean that they were blood relatives, rather fellow countrymen closely associated with Paul.

[4] It was in Tarsus that Alexander nearly lost his life when after strenuous exertion he plunged into the icy waters of the Cydnus and emerged with a violent chill.

Cleopatra's famous galley with its heavily perfumed lavender sails was equipped with a tier of silver oars which flashed in the sun as they dipped and rose to the rhythmic music of orchestrated flutes, pipes and harps.

Under an awning spangled with gold, lounged the queen dressed as Aphrodite, the goddess of love, while colorfully dressed pageboys fanned her from either side. At the helm stood beautiful slave women attired as sea nymphs.

Wildly enthusiastic crowds, waving from both shores, cheered the dazzling queen as she slowly sailed by. Conscious of her celebrated beauty, she warmly smiled and waved back. No queen was ever more theatrical or sure of her charms.

Thirty miles inland from Tarsus was the well-known pass, the Cilician Gates, chiseled out of the cliffs and threading its way through the Taurus Mountains. This was the route followed by the great armies of Shalmaneser, Cyrus, Xerxes, Alexander the Great and Julius Caesar. It provided access to Tarsus from the hinterlands of Cappadocia and Galatia from which camel caravans brought much sought-after merchandise.

Tarsus: "First, fairest and best"

Tarsus, dating back to the Neolithic period (5000 B.C.), was in Saul's day self-governing and independent. Cosmopolitan in its make-up and intellectual in its outlook, the city had reached its height of prosperity with its university recognized as the world's principal seat of learning, excelling even the universities of Alexandria and Athens.

On the coins of Tarsus was written "Tarsus, the metropolis first, fairest and best." It was indeed "no insignificant city" (Ac. 21:39) and had good reason to be proud of its many sons who had attained eminence in every field of academia. Among them was the teacher and advisor of Augustus, Athendorus Cardylion,[5] as well as other famous Stoics: Antipater, Archedmus, Nestor, and Athendorus, the son of Sandon.[6]

Tent-making and leather-working

Tarsus was famous for its tapestries, belts and saddles and particularly for its black goats, the hair of which was used in the manufacture of clothing, blankets

---

[5] Athendorus advised the emperor when tempted to vent his anger to repeat every letter of the alphabet before saying or doing anything.

[6] *The Mind of St. Paul*, William Barclay, p. 25.

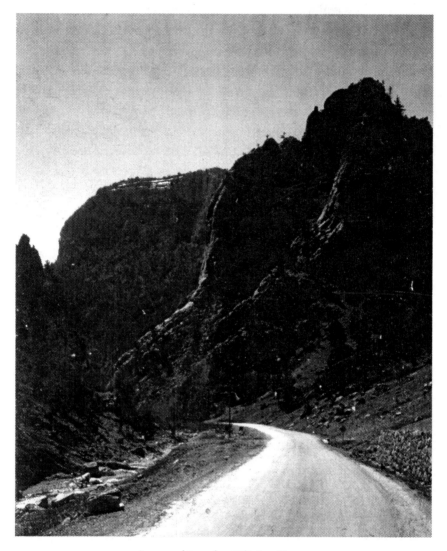

Approaching the Cilician Gates.

and tents. Saul learned early how to weave tent cloth and work with leather, and it was this knowledge that afforded him a lucrative trade throughout his life.

Early training

At the age of six Saul began his education in the synagogue of Tarsus, with the Jewish Scriptures the only textbook used. As the years went by he became thor-

Entering the Cilician Gates.

oughly familiar with the teachings of the Sacred Book and later quoted extensively from all its three divisions: the Law, the Prophets and the Writings.[7] Among his favorites appear to have been the book of Psalms and the book of Isaiah. In his letters he quoted from thirty-nine psalms and from twenty-nine chapters in Isaiah.

Educated as a Pharisee

Following his training in Tarsus, and probably at the age of twelve or thirteen, Saul was sent to Jerusalem to study at the feet of Gamaliel, the most respected rabbinical scholar of the day and the grandson of the renowned Hillel.[8] Here he con-

---

[7] Paul quoted from a total of 142 chapters in the Old Testament as well as over two hundred single verses. In addition to quoting from the Psalms and Isaiah, he quoted from all five books of the Torah, 1 and 2 Samuel, 1 Kings, Proverbs, Jeremiah, Ezekiel, Daniel, Hosea, Joel, Amos, Habakkuk, Zechariah and Malachi.

[8] Pharisaism was represented by two schools, one founded by Hillel and the other by Shammai. The school of Hillel taught a more advanced and liberal Judaism while that of Shammai held to a strict and unyielding literalism of the law. Constant rivalries prevailed between the two groups. The orthodox Jews believed that God loved only Israel of all the nations of the earth and had created Gentiles to be the fuel for the fires of hell. With this in mind these fanatics refused to help Gentile mothers about to give birth and declared that to do so was to break the rabbinical law. *The Letters to the Galatians and Ephesians*, William Barclay, pp. 4, 5.

Black goats of Tarsus.

tinued his rigorous training in the Scriptures and as the years advanced was recognized as an outstanding scholar and zealous defender of the law.

> To understand this law was the supreme object of his study; to obey this law was the supreme object of his life.… The moral law—so argued the Pharisees—relates to man's duty to his fellow-man; the ceremonial law relates to man's duty to God. Justice, mercy, kindness, are obligations due by man to his fellow-man; but to offer the appointed sacrifices, to fulfill the required ritual in worship, to perform the ceremonial ablutions, is doing man's duty to God. It is a great deal more important to do one's duty to God than to do one's duty to his fellow-man.[9]

---

[9] *The Life and Letters of Paul the Apostle*, Lyman Abbott, p. 23.

To Saul, therefore, ritual was the heart of the law and religion obedience to ritual. He fasted twice a week; on the fifth day to commemorate the day Moses climbed Mt. Sinai; and on the second day to commemorate the day he came down. Saul's year was filled with fastings celebrating the great calamities in Jewish history: the overthrow of Jerusalem and burning of the temple by Nebuchadnezzar; the murder of Gedaliah by Ishmael and the siege of Jerusalem by the Chaldeans. The Sabbath law was scrupulously kept as were the Jewish feasts. Always when in the presence of Gentiles Saul was careful to wash his hands in the basin of water that stood in every Jewish home, lest he might have touched a Gentile unknowingly and then have eaten with unclean hands and become degraded.

It is not surprising that Saul was subsequently invited to join the Pharisees who formed the national party of the Jews and considered themselves the guardians of Judaism. Never more than six thousand at a time, they maintained that as long as Israel was faithful to the law, no power on earth could conquer her.

To become a Pharisee one had to believe and promise to obey not only the law of Moses but also the oral law which comprised the interpretation of the divine oracles handed down to the fathers from generation to generation. Further, the aspiring Pharisee had to pledge that he would pay all his tithes before he bought or sold any commodity.

Saul would have been shocked and angered to learn of Gamaliel's counsel to the Sanhedrin not to interfere with the preaching of the apostles who strongly believed Jesus had risen from the dead. "[I]f this plan or action should be of men," Gamaliel predicted, "it will be overthrown; but if it is of God, you will not be able to overthrow them; or else you may even be found fighting against God" (Ac. 5:38, 39).

Saul would never have endorsed such a *laissez faire* policy, convinced as he was that the apostles were heretical and blasphemous in preaching a false Messiah. Let them be silenced immediately![10] The situation was far too serious for temporizing measures.

Saul a bachelor

Saul's advice to the unmarried and widows in Corinth that it was good for them to remain even as he was (1Cor. 7:8) clearly indicates that Saul at the time of

---

[10]See *Paul: Apostle of the Heart Set Free*, F. F. Bruce, pp. 51, 70.

writing was not married; and, since he does not address widowers, it appears he had never been married.[11]

World ready for the gospel

In the 3,000 years of recorded world history up to the first century, fewer than 150 years were without war. It was during one of these periods known as the *pax romana* that Christianity was introduced to mankind. Such a time of peace, of course, greatly facilitated the spread of the gospel.

Traveling by land in many areas was relatively easy in Saul's day with the roads constructed of closely-fitted igneous blocks and radiating from a golden marker at the center of the forum in Rome. From here they were measured off with milestones to mark the distance from the capital. All roads *did* in truth lead to Rome.

The government postal system was highly efficient with fresh horses stationed at designated points so as not to delay the mail. The post, however, was only for official use, which meant the general public was left to find its own means of communication. Letters were written on papyrus which was then rolled up and tied with string, and when privacy was desired, the knots were sealed with wax. Generally such mail was delivered by paid carriers, but in the case of Paul's epistles they seem all to have been delivered by friends and probably with no thought of remuneration.

The major language spoken throughout the empire was Greek, spread by Alexander a little less than 350 years before Saul's birth. It was the language of trade and politics. Though local languages continued, it was Greek that bound the empire together. Saul's thorough knowledge of this language, as well as of Latin, Hebrew and Aramaic (the vernacular of the Palestinian Jew), of course assisted him greatly in ministering to both Jew and Greek.

---

[11]For further discussion on Saul's celibacy, see Chapter 20, "Counseling Corinthians" on p. 141. Note: The high religious court of the Jews required each member, *after* A.D. 70, to be married and the legal father of at least one child. But since it is uncertain that this law also applied *before* A.D. 70, it cannot be said categorically that Paul was not a member of the Sanhedrin. (See footnote to 1Cor. 7:8, *Ryrie Study Bible.*) The fact that Saul as a Pharisee had voted for Christians to be put to death does not, of course, prove he was a member of the Sanhedrin (Ac. 26:10).

Chapter 2

At Ground Level

Not long after Jesus rose from the dead many Christians in Jerusalem, to commemorate the Resurrection, began meeting for worship in their homes on the first day of the week rather than in the synagogues[1] on the Sabbath. These "house churches" were labeled by the Jews as "synagogues of Satan." To claim that Jesus was the atonement for sin, let alone that He was the Son of God, was of course anathema to the Jews. But the Christians were convinced that Jesus had come forth from the tomb and were ready to lay down their lives for their faith.

Soon a strong group of believers was formed. In order to minister to the physical needs of the congregations, especially those of the Christian widows of Hellenistic Jews, seven deacons were appointed, among them a man named Stephen. He was held in high regard by the brethren and was recognized for his godliness (Ac. 6:1-5).

Stephen before the Sanhedrin

Stephen insisted that Christian fellowship be extended to Gentiles and that the church not remain an exclusive Jewish sect based only in Jerusalem. Yearning thus to reach those who had come to Jerusalem from Cyrenaica and Alexandria and from the provinces of Cilicia and Asia, he entered into vigorous debate with them, only to have them turn on him and spread false rumors that he was blaspheming "Moses and God" (Ac. 6:11.)[2] When the elders and scribes heard this, they were furious and brought him before the Sanhedrin to answer the charges.

This Jewish high court, which sat in a semicircle and was usually presided over by the high priest, comprised 70 men: 24 chief priests or heads of courses, 24 elders (Pharisees) representing the laity, and 22 scribes or lawyers. It was empowered to impose fines and to order floggings or imprisonment, but under Roman law was

---

[1] It is thought that Jerusalem at this period had 480 synagogues.

[2] Note that Moses is mentioned before God.

not allowed to carry out capital punishment except in cases affecting the sanctity of the temple.[3] The method for Jewish execution was stoning.

Before the examination of Stephen began, the Sanhedrinists could not help but be impressed with his demeanor and radiant expression. He had an inner peace they had never experienced, and his face appeared to them as the face of an angel (Ac. 6:15).

Stephen began by introducing himself as a proven son of Abraham and a veritable part of the Chosen Race. Nine times he referred to the fathers as "our fathers." He stressed God's covenant with Abraham, circumcision as the mark of the Jews, and the Mosaic law as "living oracles."

After reviewing Hebraic history from Abraham to David, a history of which the Jews were inordinately proud, he pointed out Israel's disobedience in having worshipped idols. Then he reminded his hearers of the history of the temple, but suddenly stopped and declared *de facto*, "the Most High does not dwell in houses made by human hands ..." (Ac. 7:48). To emphasize this he quoted Isaiah:

> Thus says the Lord, "Heaven is My throne, and the earth is My footstool. Where then is a house you could build for Me? And where is a place that I may rest? For My hand made all these things...." (Isa. 66:1, 2; see Ac. 7:49, 50)

It was then that Stephen openly accused the Sanhedrinists of being murderers and hypocrites:

> You men who are stiff-necked and uncircumcised in heart and ears are always resisting the Holy Spirit; you are doing just as your fathers did.[4] Which one of the prophets did your fathers not persecute? And they killed those who had previously announced the coming of the Righteous One, whose betrayers and murderers you have now become; you who received the law as ordained by angels, and yet did not keep it. (Ac. 7:52, 53)

Such an excoriation naturally outraged the Sanhedrinists and caused them to gnash their teeth. But when they heard Stephen exclaim that he saw the heavens opened and Jesus standing at the right hand of God (v. 56),[5] it was then that their

---

[3] *Paul: Apostle of the Heart Set Free*, F. F. Bruce, p. 68.

[4] Stephen shifts from "our fathers" to "your fathers" (v. 51) so as not to speak ill of the honored Patriarchs. It was not the Patriarchs who killed the prophets but the fathers of the Sanhedrinists.

[5] Jesus' standing would seem to be out of loving respect for His devoted servant about to come before Him.

wrath knew no bounds. Clamping their hands over their ears lest they hear any more blasphemies, they screamed out for Stephen's death, then seized him and dragged him out of the city to be stoned.

The death of Stephen

As the stones began to strike Stephen and knowing his life on earth was soon to end, Stephen called out, "Lord Jesus, receive my spirit!" (v. 59). Then falling on his knees and with a loud voice, he implored, "Lord, do not hold this sin against them!" (v. 60). It was then under a volley of stones that his punctured body disappeared, and when the stones were removed, he was found dead.[6]

Saul introduced

While watching this bloody execution and guarding the garments of those throwing the stones, Saul first appears in Scripture. Luke begins at ground level showing Saul's feet before revealing his face. He mentions his name and that he was a young man, but says nothing of his being a ruthless Pharisee bent on destroying every Christian he could find. Only later does Luke depict him ravaging the church, entering house after house and seizing men and women and throwing them into prison, then later witnessing against them and pressing for their deaths (Ac. 8:3; 22:4; 26:10).[7] Saul was not interested in trying to persuade Christians to abandon their faith; he was only interested in silencing them forever.

Saul embarks for Damascus

Though the Sanhedrin outlawed Christian assemblies and forbade all preaching of the gospel, most Jerusalem believers continued to remain in the city and worship in secret. Some, however, fled as far as Damascus, nearly 150 miles north. Upon learning this and realizing that from there at the hub of important trade routes Christianity could rapidly spread in all directions, Saul gained permission from the

---

[6] Stephen was probably stoned during the brief presidency of the high priest Jonathan, son of Hanan, the Sadducean priest. *The Life and Work of Saint Paul*, Frederick W. Farrar, vol. I, p. 166.

[7] Paul never forgot how he had been a violent enemy of Christians, and how he had devastated the church of God beyond measure in his attempt to destroy it (Gal. 1:13; 1Tim. 1:13). He referred to himself in his letter to the Corinthians as being "the least of the apostles," not fit to be named among them because he had persecuted the church of God (1Cor. 15:9).

high priest[8] to enter the Damascan synagogues and arrest any Christian he could find. He then planned to bring them back bound to Jerusalem to be tried before the Sanhedrin, and never envisioned he would be away long.

---

[8] Theophilus was the high priest and the son of Jonathan, the high priest who gave orders to stone Stephen. High priests represented the Sanhedrin, which had jurisdiction over world Jewry.

Chapter 3

Outside and Inside Damascus

Damascus

Damascus, the capital of Syria, was founded by Uz, the great-great-grandson of Noah, and is claimed by Damascans to be the oldest city in the world.[1] Surrounded by desert and nestled in a green oasis watered by the rivers Abanah and Pharpar, the city with its many whitewashed dwellings was once described as "a handful of pearls in a goblet of emerald."[2] But such a description is no longer befitting the capital of Syria which is a sprawling, modern metropolis vastly different from the city Saul knew. Nonetheless it retains some of its ancient ambiance with its street called "Straight" still a major thoroughfare running one mile straight through the city.[3]

The great encounter

As the walls of Damascus rose on the far horizon, Saul, eager to complete his long journey and begin his purge of Christians, would have increased the pace of his caravan. Suddenly at twelve noon, as he neared the gates of the city, an immense bolt of light brighter than the sun exploded before him. The startled animals reared back in wild terror and flung their riders to the ground, leaving them cringing in the sands and hiding under their cloaks. Then all heard a voice crying out, but only Saul understood what was being said. "Saul, Saul," came the words in Aramaic, "why are you persecuting me? It is hard for you to kick against the goads" (Ac. 26:14).[4] Saul knew that goads were the sharpened protuberances positioned

---

[1] The inhabitants of Iconium disagree, insisting that their city is the oldest. See Chapter 9, "Left for Dead," p. 60.

[2] *The Life and Work of St. Paul*, Frederic W. Farrar, p. 107.

[3] The street in Paul's day had a center section reserved for chariots and horsemen and on either side a path for pedestrians. Today the street is a roofed-over bazaar. See *In the Steps of St. Paul*, H. V. Morton, p. 37.

[4] Though Saul and his men may have been on camels, it is more likely they were on horses, in view of Jesus' reference to "goads."

Camel carrying firewood.

on the front of carts to prevent the animals which drew them from kicking back. How he must have burned with indignation at being likened to an obstreperous horse or a stubborn mule! But not knowing who it was who spoke to him and fearing the unknown, he reverently responded, "Who art Thou, Lord?"[5]

Then came the appalling announcement: "I am Jesus whom you are persecuting, but rise and enter into the city, and it shall be told you what you must do" (Ac. 9:5, 6; see 22:6-10; 26:15). Aghast at the thought that he might actually be hearing

---

[5] In Ac. 22:8; 26:15 Saul is recorded as saying, "Who are you, Lord?" after Jesus had announced it was He whom Saul was persecuting. Then in Ac. 22:10 Saul asks, "What shall I do, Lord?" Saul's use of the word *Lord* when addressing Jesus was in no way a confession of faith in Him as Lord of his life. Rather, it was only a term of respect prompted by fear.

Camel train.

the voice of Jesus whom the Christians affirmed had risen from the dead, Saul must have shuddered in utter horror. But how preposterous! Blasphemous thought! Had not the law condemned the crucified and pronounced that "he who is hanged is accursed of God" (Deut. 21:23)?[6] No, it could not be the voice of the crucified Jesus! Impossible! It must be that of a demon blocking his way.

Determined to solve the mystery, Saul lifted his cover and peered out, but to his consternation and great alarm he could see nothing! He opened his eyes wider

---

[6] Because Saul was a Roman citizen he would have looked upon crucifixion with special abhorrence and would have echoed the words of Cicero regarding it: "Far be the very name of a cross, not only from the body, but even from the thoughts, eyes, ears of Roman citizens." *A Man in Christ*, J. S. Stewart, p. 138, fn. 2.

Camels first go down on their front knees when they lie down.

but still all before him was impenetratable darkness. Then the shocking truth crashed in upon him—he was blind! Nervously he inquired of his cohorts if they could see, and upon learning that they all had their sight, and realizing he alone was blind, he frantically announced his dreadful plight.

Knowing now that he was completely dependent upon others, he had no choice but to submit to being led into the city. How he must have rebelled at the thought of being escorted through the streets a helpless, stumbling invalid with hundreds of eyes focused upon him and among them surely the eyes of Christians whom he had come to arrest! But there was no other way. He must enter the city blind and do as the Voice commanded.

House of Judas

Luke does not say why Saul was taken to the home of Judas on the street called "Straight," but probably it was because Judas (not a Christian) was a friend of Saul who would be only too honored to provide lodging for the well-known Pharisee. Then too, Saul may have counted on him to single out Christians in the synagogues and help in their arrests.

Saul's soul-searching

For the next three days Saul refused all food and drink. The terrifying awareness that he might be blind forever must have plunged him into deepest despair. Then too, the agonizing why of it all. Why, as the defender of the Patriarchs, the Temple and the Torah, had he been summarily deprived of his command and robbed of his sight? Why, when he had come to Damascus to eliminate an insidious cult whose members were blasphemously worshipping an obvious imposter who claimed to be God, deity personified and the Savior of the world? Why now was Saul thwarted at the gates of Damascus in carrying out his authorized mission? Why was he left in the grip of despair, blind and powerless to proceed?

Hour after hour Saul searched his heart and his relationship with God. The faces of the many Christians he had imprisoned and watched as they were brutally stoned to death—especially the angelic face of Stephen—would have been vividly recalled. The memory of their agony would have torn at his soul. Though he claimed he had acted in ignorance and unbelief (1Tim. 1:13), his conscience condemned him. The awful weight of his sin was unbearable. The altar he knew had no power to save. Animal sacrifices he knew were an offense to God. Who then could atone for his long record of sins? Murder and more murder of helpless men and women, heinous sins he alone had committed! Who could take away his awful guilt? Who could bring peace to his burdened soul?

It was only through the enlightenment of the Holy Spirit that Saul would ever be convinced that Jesus was indeed the Son of God. Too long had Saul regarded Him a charlatan from Nazareth, a charismatic, itinerant Jew claiming deity. He firmly believed Jesus deserved to be crucified. Had He not broken the law and blasphemed God? Why then have mercy upon Him?

But now as Saul meditated on the blinding light he had seen outside the gates of Damascus and recalled the voice he had heard calling out his name, his view of the Savior began to change radically. Was this not indeed the voice of Jesus he had heard? Was this not Jesus come back from the dead? On earth surely He had lived as God incarnate declaring His love for the world. Now His shed blood on the cross of Calvary was the perfect atonement for the sins of mankind—for all who would repent and acknowledge Him as Lord. The cross verified Jesus' love; the open tomb validated His deity. Surely the God-man from Galilee was the unblemished Lamb of God, the perfect sacrifice for sin. Now it was left for Saul to acknowledge Him as Savior and receive Him as Lord.

Visit of Ananias

In the meantime God had spoken to Ananias,[7] a devout Christian living in Damascus, and had instructed him to go to Saul and lay his hands upon him so that he might regain his sight. It is not surprising that Ananias at first rebelled. The dreaded name of Saul the persecutor was known everywhere, and word of his arrival in Damascus would have terrified the Christians scattered throughout the city and left them cringing in fear. For Ananias to come near such a man was to jeopardize not only his own life but the lives of others. But God assured Ananias that Saul had been prepared for his visit and was now ready to become a chosen servant of His.

Saul converted and baptized

It was thus in trusting obedience that Ananias approached blind Saul and laid his hands upon him. By faith he said, "Brother Saul, the Lord Jesus, who appeared[8] to you on the road by which you were coming, has sent me so that you may regain your sight, and be filled with the Holy Spirit" (Ac. 9:17). When Saul heard these words his heart was suddenly opened and he was filled with the Holy Ghost. Ineffable peace and joy flooded his soul[9] as something like scales fell from his eyes and his sight was restored. Saul was a new man with a new nature of love. He had

---

[7] In the New Testament there are two other men named Ananias, both from Jerusalem: Sapphira's husband, who lied to the church council and was struck down as a consequence; and Ananias, the corrupt high priest, who had ordered Saul (then known as Paul) smitten on the mouth. Finally, this Ananias was murdered by the Sicarii.

[8] See "Jesus' Resurrection Appearances" on p. 292 for comments on Saul's encounter with Jesus on the Damascus road.

[9] This was the peace and joy which Jesus promised to all who would believe in Him (Jn. 14:27; 15:11; 16:33).

received his physical sight, but much more, he had gained spiritual sight. Now he had become a child of God through faith in Jesus Christ.[10] Now he was forever a member of the family of God. No longer did he feel condemned under divine judgment. His sins he knew were all forgiven; Jesus had set him free. He might break the communion with God, but never the union. He might fall *on* the bridge to Heaven, but never *off* the bridge.[11] His new birth and indwelling of the Holy Spirit assured him of his eternal salvation. Paul never wavered from this conviction.

The first face he saw was that of Ananias. Three days earlier Saul would have arrested him. Now he welcomed him as his dear brother in Christ. Christians whom he once despised and wanted to kill now he considered his personal friends. His appetite was restored and he was eager to eat and drink.

Immediately he was baptized and taken into the fellowship of believers. Saul no longer wanted to remain in isolation, regarded as a notorious persecutor of Christians. He must let the world know he was now to be numbered among the followers of the Savior. He was no longer under the law but under grace. He had become a servant of Christ; Christ Jesus had become his Lord.

After spending several days with the believers, he began proclaiming Jesus in the synagogues, affirming, "He is the Son of God" (Ac. 9:20). Those who heard him were astounded and exclaimed, "Isn't he the man who raised havoc in Jerusalem among those who call on this name? And hasn't he come here to take them as prisoners to the chief priests?" (v. 21 NIV).

---

[10]A Christian is not only God's physical creation but His new creation through faith in Christ (Gal. 3:26).

[11]"The presence of the Holy Spirit, the seal, is the believer's guarantee of the security of his salvation" (Footnote to Eph. 1:13, *Ryrie Study Bible*). See Chaoter 21, pp. 147, 148.

Chapter 4

Conversion Aftermath

Saul becomes Paul

After his conversion Paul continued to be known for many years by his Hebrew name *Saul* ("strongwilled" in Hebrew), and not until he had been commissioned a missionary to the Gentiles and was well along on his first missionary journey did Luke begin to call him *Paul* ("little one" in Latin) (Ac. 13:9). Since this is the name which Saul preferred after becoming a Christian and used in all his epistles, it is therefore appropriate to refer to him from now on as Paul.

Into Arabia

The next three years of Paul's life were spent in Arabia, known as the Nabatean kingdom. The kingdom stretched 450 miles from Damascus to Mt. Sinai and was ruled by Aretas IV (9 B.C. to A.D. 40). Luke, surprisingly, records nothing of this segment of Paul's life, not even mentioning that he went into Arabia shortly after his conversion. Paul also remains silent about the matter until years later when he refers to it in his letter to the Galatians (the only place he mentions it). Here he declares that the gospel he preached was

> not according to man. For I neither received it from man, nor was I taught it, but I received it through a revelation of Jesus Christ … He who had set me apart, even from my mother's womb, and called me through His grace, was pleased to reveal His Son in me, that I might preach Him among the Gentiles, but I did not immediately consult with flesh and blood, nor did I go up to Jerusalem to those who were apostles before me; but I went away to Arabia, and returned to Damascus. Then three years later I went up to Jerusalem to become acquainted with Cephas.... (Gal. 1:11-18)[1]

---

[1] Paul's statements, "I went away to Arabia, and returned once more to Damascus. Then three years later I went up to Jerusalem …" (Gal. 1:17, 18), do not mean that he stayed in Damascus for three years and then returned to Jerusalem. Rather, it means that after Paul had spent three years in Arabia he went back to Jerusalem. The Jewish leaders in Damascus would never have tolerated Paul's vigorous preaching in their city for three years. Luke states, "when many days [not years] had elapsed, the Jews plotted together to do away with him" (Ac. 9:23).

What the "revelation of Jesus Christ" entailed Paul does not disclose, but obviously it was a very personal, spiritual experience which Paul seems to have kept to himself. He might never have mentioned it had not the Galatians questioned his apostleship.

Luke, who of course would have known of Paul's three years in Arabia, doubtless felt that they were "private" years and best left up to Paul to write of them as he would. In the meantime Luke concentrated on how Paul's ministry was launched and the reaction to his preaching from the Jews and the Gentiles, as well as from the apostles.

It is logical that Paul, long under the Mosaic law but now under grace, would have wanted to visit Mt. Sinai where the law was first given to Israel. There in the environs of the sacred mountain he could re-examine the Scriptures in the light of his newfound faith against the backdrop of Calvary and the empty tomb. The road Paul traveled to Sinai would have been the Kings' Highway, which ran from Damascus to the Gulf of Aqaba. It passed the well-marked turn-off to Machaerus, the former stronghold and palace of Herod Antipas. Here Paul would certainly have lingered and thought of the famous fortress.

Machaerus

Machaerus, about one mile from the Arab village Khirbet el-Mukawer and five miles south from the hot springs of Callirhoe,[2] was built by Alexander Jannaeus (103-76 B.C.) and destroyed by Pompey's general Gabinius in 57 B.C. Later it was rebuilt by Herod the Great (37-4 B.C.) and upon his death passed on to his son, Herod Antipas (4 B.C.-A.D. 38). Antipas ruled both the tetrarchies of Galilee and Perea, but was never given the official title of king, though he was referred to as such. After the death of Antipas, Machaerus continued to be held by Roman garrisons until A.D. 66, then was taken over by the Jews. It was recovered by the Romans circa A.D. 72, and finally totally demolished.

Situated 3,700 feet above the Mediterranean Sea and 4,970 feet directly above the eastern side of the Dead Sea, Machaerus, in its heyday, looked down into the rocky ravines of the bare, brown mountains of Moab and on to the undulating hills

---

[2] It was here that Herod the Great was frequently taken during his last illness when he was suffering from arteriosclerosis in the hope that the hot waters would heal him. He died in his 68th year.

At Machaerus, the possible cell of John the Baptist.

surrounding Jerusalem. Superbly fortified on all sides and constantly on the alert for enemy attack, Machaerus soon became known as the "Watch Tower of Arabia."

Here John the Baptist, whom Jesus claimed had no rival for greatness (Mt. 11:11), was incarcerated for his stern denunciation of the unlawful marriage of Herod Antipas to Herodias, the wife of his brother, Herod Philip. Since John ministered in Judea, it was logical that he be imprisoned at Machaerus rather than at Tiberius in Galilee.

Herod's birthday party

The outcome of Herod's memorable birthday banquet, held at Machaerus in the early days of Jesus' ministry, would have been familiar to Paul. Vividly he must have visualized, as he paused at the turn-off to the notorious fortress, the electrifying events of that birthday celebration which ended in such tragedy.

At one end of the great dining hall illuminated with blazing torches and filled with the aroma of steaming foods prepared for the hundreds of invited guests, Paul would have envisioned the inebriated king slumped on his throne surrounded with guards and military staff, among them the chief dignitaries and generals from his two tetrarchies.

Salome

Salome, Herodias's stunning daughter and an Asmonean princess,[3] was the featured dancer of the evening. Doubtless, Paul would have visualized her voluptuous performance holding enthralled her infatuated admirers and would have heard the bewitching sound of dulcimers and flutes as she danced through the night teasingly dropping her veils. Then, near the end of her exotic performance, amid the clash of cymbals and blare of trumpets, Paul surely would have imagined the fragile princess suddenly pausing and tossing back her head, then with a squeal of ecstasy and her slender arms held high above her head, spectacularly pirouetting before her intoxicated, bleary-eyed stepfather and deftly falling at his feet.

Death of John the Baptist

Thunderous applause breaks out; the king staggers to his feet. "Ask me for whatever you want," he addresses the princess, "up to half of my kingdom" (Mk. 6:22, 23). Salome blushes and rushes to her mother, Herodias, to inquire what she should ask, and returns with the chilling request, "the head of John the Baptist" (v. 24).

Though reluctant to comply, knowing the popularity of the much-loved evangelist, and acutely aware of his wrongful imprisonment, but daring not to go back on his word in the presence of his officers, Herod grudgingly summons his swordsman and orders the grisly execution.

Soon the bloodied head of John on a silver platter is delivered to Salome, who in turn, trembling, carries it to her mother. According to tradition, Herodias, fear-

---

[3] Salome, the daughter of Herod Philip and Herodias, at about nineteen years of age, became the wife of her uncle Philip the Tetrarch, the son of Herod the Great by Cleopatra of Jerusalem (not Queen Cleopatra of Egypt). Salome's name does not occur in Scripture. See *The Bible As History,* Werner Keller, p. 365.

ing that John might speak out against her even in his death, draws out a bodkin from her hair and thrusts it through his pallid tongue.

But John's cry, "Behold, the Lamb of God who takes away the sin of the world!" (Jn. 1:29) was not to be silenced. It echoed again and again throughout Paul's preaching and was at the very heart of his evangel.

Herod Antipas, whom Jesus called "that fox" (Lk. 13:32) eventually was accused by Emperor Caligula of treachery and insurrection and with Herodias was banished to Spain where they remained the rest of their lives.

Today the Mosque of Omaiydes in Damascus, previously named the Cathedral of St. John, is reputed to contain the skull of John the Baptist. This is highly probable when it is remembered that King Aretas IV, formerly of Petra, was the father of the first wife of Herod Antipas, who divorced her in favor of Herodias. Aretas would have held John the Baptist in highest regard for having vehemently denounced the unlawful marriage, and when John was beheaded, Aretas, now ruling in Damascus, might well have asked Herodias for his head. She would gladly have given it to be rid of her enemy. Aretas on the other hand would have been honored to have the saintly head and would have enshrined it in some sacred place, most probably in Damascus.[4]

Masada

Had Paul (now in his early thirties) contemplated Machaerus as he passed down the King's Highway, it stands to reason that he would also have thought of Masada across the Dead Sea, sixteen miles south. Here on its summit Herod the Great had built his heavily fortified summer palaces. Throughout most of Paul's life Masada remained under Roman garrisons, and not until A.D. 66 did Menahem and his band of Zealots succeed in capturing it. Paul, of course, would never have been allowed in Machaerus or on Masada; nor would he have imagined that in less than forty years, just after his death, Israel as a nation would cease to exist, and the place of its demise would be on Masada.

After the fall of Jerusalem in A.D. 70, 996 Jews, including children, fled to Masada's heights and refused to surrender. They were well supplied with food, water and wine—well equipped, they felt, to withstand Roman attack for however long the siege might last. But Flavius Silva, the Roman procurator, was determined to conquer them, and built a high wall around the base of the mountain and eight army encampments to prevent the rebels escaping or receiving aid.

---

[4] John the Baptist's body was taken by his disciples and laid in an unknown tomb (Mk. 6:29).

Masada from the Dead Sea.

Thousands of slaves, among them thousands of Jewish prisoners, were then made to construct a mole 645 feet long and 450 feet high to Masada's 20-acre plateau. The mole required approximately two years to complete, and because Jews were used in its construction, their brethren on the summit of Masada refused to scald them with boiling water or burning coals or to do them any harm.

Finally the time came for the attack. A huge turret, fifty feet high on wheels, had been constructed at the base of the great incline, and on top of the structure were stationed soldiers to man the battering ram and catapults. Endless regiments of slaves then dragged the massive tower to the summit, and, after an extended siege, the outer stone wall was broken through. A second wall of earth and timber proved more difficult to pierce, and finally had to be burned before it gave way. Visualize the horror of viewing the macabre sight of 989 corpses strewn everywhere! The insurgents, all but seven, had allowed themselves to be killed or had committed suicide.

The remaining mole to Masada's summit.

Found alive hiding in a cistern were the survivors, two women and five children. How they had escaped no one knows. They told the tragic story of how the fathers first killed their children and then their wives. Then ten men were chosen by lot to kill the others, and again by lot one of the remaining ten was selected to dispatch the other nine, after which he committed suicide.

Not until 1948 did the Jews return to claim their land and set up the State of Israel. Today the site of Masada has become a national monument, highly revered by Israel, and one of the most meaningful in all the world.

Petra

If Paul traveled the trade route from Syria to Egypt, it is most probable that he visited Petra, the famed "rose-red city half as old as time."[5] He would, of course,

---

[5] Dean Burgon, the Victorian traveler and poet.

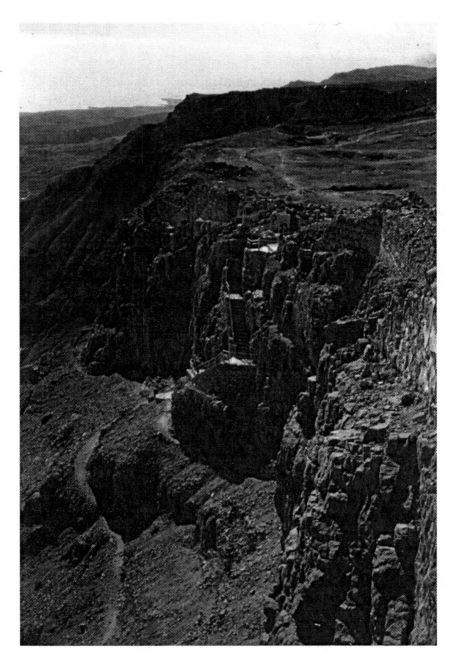

The stairs, in 1962, to Masada's summit before the cable car was built.

Roman legion enclosures from the summit of Masada.

have been familiar with its history and known that it had been the Edomite stronghold of Ishmael and Esau. Such a tie-in with Paul's race would have heightened his desire to visit it and meet its people.

The only entrance into the city was through an immense crack in Nubian sandstone over one mile long and known as the Siq. On either side are almost perpendicular rocks rising as high as three hundred feet. At certain points the rocks are scarcely twelve feet apart.

As one comes out of the winding Siq, the first object that greets the eye is Petra's most impressive monument, el Khazneh—the Treasury or "Temple of the Muses," as some call it—carved out of deep rose and chocolate-colored rocks and standing 140 feet high and 90 feet wide. There is evidence that it was once used as a royal mausoleum and may well have been the tomb of King Aretas.

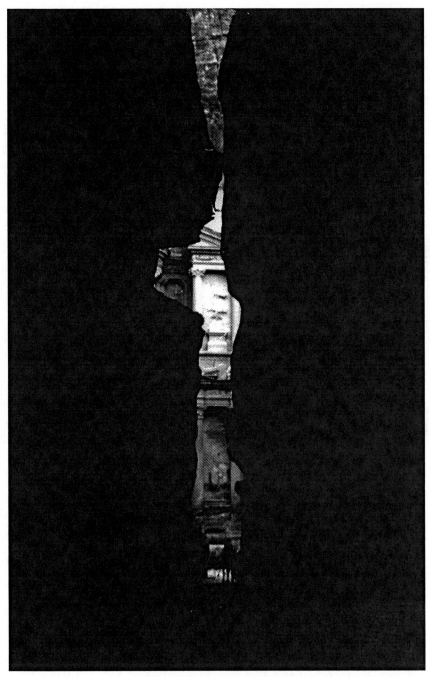

Entering Petra through the Siq.

Petra's rock temple as seen from the Siq.

Petra was first settled about 800 B.C. by a Semitic tribe from northern Arabia and became the capital of the Nabateans, and was greatly embellished through Roman help. Herod the Great, as a boy of ten, spent part of his boyhood at Petra. Its structures today include the ruins of majestic temples, palaces and bridges, and many rock dwellings and tomb-like caverns. There is a triumphal arch as well as an immense theater with thirty-three tiers of seats capable of seating at least three thousand spectators.

The hidden city continued as a center of a rich caravan trade until A.D. 200, when it fell before its rival, Palmyra. After a succession of rulers and a history of fighting and ever-increasing attacks from marauders, its caravan trade dwindled and the city was deserted. For centuries it was lost to memory and not rediscovered until 1812, when a Swiss explorer stumbled on it.

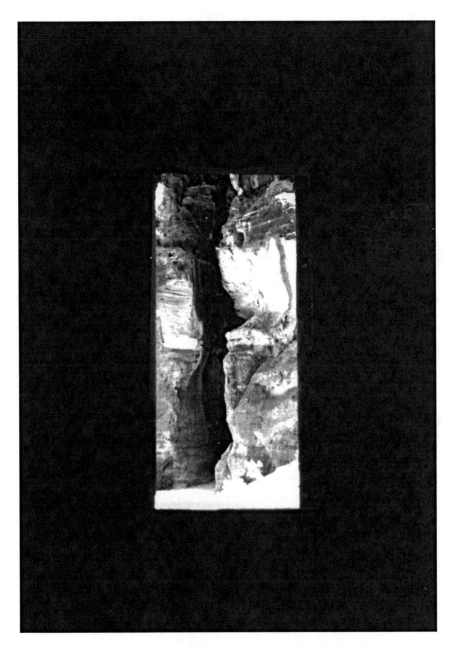

Viewing the Siq from inside the rock temple.

Chapter 5

From Sinai to Tarsus

Mt. Sinai

Had Paul visited Petra and later Sinai, he would have stayed in Petra only long enough to prepare himself for the 150-mile journey to Mt. Sinai. Once there he would certainly have climbed the famous mount where Moses had received the law. Paul knew he was no longer under Mosaic laws but under grace and under "a new covenant, not of the letter, but of the Spirit" (2Cor. 3:6).

> There in the sterile heights of Mt. Sinai he realized that the whole Pharisaic program was an equally sterile one. The people under the law were in bondage. They were the children of the slave woman. Only those who were saved by grace could claim to be free. The terrors of the law had to be supplanted to lead men to Christ.[1]

Christ had become the High Priest, and faith in Him alone was the only way into the presence of God.

All but for the fourth of the Ten Commandments were later included in the New Testament. The fourth, dealing with the Sabbath (rest), concerned only the Jews and their servants and friends who dwelt with them (Ex. 31:12-17; Deut. 5:15; Ezek. 20:12).[2] It had been given to Israel to remind her that for 430 years while in Egyptian slavery she had had no rest day, and that it was the Lord who had delivered her from bondage.

Paul no longer a Sabbatarian

Paul as a Christian was no longer a Sabbatarian and only once in all his letters did he allude to the Sabbath. This was when he wrote the Colossians: "Therefore let no one act as your judge in regard to food or drink or in respect to a festival or a new moon or a Sabbath day—things which are a mere shadow of what is to

---

[1] *Paul and His Epistles*, D. A. Hayes, pp. 32, 33.
[2] See "The Sabbath and the New Testament" on p. 288.

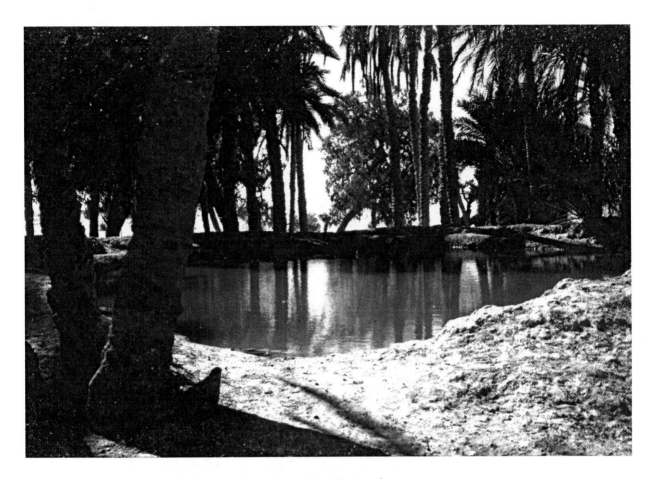

Oasis, Sinai Peninsula.

come …" (Col. 2:16, 17). The fact that Paul made it his policy, wherever he went, to visit synagogues on the Sabbath was not to uphold the law of the Sabbath, but to reach the Jews who assembled there on the Sabbath.

Paul doubtless did not remain long at Mt. Sinai but returned to some community outside of Damascus and lived with Christians there. Here he would have worshipped daily with his brethren and come to know their spiritual way of life. Here too he would have spent long hours studying the Scriptures, and seeing in them not only the Messianic prophecies now fulfilled in Christ, but also the whole plan of salvation. During this time he would have formulated the all-important doctrine of the vicarious atonement of Christ at the Cross, verified by the equally

The arid Sinai Peninsula.

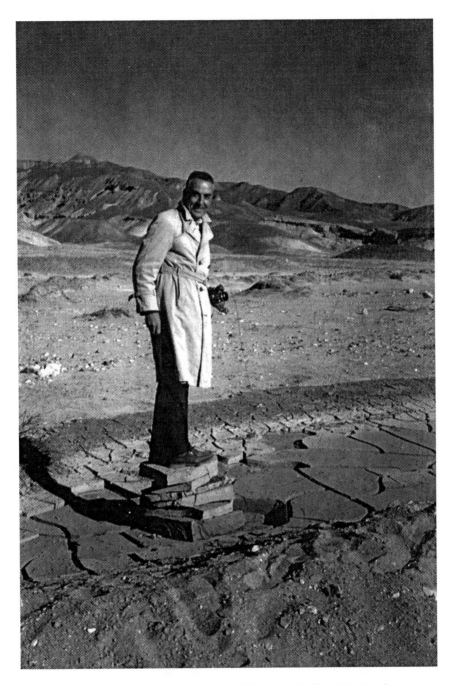

The author standing on cakes of dried mud, Sinai Peninsula.

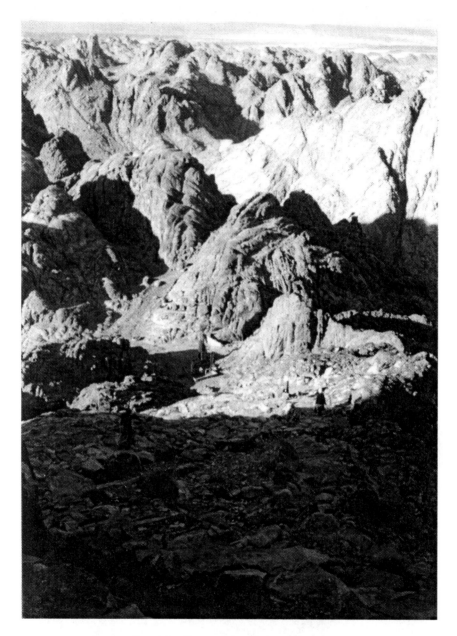

Descending Mt. Sinai to St. Catherine's monastery.

The summit of Mt. Sinai.

important doctrine of Jesus' resurrection, without which His death would have no meaning.

The eschatological teachings too, which appear in Paul's letters embracing the Second Coming, the Rapture, and the bestowal of rewards and future judgments, would have been carefully pondered and written down during this period. It was therefore with a clear understanding of the gospel that Paul again entered the synagogues of Damascus and began to preach the risen Christ.

Escape from Damascus

After many days Paul's fervent proclamation of Jesus as Messiah and Savior stirred up so much opposition among the Jewish leaders that they determined to murder him. The governor of the city was persuaded to station guards at all gates of the city to arrest him if he tried to escape. This left Paul with no choice but to accept the kind offer of friends, whose home was on the wall, to conceal him in a basket, and while the city slept, lower him to the ground. The fact that they were willing to risk their lives in doing this shows how much they thought of Paul (Ac. 9:23-25).[3]

As Paul stole away in the darkness and started on his long journey to Jerusalem, he would have vividly recalled his dramatic approach to Damascus three years earlier. How incredible now to be returning to Jerusalem, no longer the persecutor of Christians but the proclaimer of the risen Christ whom he loved and now was serving!

Paul's first Jerusalem visit as a Christian

One of Paul's reasons for returning to Jerusalem was to become acquainted with Peter whom he probably had never met, inasmuch as the two men traveled in different circles, Paul with the intelligentsia and Peter with the laboring class. Now as a Christian, Paul was eager to come to know Peter along with the other apostles. They, more than any others, could bring him firsthand information about Jesus.

How disappointing it must have been to find upon his arrival in Jerusalem that the laymen of the church were unwilling to associate with him. They had not forgotten his notorious reputation as a murderer of Christians and refused to believe he had changed. Though Paul affirmed he had repented of his evil and had surrendered his life to Christ, they remained skeptical and banned him from their fellowship.

Support from Barnabas

It was then that Barnabas, highly respected in the church and known for his compassion, brought Paul to Peter and James, the half-brother of Jesus and president of the council. Paul remained with them for two weeks before they were will-

---

[3] Paul would certainly have thought of David who had been let down from a window in Jerusalem and fled for his life when threatened by Saul (1 Sam. 19:11, 12). Paul never forgot his humiliating escape from Damascus and includes it at the end of his list of sufferings recorded in 2Cor. 11:23-33.

ing to introduce him to the rest of the Twelve[4]; they wanted time to evaluate him to be sure he had been converted. Finally Paul was brought before the other apostles who were assured by Peter and James that he had indeed become a Christian. Upon hearing this they threw their arms around Paul and welcomed him into their midst. His previous reputation was now no longer important to them; it was what he had become that mattered.

Jesus' first appearance to Paul; Paul sent to the Gentiles

It was while Paul was praying in the temple that he fell into a trance and saw the Lord Jesus, who instructed him to flee Jerusalem because of its hostile Jews. "Go!" Jesus said, "for I will send you far away to the Gentiles" (Ac. 22:21). This was the first time Paul had actually seen the risen Christ and the first time he had received His commission to minister to the Gentiles. Never would he forget the face of Jesus nor His marching orders (vv. 17, 18, 21).[5]

Paul in Paradise

It may also have been during this visit to Jerusalem that Paul experienced his transport into Paradise, of which he informed the Corinthians fourteen years later. Unlike his encounter with Jesus outside the walls of Damascus, the sights and sounds and very words of which he was able to describe years later, his entrance into Paradise[6] was too glorious, too wrapped in holy mystery for him to express in words. Paul even removed his name when telling of it, so unworthy he felt of the sacred experience. "I know a man in Christ," he wrote,

> who fourteen years ago was caught up to the third heaven. Whether it was in the body or out of the body I do not know—God knows. And I know that this man—whether in the body or apart from the body I do not know, but God

---

[4] See Ac. 9:27 and Gal. 1:18, 19. James, Jesus' half brother, though not actually an apostle, was considered as such because of his relationship to Christ and his close association with the other apostles.

[5] See "Jesus' Resurrection Appearances" on p. 292.

[6] The word *paradise* comes from a Persian word meaning "walled-in garden." When a Persian king wished to confer a special honor upon someone, he granted him the right to walk with him in the royal gardens. Paul in much the same way experienced such a privilege when he was invited to visit Paradise. *The Letters to the Corinthians*, William Barclay, p. 288. For discussion on Paul's sharing this experience with the Corinthians, see Chapter 23, "Paul's Heart Revealed" on p. 159.

knows—was caught up to paradise. He heard inexpressible things, things that man is not permitted to tell. (2Cor. 12:2-4).

Paul returns to Tarsus

Paul's vigorous preaching in Jerusalem infuriated the Pharisees and Sadducees, and soon another plot on his life was discovered. Upon learning of it, Paul's friends quickly hurried him out of the city and accompanied him to Caesarea where he was placed on a ship and sent off to Tarsus (Ac. 9:29, 30).[7]

A curtain now descends over the next period of Paul's life, possibly as long as ten years. Though nothing is known of how Paul spent these years except that he went into the regions of Syria and Cilicia (Gal. 1:21), it would be expected that he remained very active in evangelizing. Little did Paul realize that he was being prepared for a ministry far greater than he ever dreamed. It was a ministry that would reach the whole of the Roman empire and eventually the entire world.

---

[7] There is no indication of how Paul was received in his home city. Probably his father, as a Pharisee, had immediately disowned him when Paul became a Christian and never welcomed him home again.

Chapter 6

Antioch, Syria, "Queen of the East"

Antioch, Syria

The great city of Antioch, with an estimated population of 700,000, was located on the northeast corner of the Mediterranean about fifteen miles inland on the broad, navigable river Orontes. It was here that Christians fled after the martyrdom of Stephen and established what became one of the strongest missionary outreaches of the church.

It was not long before zealous Jewish converts from Cyprus and Cyrene came to Antioch and joined with the Christians in an all-out attempt to evangelize the city. As a result many Greeks were converted and added to the church.

Barnabas brings Paul to Antioch

Upon learning of this large Greek influx into the church, the Jerusalem council sent Barnabas to Antioch, about three hundred miles from Jerusalem, to assess the situation. When he found the Gentile believers there very much alive in Christ and saw how hungry they were to be taught more of the gospel, he realized the paramount need for more Christian teachers. It was this that inspired him to travel to Tarsus and find Paul. It would not have been difficult to locate him, for Paul by now would have been well known as a Christian evangelist and a highly respected teacher. If not preaching and teaching in his home city, he would have been ministering in the provinces nearby.

When Paul learned from Barnabas of the great need in Antioch for Christian teachers, he readily accepted the invitation to go with him to Antioch. There then followed for both men a most fruitful ministry that lasted for one year (Ac. 11:26).

"The Queen of the East"

Antioch was founded in 301 B.C. by one of the generals of Alexander the Great, Seleucus Nicator, who named the city after his father Antiochus. In Paul's day the city was a thriving center of trade and commerce and was regarded as "the Queen

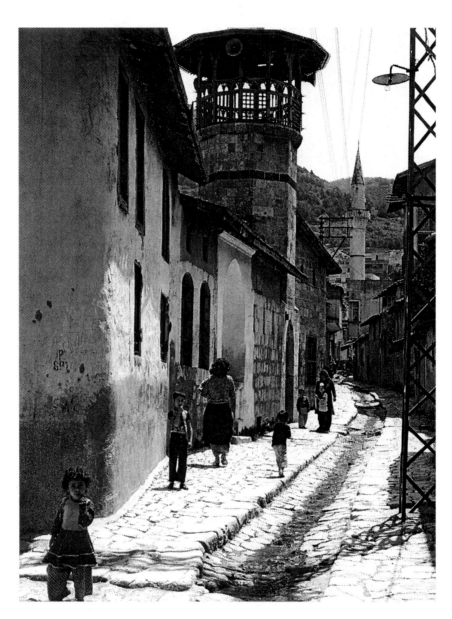

Antioch (Antakya), Syria.

of the East." After Rome and Alexandria, it was the most important city in the empire.

With its excellent location and salubrious climate, Antioch was a haven for aristocrats and *nouveaux riches* as well as thousands of well-to-do. The city's town planning revealed the genius of its architects with a four-and-a-half-mile street through its center flanked by covered colonnades. At right angles along this "Broadway of the ancient world" stretched, on the gridiron principle of Alexandria, miles of streets, some of them paved with marble and lined with temples, public buildings, and markets and spanned by triumphal arches.

The Antiochians' passion for drama and music and sporting events is confirmed by the thousands who regularly attended the theaters and music halls of the city as well as its great amphitheater and popular racetrack. The city was consequently inundated with tipsters, jockeys, actors and dancers and the best of professional athletes.

Though notorious for its licentious and profligate lifestyles, Antioch was considered a religious city. Here, like Athens, were temples of Apollo, Daphne, Artemis and particularly of Jupiter whose giant statue towered on the highest peak of Mt. Silpius, 1,455 feet above and directly behind the city. From its summit could be gained a panoramic view of the expansive metropolis, which at night was a dazzling network of street lighting, one of the most effective and elaborate in the ancient world.

Antioch prided itself on its emancipation from tradition and on its impressive scientific achievements, many of them invented to make life easier.

> An up-to-date man would install an automatic door-opener for the doorkeeper of his house, and a washing machine which delivered water and mineral soap as needed. Outside the temples the priests set up automatic dispensers of holy water, while a water sprinkler operating by water pressure reduced the danger of fire.[1]

Jewish community

In such a city the Jews formed one of the most prosperous communities in the Diaspora and possessed:

> not only civil rights, but also self-government by an elected body similar to the Sanhedrin in Jerusalem. They seemed to have lived on easier terms with the Gentiles than their fellow-Jews in Alexandria, who existed in an atmosphere of intermittent pogroms. In order to show his appreciation for the good will existing

---

[1] *In the Steps of St. Paul*, H. V. Morton, p. 85.

between Gentile and Jew, Herod the Great paved with marble two and a half miles of Antioch's streets, and erected a covered colonnade beneath which the citizens could seek shelter from sun or rain.[2]

Seleucia

Antioch's port, Seleucia, was some fifteen miles from Antioch and connected with a high wall, similar to Athens and its port Piraeus in the fifth century B.C. In order to keep Antioch's bustling port open, Constantine in the year A.D. 338 began excavating through solid rock a conduit more than four thousand feet in length. It was designed to scour the inner port and the waterway by periodically releasing torrents of water from a reservoir high in the mountains. This proved most effective until an earthquake destroyed the conduit. No longer able to be flushed, the harbor soon became choked with mud and eventually had to be abandoned.

Today Seleucia, once the celebrated harbor second to none, is a vast quagmire of swamp grass. Gone are its massive bulwarks which once defied the sea, and gone is the thunder of its traffic and the welter of its many languages. Only the sound of croaking bullfrogs or screeching seagulls on their way out to sea disturb the solemn silence of Seleucia as it slumbers in its grave.

The name Christian coined

It was at Antioch that the followers of Christ were first called "Christians,"[3] a name, however, not originating with the Christians who called themselves followers of the "Way,"[4] "Disciples," "Brethren" or "Saints." The Jews called them "Nazarenes" but never spoke of them as "Christians," since the word embodied the name *Christ* (Messiah) whom the Christians equated with Jesus the Messiah. This the Jews viewed as sheer blasphemy.

Surprisingly, it was the pagans of Antioch known for giving nicknames[5] who coined the word *Christian,* derived from the Greek word *christianos* ("follower of

---

[2] Ibid.

[3] The name *Christian* appears in only two other places in the New Testament: Ac. 26:28 where King Agrippa exclaims to Paul, "In a short time you will persuade me to become a *Christian*"; and in 1Pet. 4:16, where Peter instructs the early followers of Jesus, "if anyone suffers as a *Christian*, let him not feel ashamed, but in that name let him glorify God."

[4] The *Way* is mentioned twice in the book of Acts (9:2; 22:4).

[5] The Antiochians nicknamed Emperor Julian "the goat" because of his long beard; and since he wanted to revive the sacrifices of animals in heathen temples, they also dubbed him "the butcher."

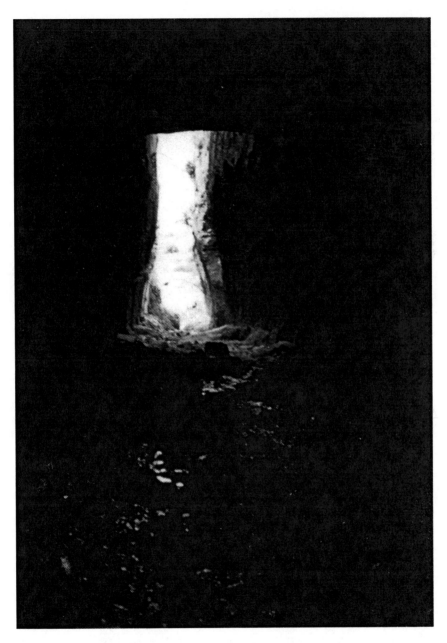

Looking out of the ruined conduit, Seleucia.

Seleucia's filled-up harbor.

Christ"). Because the believers declared they were Christ's followers, they therefore became known by this unique name.

Second Jerusalem visit

During the severe famine in Palestine in the reign of Claudius Caesar, the Christians at Antioch sent Barnabas and Paul with an emergency offering to the brethren in Jerusalem. There the Christians were not only undergoing a critical shortage of food but were also suffering under the harassment of King Herod Agrippa. He had recently beheaded James, the brother of John, the first of the apostles to be martyred. Though Paul was well aware that to remain a prominent spokesman of the Christians was to place his life in jeopardy, there is no evidence that he ever once renounced his call.

Missionary teachers

When Paul and Barnabas, now accompanied by Mark, Barnabas's cousin (Col. 4:10), arrived back from Jerusalem, they were assisted by three teachers: two from Cyrene, Lucius and Simeon; and Manaen, the foster brother of Herod Antipas. To find Manaen, a member of Herod's family, now a teacher of the gospel in Antioch is as astounding as finding Joanna, the wife of Chuza, the steward of Herod Antipas, at the tomb of the Resurrection (Lk. 8:3; 24:10). Very possibly both Manaen and Joanna were converts of John the Baptist while he was imprisoned at Machaerus.

Barnabas and Paul commissioned as missionaries

The church at Antioch, after earnest prayer, was led to choose Barnabas and Paul to be their first foreign missionaries. The fact that the Christians at Antioch were willing to part with these two esteemed leaders, leaves no doubt as to the high priority they placed on obeying the Great Commission (Mt. 28:19, 20).

Chapter 7

Desertion at Perga

First missionary journey

Barnabas and Paul, having been solemnly commissioned as the first foreign missionaries of the church at Antioch, chose young John Mark, the cousin of Barnabas (Col. 4:10), to accompany them. Their first destination was Cyprus, the birthplace of Barnabas, and the third largest island in the Mediterranean. It was 140 miles long and ranged in width from five to sixty miles. Often it was referred to as an "ox-hide flung upon the sea" or as "the island with the long tail." Blessed with a pleasing climate, heavily forested mountains and deep, fertile valleys, it was known as "Makaria" ("the happy one"). The Phoenicians were the first of nine kingdoms to govern it, and in Paul's day it was an imperial province well known for its copper mines and the manufacture of salt. It also served as an important shipbuilding center.

Salamis

Salamis on the east coast was the first city visited and the largest on the island. Here on the Sabbath, as was his custom, Paul entered the synagogue. Though no longer adhering to the Sabbath law, he still maintained an amicable relationship with synagogues wherever he went, for here was an excellent opportunity to proclaim Christ to his own race. Always initially he received a warm welcome as the Jews were eager to listen to itinerant evangelists.

Great numbers of synagogues had been established across the Greco-Roman world, attended not only by Jews but also by Gentiles willing to be circumcised. They were accepted as *bona fide* adherents to the Jewish faith. But there were also other Gentiles, who, though refusing to be circumcised, attended the synagogues. They subscribed to the ethical and moral teachings of Judaism and to its staunch belief in one God. They were known as "God-fearers" or "God-worshippers." With such groups attending the synagogues, Paul was relieved of having to teach

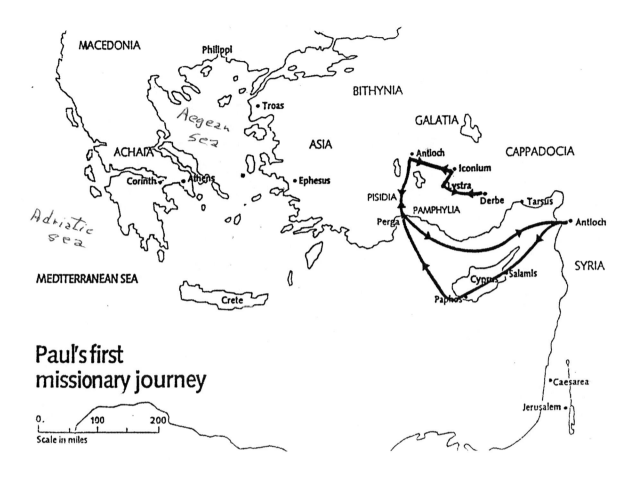

Paul's first
missionary journey

0.   100   200
Scale in miles

the basics of morality and monotheism, and could immediately concentrate on presenting the unique claims of Christ.[1]

Paphos

How long the missionaries ministered in Cyprus is not known, but it appears they were well received until they reached Paphos in the far southwest of the island. Here lived a proconsul by the name of Sergius Paulus, described as a "man of intelligence" who summoned Paul and Barnabas to proclaim to him the Word of God. Obviously the nearby temple of Aphrodite Pandemos with its gross immoralities and shocking orgies had not satisfied him.

---

[1] *The Origin of Paul's Religion*, J. Gresham Machen, pp. 10, 11.

Salamis, Cyprus.

Attending the proconsul was a Jewish sorcerer, Elymas (Bar-Jesus), who, it is not surprising, reacted vehemently against the missionaries' message and did his best to dissuade the proconsul from listening to them. Finally, in utter exasperation, Paul glared at him and rapped out,

> You who are full of all deceit and fraud, you son of the devil, you enemy of all righteousness, will you not cease to make crooked the straight ways of the Lord? And now, behold, the hand of the Lord is upon you, and you will be blind and not see the sun for a time.... (Ac. 13:9-11)

Immediately the startled magician felt a mist and darkness settle over him and realized Paul's words had literally come true. Frantically he pleaded for someone to lead him by the hand. In the meantime, Sergius, deeply impressed by what he had seen, listened more intently than ever to what Paul had to say, and eventually was won to Christ.

This is the first recorded incident of Paul venting his anger in behalf of the gospel; and though he was wrong to have lost his temper, it was quite understandable. Paul's intense desire to minister to the proconsul and his immense annoyance at being obstructed by the obnoxious intruder prompted him to lash out as he did. But it is hard to believe that Paul thought God would strike Elymas blind, and must have been as shocked as the sorcerer was when he lost his sight. How relieved Paul would have been when Elymas again could see!

Paul becomes team leader

Up to this point Barnabas seems to have been in charge of the missionary team, since his name appears first whenever he is mentioned with Paul (Ac. 14:14; 15:12). But after the conversion of Sergius Paulus, the names of Barnabas and Paul are reversed and remain so whenever appearing together, with the exception of when they visited Lystra, and later at the Jerusalem council. Paul definitely had become the new leader.

Mark

The first suggested reference to Mark is found in his own Gospel where he writes of a boy dressed in a linen cloth following Jesus into the Garden of Gethsemane on the night of His betrayal. When an attempt was made to seize the lad and rough hands pulled off his garment, he fled away naked into the night (Mk. 14:51, 52). Since Mark alone records this incident, most probably he was referring to himself.

Mark lived in Jerusalem with Mary, his mother, in whose home the disciples often met (Ac. 12:12). After traveling with Mark back to Antioch, Paul and Barnabas would have come to know him well, and being impressed by his behavior and youthful enthusiasm, subsequently invited him to accompany them on their first missionary journey (13:5).

Attalia and Perga

It appears Mark proved a reliable helper all through Cyprus and gave no indication that he was not happy to be traveling with Paul and Barnabas. Missionary life

The harbor of Attalia backdropped by snow-covered mountains.

he found exhilarating and relatively easy with well-built roads over which to travel and warm hospitality accorded him wherever he went. Cyprus, being the home of Barnabas, had brought him a host of friends and he wanted for nothing.

Sailing out of Paphos the team crossed to Asia Minor and entered the picturesque little harbor of Attalia with its backdrop of silvery-grey mountains reflected in tranquil blue waters. The harbor has remained the same for centuries, a popular haven for small vessels, and is watched over by a quaint little village. How thrilled Mark must have been as he stepped ashore and realized he was soon to explore the exciting interior of Asia Minor, all the way to Antioch, Pisidia!

Viewing the Taurus Mountains from Perga.

Mark deserts

But when Mark reached Perga, sixteen miles inland, his attitude suddenly changed and he refused to go further. Luke offers no reason for Mark's decision, but it appears he had become deeply apprehensive. Doubtless, upon reaching Perga he had heard many harrowing tales of wayfarers who had entered the Taurus Mountains, which loomed just ahead, and through which Paul and Barnabas were planning to travel. Many traveling on this route had been robbed and beaten and some were brutally murdered or never seen again.

Being young and obviously no longer committed to the missionary enterprise, Mark was not willing to risk his life. He lacked the zeal and dedication of Paul and

Barnabas, and knew he would never be able to walk with them to the edge by faith. He had made the wrong decision to team up with them; he knew it. Nothing Paul or Barnabas could say would change his mind. He was determined to go back to Jerusalem and his mother, and it was not long before he was on his way (Ac. 13:13).

Mark's most unexpected desertion at Perga would have shocked Paul and Barnabas who had counted on him to help carry the luggage and lend a helping hand. Now for him to leave, when he was more than ever needed, would have tempted Paul and Barnabas to label him a coward and a veritable traitor. Barnabas especially would have resented Mark's untoward behavior, since, as his cousin, he would doubtless have vouched for his loyalty.

But both Paul and Barnabas were not above prayerfully considering Mark's callow youth and the fact he had come at their invitation obviously with little serious thought of what this might involve, even though Paul and Barnabas would surely have pointed this out. It was apparent now that Mark had become genuinely frightened. He was obviously not emotionally prepared to accompany them further. Paul and Barnabas would readily have sensed this as well as admitting their error in bringing Mark with them. They would not have berated the young man, but rather would have prayed with him and assured him of their love for him. Then they would have fervently committed him to the Lord's care as he started off alone back to Jerusalem.

As for themselves, they had no thought of turning back, remembering the edge-by-faith principle and the words of Jesus: "No one, after putting his hand to the plow and looking back, is fit for the kingdom of God" (Lk. 9:62).

Chapter 8

Shaking Off the Dust

On to Antioch, Pisidia

The 120 miles to Antioch, Pisidia, through the Taurus Mountains required many days of hiking and would have proved one of the most dangerous and difficult journeys Paul had ever attempted. The mountains were steep, the trails rugged and the rivers fast-moving and treacherous to ford. Strabo, Xenophon and Zosimus all relate tales of lawlessness in these mountains, and here Alexander the Great met with some of his stiffest resistance. It must have been this journey among others Paul had in mind when he wrote, years later,

> I have been on frequent journeys, in dangers from rivers, dangers from robbers ... dangers in the wilderness ... through many sleepless nights, in hunger and thirst, often without food, in cold and exposure. (2Cor. 11:26, 27)

Antioch, Pisidia

Upon arriving in Antioch, Paul and Barnabas found it a city built on a plain stretching one hundred miles from Mt. Taurus to Mt. Olympus, and at an altitude of 3,600 feet. Surrounding the city were many crystal lakes noted for wild swans and storks and many other fowl.[1] Even today these charming lakes provide nesting places for thousands of birds.

Antioch was founded in about 300 B.C. and named after Antiochus Epiphines, as were sixteen other cities scattered throughout the empire. The city became a Roman outpost in 6 B.C., and was famous for its temple dedicated to the god Men, an idol with the head of a bull and associated with the fertility goddess Artemis. In Paul's day the official language of the city was Latin and its population comprised Greeks, Jews, Romans and many Phrygians.

Though the bustling city of Antioch, is now replaced by an insignificant village, much of its impressive aqueduct remains. Paul would certainly have walked

---

[1] There are also salt lakes in the area.

Ruined aqueduct, Antioch, Pisidia.

beneath its towering arches and drunk of its cool, clear water. It is not improbable that as he drank from the waterway in the sky he would have been reminded of the Water of Heaven he was bringing to this far-inland, heathen city not yet introduced to the gospel.

Antioch's synagogue

As there were many Jews in the city, Paul and Barnabas rejoiced in the opportunity of meeting them as they assembled in the synagogue on the Sabbath. The square, low-ceiling house of worship faced Jerusalem—a characteristic of all synagogues—and was unadorned and devoid of anything which might resemble an idol. In the front were chairs for rabbis and Pharisees, and behind them, screened off by a curtain, were the sacred scrolls. At the rear of the room was a balcony provided with a lattice, behind which the women worshippers sat. They were forbidden to have any part in the service and were required to be veiled.

The service began with a liturgy that included prayers followed by readings in the Law and the Prophets. These were always read in the original Hebrew and were translated into the local languages. So revered were the Scriptures that before they were expounded, each verse had to be checked by a translator before the next verse was read, lest the Scriptures in any way be altered.

The principal officers, known as *rulers*, were generally the ones who preached and maintained order. Sometimes this reached the point of inflicting scourgings for misbehavior. The rulers were also responsible for giving permission to members of the congregation and to visitors to expound the Scriptures.

When Paul was introduced (probably as a Pharisee) and invited to speak, he rose to his feet, as would a Greek orator, rather than remain seated and speak from his chair, as was the custom of the rabbis. This he did because he was to proclaim the gospel and not the Jewish law. It would certainly have caused considerable murmuring among the orthodox Jews present, who would have insisted that as a Pharisee he remain seated. Luke's comment that Paul motioned with his hand before commencing to preach may very probably have been his attempt to restore order (Ac. 13:16; see 21:40; 26:1).

Justification by faith

Paul began his sermon[2] by tracing the history of the Jewish nation from its days in Egyptian bondage to the era of its kings. He then recounted the origin of Christianity from the birth of John the Baptist to the birth of Christ, whom Paul adamantly pronounced as the promised Messiah and the Son of God risen from the dead. Quoting Habakkuk—"the righteous will live by his faith" (Hab. 2:4)—Paul shocked his audience by declaring that it was only through faith in Christ as the atonement for sin that man can be justified before God.

Here Paul used the language of the law courts, where a judge pronouncing the accused innocent was understood as having him *justified* and restored to society.

> Paul transferred this familiar legal language of Judaism to the personal realm and supremely to the soul's personal relationship to God. He had been seeking [before

---

[2] This is the first extant record of Paul's preaching.

he was converted] strenuously to become acceptable to God (justified) through his meticulous observance of the Law (Torah), which for him embodied the holy will and purpose of God for every aspect of human life. Only through such observance could he meet God's moral requirements and thus be at peace. The more sincere his desire and effort to find peace in this fashion, the less capable he found himself of achieving it. He concluded that no man could find himself in right relationship with God simply by moral striving.[3]

Having stated the above, Paul enthusiastically announced that he had found a completely new way into the presence of God, not dependent on man's moral effort.

God did not expect man by long and arduous ethical struggle to make himself fit for divine acceptance. On the contrary, the act of God in Jesus Christ means that, even while man remains in his sinful state, God manifests his love to him [Rom. 5:7-11], indeed shares his love with him, and thus creates in him a new 'life in the Spirit' in which man walks pleasing to God because he walks in love, partaking of the very nature of God himself. God is not, therefore, a moral judge standing over man with a moral lash and demanding ethical goodness. He is rather a heavenly Father, eager to welcome wandering sons, to confer upon them the gift of his grace, desiring only that they share a new righteousness, his righteousness of love.[4]

Christ Jesus had fulfilled the law and what the law could not do had been done by the gracious action of God in Christ (Rom. 8:1-4).

Such teaching, which completely abrogated the sacrificial system of the Mosaic law and annulled the Levitical priesthood, naturally startled the congregation with the result that nearly the whole city assembled the next Sabbath to hear Paul preach. This would have necessitated in having an outdoor mass assembly (Ac. 13:44). Then followed a succession of Sabbaths with an ever-increasing interest shown in Paul's message, until news of his gospel had spread throughout a large area surrounding the city.

The guardians of the Torah, noting many Jews were turning to Christ, as well as many Gentiles, became alarmed and finally rose up in violent opposition. Supported by Jewish leaders and devout influential Jewish women, they stirred up a persecution against the missionaries and promptly expelled them from the city.

---

[3] *Encyclopaedia Britannica*, vol. 17, 1964. p. 392.

[4] Ibid.

As Paul and Barnabas departed, they obeyed Jesus' instruction to His disciples: "as for those who do not receive you, as you go out from that city, shake off the dust from your feet as a testimony against them" (Lk. 9:5; cf. Mt. 10:14; Mk. 6:11; Lk. 10:10, 11). But though they followed Jesus' instructions, they showed no bitterness toward their antagonists. At the end of Paul's life, when writing to Timothy (2Tim. 3:11), he mentions the persecutions he had suffered at Antioch but again shows no hostility towards his persecutors. Though he had shaken off the dust of his shoes against them, he had not shaken them out of his heart.

Chapter 9

Left for Dead

Iconium

After being driven out of Antioch, Paul and Barnabas traveled to the Greek city of Iconium, about 100 miles southeast of Antioch. It served as the capital of Lycaonia, an independent tetrarchy of fourteen towns encircled by mountains, except on the eastern side where a wide plain stretched as far as the eye could see. Today the city still thrives as a large metropolis with its inhabitants insisting that their city, not Damascus, is the oldest city in the world. Nannacus was one of its earliest kings, and the proverb is still heard, "since the days of Nannacus," meaning "since the beginning of time."

When Paul and Barnabas arrived in Iconium, they went as usual into the synagogue on the Sabbath and proclaimed the gospel. It was not long, as proved true in Antioch, before great numbers of Jews and Gentiles were won to Christ. Paul's ministry had such an impact that the city actually became divided, half siding with the missionaries and half with the Jews and their supporters.

In the hostile group were some who at first were willing to enter into debate with the missionaries but finally lost all patience and began a concerted effort to destroy them. Realizing that the ruling authorities of the city were behind this plot and fearing that to remain might incite a riot accompanied by stoning, Paul and Barnabas decided it was best to leave quietly. Thus they traveled southwest twenty miles to the Roman colony of Lystra[1] where they found people willing to listen to them.

Mythology in Lystra

The people of Lystra, long influenced by Greek mythology, were well acquainted with the legend of Zeus (Jupiter) and Hermes (Mercury) who it was

---

[1] Probably, as in Antioch, the missionaries repeated the ritual of shaking off the dust of their sandals as they departed.

believed had once visited Lystra to see if it was as wicked as reported. While Zeus was on his way to dine with the king of the city, the citizens recognized him as a god and paid him homage. The king, however, not convinced that his guest was a deity, decided to test him to see if he could discern what food he was about to be served.

The menu included the roasted flesh of a messenger who had just arrived at the palace and who had been killed for the main course of the meal. Zeus, however, immediately recognized the feast as cannibalistic and, furious with the king for having tried to deceive him, promptly turned him into a wolf.

Ovid, in his *Metamorphosis,* describes the grisly scene:

> He would have spoke, to speak in vain he tried;
> A savage howl was all the tongue supplied;
> With hungry jaws that gathered foam he churns,
> And on the bleeding flock his fury turns.
> His mantle, now his hide, with rugged hairs,
> Cleaves to his back, a famished face he bears;
> His arms descend, his shoulders sink away,
> To multiply his legs for chase of prey.
> He grows a wolf, and in the wolf you can scan
> The hoariness and rage that mark the man.
> His eyes still sparkle in a narrower space,
> And still a horrid grin distorts the face.[2]

Such was the frightening legend associated with Lystra at whose gates stood the temple of Zeus, the guardian deity of the city.

Since Lystra had few Jews and no synagogue, the missionaries preached wherever they could gain a hearing, and in their audience one day sat a man crippled in both feet from birth. As the man was listening carefully to what Paul was saying, Paul gazed intently at him and, perceiving he had faith to be healed, commanded him to stand up. The invalid, longing to walk and willing to do all he could to help himself, determined to obey. With utmost belief in the possibility of the seemingly impossible, he stretched out his legs to their fullest, then with a surge of faith pulled them back and leapt to his feet and began walking!

---

[2] Ovid, *Metamorphosis* VIII, pp. 626, 627.

Mistaken for gods

When the people of Lystra saw the miracle, they recalled the legend of Zeus and Hermes and shouted in the vernacular, "The gods have come down to us in the likeness of men!" (Ac. 14:11). They compared Barnabas to Zeus, the chief of the gods, perhaps because of his commanding appearance; and Paul to Hermes, the eloquent messenger of the gods, doubtless because of Paul's oratory.

When Paul and Barnabas learned that the Lystrians considered them deities and that the priests in the temple of Jupiter were actually preparing to sacrifice to them oxen decorated with garlands, they tore their outer garments and rushed into the crowd. Vehemently they denied that they were gods, and only after much exhortation did they finally persuade the priests to desist with the sacrifice.

Paul stoned

In the meantime hostile Jews arrived from Iconium and Antioch and began to inveigh against Paul and Barnabas, declaring that indeed the men were not gods but false prophets who ought to be eliminated. The Lystrians soon were convinced and started hurling stones at them. One of them struck Paul with such force that he fell unconscious. The Jews, believing him dead, dragged him outside the walls of the city and left him for the dogs to devour. But Paul, with his disciples gathered around, got up and went back into the city (Ac. 14:20).

The next morning, despite his injuries and severe pain, Paul in the company of Barnabas walked thirty miles to Derbe. To have made this journey so soon after the brutal attack speaks loudly for Paul's incredible stamina. He would let nothing, absolutely nothing, master him (1Cor. 6:12b)!

On to Derbe

Little is known of Derbe except that it was a Lycaonian city, half Greek and half Asian and of some military importance. Gaius lived there and was with Paul on his final journey to Jerusalem. When Paul and Barnabas arrived in Derbe, it was at the height of winter with the ground heaped with snow. It is reasonable to believe therefore that they remained there until spring before deciding to return to their home church in Antioch, Syria.

The direct route via the Cilician Gates was about 260 miles. The missionaries, however, chose to return the same way they had come, visiting on the way Lystra, Iconium, Antioch, Perga and Attalia, and then boarding a ship to their home port.

It was a distance of about 600 miles! Why would Paul and Barnabas have chosen the longer and much more dangerous route when they could easily have traveled the shorter and safer way? This is incomprehensible to the non-Christian world.

But to those who have the burning heart of Paul and Barnabas, and who have walked in their footsteps, the decision to return to their new converts is well understood. More important to the missionaries than their own safety was the welfare of their spiritual children. It was love for them that turned them back, and faith that led the way.

Chapter 10

Peter Rebuked

Third Jerusalem visit

Soon after Paul and Barnabas had returned to Antioch, Syria, some teachers arrived from Judea declaring that unless Gentile Christians were circumcised they could not be saved.[1] Such false teaching, of course, could not be left unchallenged, and the church at Antioch promptly sent Paul, Barnabas and Titus to Jerusalem to obtain from the apostles and elders a firm ruling regarding the requirements for becoming a Christian.

The council

Peter was the first to speak before the council and emphasized that it was by grace alone through faith in Christ that all (both Jews and Gentiles) were saved. This, of course, supported Paul's teaching that Gentile Christians were not required to be circumcised and that those who insisted on this were false teachers (Gal. 2:1-6). Christianity, he vowed, must not be regarded a sect of Judaism, nor Christ only the Messiah of the Jews. Jesus was the Savior of all who believed in Him whether Jew or Greek, bond or free, male or female. Faith in Christ was the only way into the Kingdom of Heaven.

After the council had discussed the matter thoroughly, James, the president, proposed that the apostles and elders draft a letter to the Gentile believers in Antioch and the provinces of Syria and Cilicia, and that it be delivered by Paul and his party. The letter read:

The apostles and elders, your brothers,

---

[1] "The notion of God's love coming to us free of charge, no strings attached, seems to go against every instinct of humanity. The Buddhist eight-fold path, the Hindu doctrine of *karma*, the Jewish covenant, and Muslim code of law—each of these offers a way to earn approval. Only Christianity dares to make God's love unconditional." *What's So Amazing About Grace?* Philip Yancey, p. 45.

To the Gentile believers in Antioch, Syria and Cilicia:

Greetings.

We have heard that some went out from us without our authorization and disturbed you, troubling your minds by what they said. So we all agreed to choose some men and send them to you with our dear friends Barnabas and Paul—men who have risked their lives for the name of our Lord Jesus Christ. Therefore we are sending Judas and Silas to confirm by word of mouth what we are writing. It seemed good to the Holy Spirit and to us not to burden you with anything beyond the following requirements: You are to abstain from food sacrificed to idols, from blood, from the meat of strangled animals and from sexual immorality. You will do well to avoid these things.

Farewell. (Ac. 15:23-29 NIV)

The fact that the council says nothing in its letter regarding circumcision of Christian Gentiles is at first puzzling when it is remembered that one of the major reasons for the Antioch church sending Paul and his company to Jerusalem was to obtain the council's ruling on the matter. But after reviewing the letter, it is clear that the council agreed with Paul and Barnabas and the others that Gentile Christians were not under the law and need not be circumcised.

As for the council forbidding Gentile Christians to eat food sacrificed to idols and to refrain from drinking blood and eating flesh of animals strangled and from committing sexual immorality, this calls for clarification. Why would the council have issued such instructions? And why would Paul and Barnabas and Silas and Judas (Barsabbas) have consented to deliver such instructions to the Gentile Christians in Antioch, Syria, and Cilicia?

First, it is important to remember that the council was in perfect agreement with Paul and his party as to the requirements for becoming a Christian. Paul years later emphasized this when he expressed to the Galatians that the council had nothing more to add to his message (Gal. 2:6).[2]

Second, it is important to remember that many Jewish believers felt that as Jews they were not wrong in continuing to observe ceremonial laws not directly opposed to the spiritual or ethical teachings of Christianity. Paul agreed but forbade these Jewish converts from insisting that Gentile Christians adhere to these laws (Gal. 2:1-5).

---

[2] See *The Origin of Paul's Religion*, J. Gresham Machen, pp. 92, 93.

Further, it should be noted that Jews from birth were taught that Gentiles were not their equals and very much inferior to them. This left the Jewish believers with the perplexing question as to how to work and worship with their Gentile brethren in Christ. The council obviously attempted to solve this problem by instructing the Gentile Christians to abstain from the four things mentioned, which, if participated in, would greatly offend the Jewish believers.

While abstaining from eating food offered to idols and avoiding sexual immorality were in accord with Christian teaching, abstaining from drinking blood and eating flesh from things strangled was definitely not Christian teaching and placed the Gentile believers under the Mosaic law. This Paul would never have countenanced. Then why did he carry the letter with these provisions in it back to the Gentile Christians in Antioch, Syria, and Cilicia?

The query is easily answered when it is pointed out that abstaining from eating flesh of things strangled is most probably *not* in the original text (autographs). According to the "Western text" of the book of Acts, attested by the *Codex Bezae*, Acts 15:28, 29 reads as follows: "For it has seemed good to the Holy Spirit and to us to lay no further burden upon you except these necessary things—that you refrain from things offered to idols and from blood and from fornication, and that you do not do to another whatsoever things you do not wish to be done to you." (Scholars generally agree that the Golden Rule, negative in this case, had been added by a copyist.)

If this "Western text" (*without* "things strangled") is the correct translation, then the provisions of the decree need not be regarded as ceremonial but only as moral. "Things offered to idols" would refer to idolatry in general; "blood" to murder; and "fornication" to all forms of sexual misconduct.

In light of the above it then seems safe to say that the council in Jerusalem had no intention of imposing any Jewish ceremonial laws on their Gentile brothers in Christ, only instructing them morally. In this way both Jewish and Gentile converts would be at one in upholding Christian principles.

The arrival of Peter in Antioch

Soon after Paul had returned to Antioch, he was followed by Peter, who must have told him in Jerusalem of his plan to come. Paul of course counted on him to renounce the Judaizers' false teachings and to stress that Christians, no matter whether Jew or Gentile, were one in Christ. They were free to dine together and could eat anything they wished in accord with Jesus' teaching that all foods were clean (Mk. 7:19; refer to 1Cor. 10:25; Rom. 14:14, 20; 1Tim. 4:2-4).

It should be stressed here again that Jews had long been reared in the belief that Gentiles were their inferiors, and the thought of eating with them therefore was quite unthinkable. The Gentiles also ate many foods strictly forbidden by Mosaic law, and this included pork, considered by Gentiles a delicacy, but by Jews the most detested of all meats. Jews never mentioned the pig by name but referred to it as *dabhar acheer*, "the other thing."

Pirke Rabbi Liezer vehemently exclaimed, "He who eats with an uncircumcised person eats, as it were, with a dog; he who touches him touches, as it were, a dead body; and he who bathes in the same place with him bathes, as it were, with a leper."[3]

Peter and Barnabas rebuked

With this in mind, Peter, upon arrival in Antioch, was unwilling to eat with the Gentile believers. His reason was that he did not want to offend the strict Jewish Christians who insisted on Jews and Gentiles dining separately (Gal. 2:11, 12). Paul, as would be expected, was shocked at Peter's withdrawal and even more so by Barnabas's who followed Peter's example (v. 13). Barnabas, known as a devoted evangelist to the Greeks, and having worked closely with Paul in their ministry to the Gentiles, had never once shown any evidence of segregating himself from Gentiles. Paul, therefore, felt he had no choice but to speak out against him as well as against Peter.

First, he followed Jesus' instruction and reproved Peter in private (Mt. 18:15-17), but not finding him repentant, criticized him openly before the whole church (Gal. 2:11-14). This was surely one of the hardest things Paul ever felt led to do, but when it was a matter of defending the Christian doctrine of oneness in Christ, he could not remain silent.

Peter, it appears, admitted he was wrong and held no resentment towards Paul for rebuking him. Indeed, later Peter referred to Paul as "our beloved brother Paul" (2Pet. 3:15). Though Peter found in Paul's letters "some things hard to understand" (v. 16), he viewed his writings just as inspired as those of the Old Testament.

---

[3] *The Life and Work of St. Paul*, Frederic W. Farrar, vol. 1, p. 282.

It is significant that Luke records nothing of Paul's harsh criticism of Peter and Barnabas, and had Paul not mentioned it in his letter to the Galatians, the incident would never have been known. Probably Luke felt that since Peter (and probably Barnabas) had repented publicly for his un-Christian behavior, it would be both un-Christian and unnecessary to include the shameful matter in his chronicle.

Chapter 11

Called at the Edge

Paul and Barnabas separate

A few years after returning from Asia Minor, Paul was ready to embark on another missionary journey and would have traveled again with Barnabas, had Barnabas not insisted upon taking Mark. Obviously Barnabas was convinced that Mark had truly repented for having turned back at Perga and from now on could be trusted completely.

But Paul refused to travel with him again, and nothing that Barnabas could say would change his mind. Finally, in sharp disagreement the two leaders separated, Barnabas departing with Mark for Cyprus and Paul remaining in Antioch until a replacement for Barnabas could be found. No more is heard of Barnabas except in two references where Paul mentions his name in discussing the right of Christian workers to be supported by churches they represent (1Cor. 9:6; Gal. 2:9).

Though Paul has been criticized for not giving Mark a second chance to accompany him, Paul's decision was not a matter of not forgiving Mark but simply a matter of not accepting him as a co-worker at this time. Paul was predominantly "people-oriented," always thinking of evangelizing the masses and hence not willing to have anyone accompany him who was not of the same mind. Barnabas, on the other hand, in this situation was "person-oriented," thinking more of not offending his cousin by leaving him behind than of the fields white for harvest. Even at the risk of Mark deserting again, Barnabas insisted that he be allowed on the team.

Mark in later years

If Mark, as it appears, was not a Christian when he left Paul and Barnabas at Perga, then in all probability it was Peter who won him to Christ. Peter refers to him as "my son" (1Pet. 5:13). Eventually Mark was reconciled with Paul and was with him in Rome when he wrote to the Colossians (4:10). Paul calls him his "fellow worker" in his letter to Philemon (1:24); and in Paul's last letter, while awaiting his execution, he requests Timothy to bring Mark back to Rome, "for he is useful to me for service" (2Tim. 4:11).

Eventually Mark emerged as one of the chief evangelists of the early church and, according to many biblical scholars, was believed to be the first of the four Gospel writers to record many of the events in Christ's life and ministry. Mark was so highly respected by both Matthew and Luke that both evangelists incorporated much of what he had written into their own Gospels. This must not be seen as plagiarism as both writers of course would have gained permission from Mark to duplicate his material.

Mark's character should never be judged by his one-time defection at Perga, but rather assessed after a review of his life. Such a study reveals him anything but pusillanimous. According to tradition, he was one of the bravest Christian leaders of the first century and became the first bishop of Alexandria, Egypt. After years of serving his Lord there in a very hostile environment, he finally was martyred for his faith.

Silas replaces Barnabas

Paul's replacement for Barnabas was Silas, known also as Silvanus. He was a Roman citizen and a prominent member of the church in Jerusalem. Luke always refers to him as "Silas," while Paul in his letters knows him as "Silvanus."

The church at Antioch approved of Paul's choice and committed the two missionaries to the grace of the Lord before they embarked for Asia Minor (Ac. 15:40). Nothing, however, is recorded of the church commissioning Barnabas and Mark before they set sail for Cyprus. Whether Barnabas and Mark were successful in evangelizing Cyprus is not known.[1]

Second missionary journey

Paul's journey this time did not include Cyprus, doubtless because of the recent disagreement with Barnabas. Paul probably reasoned it was best to let Barnabas and Mark evangelize the island alone.

---

[1] According to tradition, Barnabas was martyred in Cyprus and buried in Salamis.

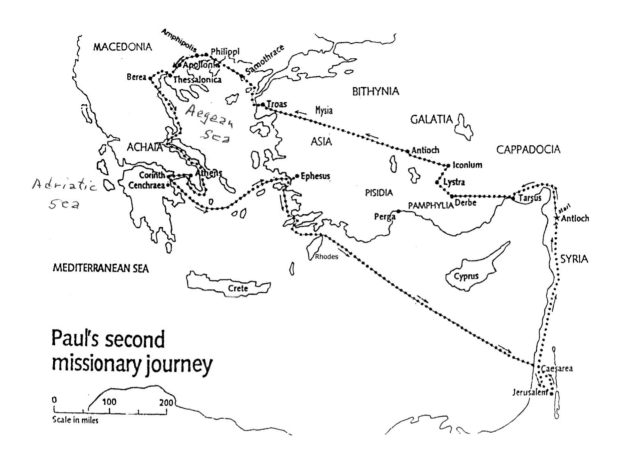

Paul's second
missionary journey

0   100   200
Scale in miles

Timothy replaces Mark

The route Paul and Silas chose was overland to Tarsus, and then via Derbe to Lystra, where they met Timothy who lived with his mother, Eunice, and grandmother, Lois, both of whom were Jewesses converted to Christianity. Timothy's Gentile father, it appears, had died. Paul on his first missionary journey had doubtless been instrumental in Timothy's conversion as he speaks of him as his "true child in the faith" (1Tim. 1:2)[2] and as his "beloved son" (2Tim. 1:2). To the Philippians he declares "I have no one like him" (Phil. 2:20).

---

[2] Paul circumcised Timothy to prevent his offending the Jews to whom he would be witnessing.

Finding now that Timothy was well versed in the Scriptures through the teaching of his godly mother and grandmother, and that he had become a strong Christian, Paul invited him to replace Mark and travel with him. The fact that Timothy accepted the challenge speaks well for his courage for he would have realized that to travel with Paul, known for his vigorous and often controversial preaching, could easily result in bitter persecution or even the loss of his life. Timothy would not have forgotten Paul's first visit to Lystra and how his preaching there had stirred up the crowds and ended in Paul's brutal stoning to the point where his body was dragged out of the city and left for dead (Ac. 14:19).

Though Timothy, it appears, was not physically robust and was often ill (1 Tim. 5:23), he was anything but weak spiritually. Paul depended heavily upon him and included his name in the salutation of six of his thirteen letters.[3]

Thwarted south and north

Departing from Lystra, Paul, Silas and Timothy returned to the Christian communities at Iconium and probably at Antioch, Pisidia, and would have preached in the sprawling province of Asia had they not been forbidden by the Holy Ghost (Ac. 16:6). Here were many great cities, among them Sardis, Philadelphia, Smyrna and Ephesus. Luke never intimates why they were not allowed to enter this fruitful field, but Paul and his companions accepted it without question as the will of God.

It was now that they must have entered the northern parts of Galatia with the intention of reaching its tribes with the Good News. There Paul contracted a serious illness and was slowly nursed back to health by the warm-hearted Galatians. It was during this time of convalescence that Paul planted the gospel in their hearts and established a strong community of believers.

The nature of Paul's malady is not known but appears, from his letter to the Galatians written months later, to have affected his eyesight. "As you know," he wrote,

> it was because of an illness that I first preached the gospel to you. Even though my illness was a trial to you, you did not treat me with contempt or scorn. Instead, you welcomed me as if I were an angel of God, as if I were Christ Jesus himself.... I can testify that, if you could have done so, you would have torn out your eyes and given them to me. (Gal. 4:13-15 NIV)[4]

---

[3] 2 Corinthians, Philippians, Colossians, 1 and 2 Thessalonians and Philemon.
[4] See pp. 160-62 for further discussion of Paul's maladies.

The silted-up harbor of Troas.

When Paul had recovered, he, Silas and Timothy proceeded on to the borders of the province of Mysia. From here they decided to go north into the province of Bithynia with its thriving cities of Nicaea, Nicomedia and Chalcedon, and those along the Black Sea, but again "the Spirit of Jesus did not permit them" (Ac. 16:7).

On to Troas

Where now to proceed? Back to the home church in Antioch where they knew awaited them a fruitful and growing ministry, or onward in pioneering faith as far as they could go? They chose to adhere to the edge-by-faith principle and continue

Buried Troas.

traveling west until they had reached the city of Troas on the edge of the Aegean Sea.

Troas, first known as Troas Antigonia in honor of its founder, bore its name for 330 years. Then its name was changed to Troas Alexander in honor of Alexander the Great. The city's harbor was one of the finest on the west coast of Asia Minor and was frequently crowded with ships sailing to and from Macedonia. No one in Paul's day would have imagined that such an important port would ever be closed, but today all that remains of it is a shrunken basin choked with sand. Most of Troas remains buried with only a few of its grey, granite pillars protruding from the earth—silent sentinels of its past.

It was at Troas that Paul and Luke first met and formed a strong friendship which continued to the end of Paul's life. Luke was a highly educated Greek physician and a devout Christian, and may well have been the one who planted the church at Troas, which seems to have been in existence when Paul and his company arrived. How long the missionaries remained in Troas is not known, but however long, one may be sure Paul, Silas and Timothy, working with Luke, would have been very active in missionary work.

When Paul, living by his edge-by-faith principle, arrived at the busy port of Troas, he may have believed that this was where God wanted him to minister and remain. But it is much more probable that Paul believed God would call him over into the unevangelized fields of Macedonia. With this in mind he must often have strolled the beaches alone, focusing his attention on the far-off horizon and yearning to hear God's call to cross over into Macedonia and start proclaiming the gospel.

The Macedonian call

Then one night, while Paul slept, God spoke to him in a vision and showed him a man standing in the moonlight on the far-off shore of Greece calling out, "Come over to Macedonia and help us" (Ac. 16:9). The call was so vivid and personal, so compelling and urgent that Paul had no doubt that God had called him over into Greece.

In the morning he shared his vision with his companions who all agreed that it was Paul's divine call to Macedonia. As fellow missionaries, they assured him they would enthusiastically accompany him and were willing to set sail whenever he was ready. Luke was among them willing to go as indicated by his use of the first per-

Sailing across the Aegean from Troas.

son plural in his chronicle, "we sought to go into Macedonia, concluding that God had called us to preach the gospel to them" (Ac. 16:10).

Troas will always be remembered not only as the launching place for the first Christian missionaries to Europe, but as the place where Brutus, the great republican, and Paul, the great apostle, spent the night before embarking on their respective missions.

Brutus

According to legend, in the year 42 B.C. Brutus was alone in his tent on the eve of his departure to join Cassius on the plains of Philippi in the struggle against the triumvirate.[5] While brooding over the forthcoming conflict, suddenly Brutus was approached by an apparition. "What are you, of men or of the gods, and upon what business are you come?" demanded the startled general. "I am your evil genius," came the reply, "and you shall see me again at Philippi."[6]

The next day outside Philippi the scheduled battle took place, with Brutus scoring victory over Octavius but with Cassius yielding before Antony. Believing all was lost, Cassius covered his face in his tent and commanded his freedmen to strike the fatal blow.[7] Three weeks later Brutus's army too was routed, and Brutus, likewise unwilling to accept defeat, committed suicide.[8]

---

[5] The members of the triumvirate were M. Aemilius Lipidus, Mark Antony and Octavius.

[6] Shakespeare, *Julius Caesar*, Act 4, Scene 3.

[7] *The Life and Letter of St. Paul*, W. J. Conybeare and J. S. Howson, p. 237.

[8] Among many other suicides linked with biblical and ancient history were: King Saul (1Sam. 31:4), Ahithopel (2Sam. 17:23), Abimelech (Judg. 9:54), Samson (Judg. 16:30), Saul (1Sam. 31:4), Zimri (1Ki. 16:18), Judas (Mt. 27:5). Mark Antony after believing false reports that Cleopatra had died; Cleopatra fearing capture, allowing an asp to sting her to death; Pontius Pilate, according to tradition, leaping into a fiery volcano; brothers Gallio and Seneca (see p. 245, fn. 4).

Chapter 12

The Lady from Thyatira

Neapolis via Samothrace

The voyage from Troas to Neapolis (Kavalla), the port of Philippi, required in good weather only one day, but Paul's voyage required two days. This may have been because of inclement weather or more probably because Paul and his companions spent a day on the island of Samothrace, perhaps visiting friends of Luke or just to relax and explore the island.

Samothrace, once under the mercantile empire founded by the Phoenicians and inherited by the Athenians and later the Romans, was thirty miles square and boasted the highest mountain (except Mt. Athos) in the north Aegean (5,240 feet). From its summit Virgil, in his *Iliad* (xiii, 12) represents Poseidon surveying the plains of Troy some one hundred miles distant. Because of its mountainous terrain and absence of large harbors, Samothrace never proved politically important, though always enjoying autonomy probably because of its fervent worship of the Cabeiri and other idols.

It was on Samothrace, ca. 305 B.C., that Demetrius Poliorcetes, the "Taker of Cities," set up his celebrated statue, the "Victory of Samothrace," known also as the "Winged Victory," and which was discovered, still on the island, in 1863.[1] Whether Paul viewed the headless, marble image, or had any interest in seeing it, is not known, but it is highly unlikely. This would be because of his Jewish background and inherent aversion to anything associated with idols.

Alexander the Great

As the dawn seeped into the sky the next morning and Paul's ship neared Neapolis, Philippi's harbor, thoughts of Alexander the Great must have coursed through Paul's mind. It was in 333 B.C. in Macedonia that Alexander was born and at the early age of twenty began his phenomenal career. Paul would certainly have been

---

[1] The statue is now in the Louvre in Paris.

Neapolis (Kavalla), Philippi's port.

familiar with his eventful life and well aware of his desire to "marry the East with the West." Alexander's dream was to establish a common currency and international market, to promote the Greek language worldwide and, above all, to establish universal peace. His dream was rapidly being fulfilled when suddenly in Babylon at the young age of thirty-two he died, possibly from disease (some conjecture malaria) or from poison at the hand of an enemy. This left his vast empire to be divided among his four generals, Cassander, Lysimachus, Ptolemy, and Seleucus.[2]

---

[2] Alexander's empire included Macedonia, Thrace, Egypt and the whole of the Seleucid kingdom. Wherever Alexander's armies went the Greek language and all aspects of life in a Greek state were taught. Schools, libraries, gymnasiums and open-air theaters were built, and many of the subjugated people adopted Greek dress and used Greek names.

Alexander's vision of uniting mankind and breaking down the barriers between Jew and Greek, bond and free, and male and female and to raise the moral and living standards of the world would all have met with the hearty approval of Paul. He too decried discord and divisions and particularly among those who claimed to be Christians.

But Alexander's concept of peace and that of Paul's were totally different. Alexander's peace was but an earthly peace maintained by the sword, while Paul's peace was spiritually oriented and sustained by the Spirit. It was a peace unknown to the pagan world, the peace of the Holy Spirit which Jesus had promised to all who would believe in Him (Jn. 14:27).

Philippi

Philippi now was the missionaries' next destination as they traveled inland twelve miles along the great Egnatian Way. Philippi was founded in 385 B.C. by Philip of Macedonia, father of Alexander the Great. The original name of the city was Crenides, meaning "The Fountains" or "The Springs," because of the numerous springs in the area. Philip, however, egotistically named each fountain after himself, with the result that soon the city was known as *Philippi*—Philip in the plural!

After the defeat of Brutus, Augustus bestowed upon the city the privilege of being a *colonia* which exempted its colonists from all poll and property taxes and allowed them to become Roman citizens. Latin was generally spoken and Roman dress observed. The city's coinage was inscribed in Latin rather than Greek so as to distinguish it from coins of Greek cities. More than half of Philippi was Latin by race and aped Rome in its worship of Diana, Dionysus, and Silvanus. The remaining population was of Macedonian stock with a sprinkling of other nationalities.

Philippi at this time had but few Jews, most of them women; and since Jewish law required a minimum of ten Jewish men before a synagogue could be built, the small Jewish community worshipped by a riverside.[3] Such places for Jewish worshippers deprived of synagogues were known as *proseuchas* (gathering places), and generally these were by a river or by the sea.

---

[3] This would be the Gangites River which flows one mile west of the ruins of Philippi.

The Egnatian Way to Philippi.

Lydia

Here on the Sabbath Paul and his fellow missionaries found a group of Jews, among them a woman named Lydia from Thyatira in Asia Minor. It is believed she was a widow who had migrated to Philippi to continue her husband's trade. This was the selling of cloth dyed in the coveted purple fluid from the murex sea snail found on the beaches of Tyre. This dye was highly prized by the Romans, especially for coloring the hems of their togas[4]; Lydia's business would surely have been flourishing.

---

[4] A pound of wool dyed in this purple liquid could sell for as much as $80.

The Gangites River outside Philippi.

As Paul shared the gospel week after week with this little group, the Lord opened Lydia's heart and she became a Christian (Ac. 16:14). After Paul baptized her and the believers in her household, she invited the four missionaries to reside in her home. At first they declined, doubtless feeling it would be an imposition to accept such hospitality, but upon perceiving how sincere she was in wanting them, they finally consented. It was out of this fellowship that grew the strong house church of Philippi which was to prove one of Paul's most missionary-minded congregations and which was to remain very dear to his heart to the end of his life.

Paul's letter to the Philippians, written from prison in Rome, clearly reveals how much Paul loved the Philippians as well as showing how much they in turn loved him and of their willingness to support him.

The Gangites River; Lydia was baptized here.

Paul and Timothy, servants of Christ Jesus,

To the saints in Christ Jesus at Philippi, together with the overseers and deacons:

Grace and peace to you from God the Father and the Lord Jesus Christ.

I thank my God every time I remember you. In all my prayers for all of you, I always pray with joy because of your partnership in the gospel from the first day until now....

It is right for me to feel this way about all of you, since I have you in my heart; for whether I am in chains or defending and confirming the gospel, all of you share in God's grace with me. God can testify how I long for all of you with the affection of Christ Jesus. (Phil. 1:1-8 NIV)

Yet it was good of you to share in my troubles. Moreover, as you Philippians know, in the early days of your acquaintance with the gospel, when I set out from Macedonia, not one church shared with me in the matter of giving and receiving, except you only; for even when I was in Thessalonica, you sent me aid again and again when I was in need. Not that I am looking for a gift, but I am looking for what may be credited to your account. I have received full payment and even more; I am amply supplied, now that I have received from Epaphroditus the gifts you sent me. They are a fragrant offering, an acceptable sacrifice, pleasing to God. (4:14-18)

Women always worked closely with Paul wherever he went; they were an integral part of his ministry. Their names abound throughout his epistles: Lydia in Philippi; Priscilla in Corinth, Ephesus and Rome; Chloe in Corinth; Phoebe in Cenchrea; and Nymph and Apphia in Colossae. Nearly one-third of the twenty-eight Christians, to whom Paul sends greetings in the last chapter of his letter to the Romans, are women (Rom. 16:1-16).

It is significant to note that it was a man who called Paul into Macedonia, but a woman who first believed the gospel in Europe. Noteworthy, too, is the fact that though the Great Commission was first given to men, women have been the most effective in spreading the gospel to the world. "The Lord gives the command; the women who proclaim the good tidings are a great host ..." (Ps. 68:11).

Chapter 13

Terror at Midnight

The pytho

As Paul and his companions continued week after week to share the gospel with Lydia and her friends at the riverside, they were frequently confronted on the way by a demon-possessed girl who hysterically cried out, "These men are bond-servants of the Most High God, who are proclaiming to you the way of salvation" (Ac. 16:17). The girl was being used as a fortune-teller by unscrupulous men to gain large revenues from her soothsaying. She was thought to be imbued with the spirit of Python, a huge serpent famous in Greek mythology for predicting the future. The god Apollo was believed to have slain this reptile but its spirit, Pythias, continued to possess people; anyone who claimed to predict the future was thought to be empowered by it. The demented girl was thus known as a *pytho*.

Paul recognized that the girl had a spirit of divination and was quite helpless to control herself. Not wanting the way of salvation to be associated with her rantings, he finally felt led to command the demon in the name of Jesus to come out of her. Immediately it departed and the girl was restored to her right mind.

Thrown into prison

The masters of the pytho, realizing that the girl was no longer under their control and had been influenced by the preaching of the missionaries, angrily seized Paul and Silas and dragged them through the marketplace to the chief magistrates. There the two missionaries were accused of throwing the city into confusion and teaching customs unlawful for Romans to observe. Though the allegations were vague and unsubstantiated, the magistrates ordered the lictors to beat Paul and Silas with heavy rods and then throw them into the inner cell of the city's prison. This windowless dungeon, from which it was impossible to escape, was used as maximum security for high-risk criminals and those awaiting execution. Here the legs of Paul and Silas were locked in stocks fastened to the floor and very probably their necks clamped and their bodies twisted into agonizing positions.

But Paul and Silas, though tortured and confined to such foul quarters, were convinced that nothing occurs but by the direct or permissive will of God. All things, the good and the bad, they believed "work together for good to those who love God and are the called according to His purpose" (Rom. 8:28). It was with this conviction that they started to pray and sing hymns. That they could do this after their brutal beating must have astounded their fellow prisoners who were listening. What was the secret of the valor of these two inmates and who was it that they were extolling? (Ac. 16:25).[1]

The earthquake

When the midnight hour had been reached, presumably under a full moon, and while Paul and Silas were praising God, suddenly a violent earthquake shook the prison and tore all the chains from the walls. Every prisoner was loosed from his shackles and all gates swung open.

The jailer, jolted from sleep and not waiting for a torch, rushed to the dungeons nearby only to find to his horror all the cells unlocked. Hearing no sounds from within, he immediately concluded that all his prisoners had fled and knowing by law he would be held responsible for their escape and required to pay with his life, drew out his sword to commit suicide.

Jailer converted and baptized

But Paul, realizing the jailer's intention, shouted out, "Do yourself no harm, for we are all here!" (Ac. 16:28).[2] Startled, the jailer sheathed his weapon and called for torches, then upon seeing Paul and Silas unshackled and standing before him, trembled and fell at their feet. Only a few hours before he had confidently looked down at them locked in their stocks; now they were confidently looking down at him!

---

[1] It is mentioned that the prisoners were "listening" to Paul and Silas. The word *listen* connotes listening with pleasure. *The Great Physician*, G. Campbell Morgan, p. 362.

[2] The fact that the other prisoners remained in their cells and made no attempt to escape or to harm the jailer can be attributed only to the powerful influence exerted over them by Paul and Silas. The missionaries must have convinced the prisoners that the God of the Christians was all-powerful, and believing this the prisoners were willing to remain in their cells and trust Him.

But sensing Paul and Silas were men of another kind—men who exuded love and compassion, he soon was on his feet leading them out into the night. There in the moonlight he looked earnestly into their faces and asked the searching question, "Sirs, what must I do to be saved?" (Ac. 16:30). "Believe in the Lord Jesus, and you shall be saved, you and your household ..." (v. 31), came the reply. Eager to know what this meant, the jailer invited the missionaries to his home and there he and his family were taught the way of salvation. Soon, under the conviction of the Holy Spirit, they surrendered their lives to Christ and, after treating the wounds of Paul and Silas, all were baptized.[3]

Refusal to leave

In the morning the chief magistrates learned to their consternation, probably from Luke and Timothy, that Paul and Silas were Roman citizens. Since the citizenship law forbade upon pain of death the beating of Roman citizens, the judges quickly ordered the missionaries released. But Paul and Silas refused to leave, insisting that the magistrates first come and explain their unlawful behavior.

Afraid that the incensed men might report them for having flogged them illegally, the magistrates rushed to the prison and explained that had they known Paul and Silas were Roman citizens, they would never have ordered them whipped. Earnestly they begged them to forgive them and to leave quietly. But Paul and Silas, their backs ripped into shreds and still throbbing with pain, were in no mood to accept their apologies. Let the magistrates agonize over having flogged Roman citizens and then let them tremble as they contemplated the dreadful consequences.

But why did Paul and Silas not announce at the outset their citizenship status? Was it not to protect Luke and Timothy who were not Roman citizens? Had it become known that Paul and Silas were exempt from beatings, then their copartners might well have been seized and whipped in their stead. The fact that Paul and Silas were willing to suffer in behalf of their co-partners is of course commendable and a clear example of Christian love. But how disappointing to find such love lacking in their dealings with the magistrates.[4]

---

[3] Baptism here was doubtless performed by effusion as there probably would have been no way to immerse.

[4] How differently Jesus would have reacted under the same circumstances! (See 1Pet. 2:23 and Lk. 23:34.)

Amphitheater at Philippi.

Five years later when Paul described the attributes of Christian love in his letter to the Corinthians, he must have been ashamed to remember how he had dealt with the terrified magistrates.

"Love is patient," Paul wrote. "[L]ove is kind ... not arrogant, does not act unbecomingly, does not seek its own, is not provoked, does not take into account a wrong suffered ..." (1Cor. 13:4, 5). Beautiful words from the pen of Paul—not hard to write, but often so hard to practice!

Chapter 14

"Upsetting the World"

Amphipolis and Apollonia

Leaving Luke to oversee the infant house church at Philippi,[1] Paul, Silas and Timothy started out for the free city of Thessalonica, one hundred miles southwest. They followed the great Egnatian Way and passed through Amphipolis and Apollonia, cities which had long since passed their prime. Though no mention is made of Paul ministering in either of them, it would be unlike him not to have spent some time with their people and to have familiarized himself with the history of their cities.

Amphipolis, the more interesting of the two, was founded in the fifth century B.C. and was located on the river Strymon. The city was dependent for her life on the large deposits of gold nearby on Mt. Pangaeus. Nine major thoroughfares converged on the city prompting her to be known as "Nine Ways."

Then came the sad day when the gold mines were exhausted and the city was no longer a commercial hub. Business houses closed and the streets became empty as steadily the city was by-passed. It then changed its name to "Roundabout Town."

Finally, after being successively conquered by Spartans, Macedonians and Romans, the forlorn city once again altered its name, this time to *Amphipolis,* "a city pressed on all sides." Paul must often have referred to it as a tragic example of depending on riches laid up on earth.

Thessalonica

Thirty-seven miles south was the bustling port city of Thessalonica, known also as Salonica, with half of its population of 200,000, Jewish. Back-dropped by the

---

[1] Luke did not rejoin Paul until seven years later in Philippi on Paul's third missionary journey (Ac. 20:6). He then remained with him for the rest of Paul's life.

Thessalonica (Salonica), "the mother of all Macedonia."

mystic grandeur of Mt. Olympus, the fabled home of the gods, it was the largest city Paul was yet to visit.

Originally named Therma for the hot springs in its environs, it was completely destroyed by Cassander in 421 B.C. He then rebuilt it and changed its name to Thessalonica in honor of his wife. She was the daughter of Philip of Macedon and the stepsister of Alexander the Great.

In 42 B.C. Antony and Augustus made it a free city with a resident Roman pro-consul and the privilege of electing its own magistrates, known also as *politarchs*. It became a great center of commerce by land and sea and was heralded as "the mother of all Macedonia."[2]

---

[2] *Paul and His Epistles.* D. A. Hayes, p. 139.

Paul's self-reliance

Paul throughout his ministry insisted that he and his co-workers earn their own living and not be dependent on others for their livelihood. With this in mind, the first thing Paul did upon arriving in Thessalonica was to look for work. Since the Thessalonians were renown for manufacturing coarse cloth for tents and since Paul was a professional tentmaker, he would have had little difficulty in finding employment.

Paul stressed the principle of self-reliance to his converts in Thessalonica when he wrote them some months later from Corinth:

> Make it your ambition to lead a quiet life, to mind your own business and to work with your hands, just as we told you, so that your daily life may win the respect of outsiders and so that you will not be dependent on anybody. (1Thess. 4:11, 12 NIV)

From this it is clear that Paul strongly opposed the custom of plebeians (the lower classes) becoming clients of wealthy patrician patrons and living on their daily doles.[3] This "hand-out mentality" was abhorrent to Paul. "[I]f anyone will not work," he exclaimed, "neither let him eat" (2Thess. 3:10).

Persecution arises

Following his custom, Paul first visited the synagogue and preached for three Sabbaths, with the result that some of the Jews and a large number of God-fearing Greeks and leading women of the city were deeply moved by his message. But the rulers of the congregation reacted quite to the contrary and soon forbade Paul to continue preaching in the synagogue. This forced him to turn to the Gentiles who were eager to listen to him.

How long Paul remained in the city is not known, but he stayed long enough to build up a sizable following. Paul insisted that he was bringing the gospel "not simply in words, but with power, and with the Holy Spirit and with deep conviction" (1Thess. 1:5 NIV).

But the antagonistic Jews rounded up some bad characters from the market place and formed a rowdy mob and started a riot in the city (Ac. 17:5). Rushing to the house of Jason, where it was thought Paul, Silas and Timothy were staying, they searched it diligently, but all in vain; the missionaries had disappeared. Frus-

---

[3] See Chapter 34, "Rome's Glitter and Gore" on p. 233.

trated to the extreme, they dragged Jason and some of the brethren before the city authorities and shouted, "These men who have upset the world have come here also and Jason has welcomed them, and they all act contrary to the decrees of Caesar, saying that there is another king, Jesus" (vv. 6, 7). After carefully questioning Jason, but finding him ignorant of the missionaries' whereabouts, the magistrates released him on bail with the understanding he would cause no trouble. What became of him is not known.

Disturbing the status quo

Though Paul never openly spoke against the laws of the state and when dealing with the laws of Moses sought only to expound them, the Jews were correct in saying that Paul's preaching was disrupting. It did upset the status quo. People could not remain the same once they had listened to him. "He was a volcano of a man and his words sometimes flowed like molten lava."[4] From the beginning of his ministry on the streets and in the synagogues of Damascus, Paul was an *edge-by-faith* agitator for Christ. He called for a verdict and revolutionized men's relationships, not only with God but with one another. His teachings established the sacredness of marriage and emphasized the equal rights of men and women. The ethical stress of his high moral pronouncements hewed at the very roots of slavery, avarice and corruption. City after city was visibly stirred soon after he entered, and remained disturbed long after he departed. Paul was not content merely to exhibit the facets of Christian doctrine, turning the gem of the gospel for the pagan world to examine. He wanted more than to convey truth; he wanted to convert to truth.

Berea

The believers, alarmed at what was happening, secretly hurried Paul, Silas and Timothy out of the city at night and traveled with them sixty miles southwest to the little town of Berea. Here they knew were Jewish friends who were noted for their daily study of the Scriptures and who would be only too glad to receive the missionaries. Paul would have been asked to expound the Messianic prophecies,[5] and with his thorough knowledge of the Scriptures and years of formulating Christian doctrine, it is not surprising many of the Bereans were won to Christ.

---

[4] *The Character of Paul*, Charles Jefferson, p. 140.
[5] See "Messianic Prophecies" on p. 290.

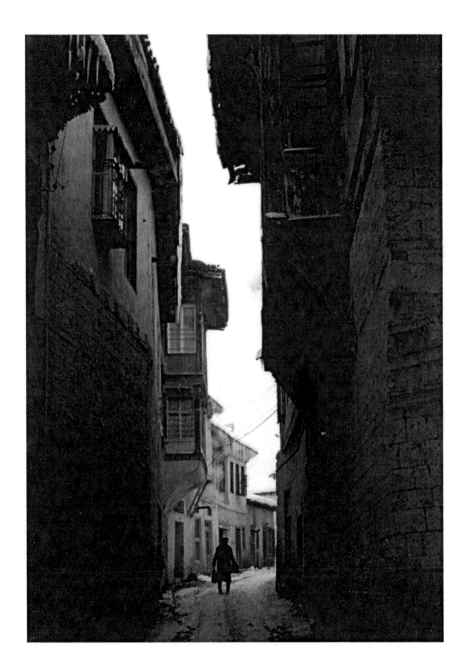

Berea.

News of Paul's very fruitful ministry at Berea eventually reached the ears of his enemies in Thessalonica who, determined to thwart his preaching, traveled to Berea and agitated the crowds against him. Fearing for Paul's life, the Bereans, leaving Silas and Timothy behind, rushed Paul out of the city and sixteen miles west to the port of Dium.[6] There with Paul they boarded a ship destined for Athens 140 miles away.

When Paul bade farewell to Silas and Timothy back at Berea, he must have fought back the tears realizing what devoted men they were willing to remain with the Berean brethren with the full anticipation of imminent persecution. Paul too would have stayed with them had not Silas and Timothy and the concerned Bereans insisted that he flee the city. They considered his welfare far more important than theirs, and saw themselves as his bodyguards.

---

[6] Unger thinks it may have been Pydna, twenty-five miles from Berea, from which Paul sailed. *Archaeology and the New Testament*, Merrill F. Unger, p. 232.

Chapter 15

Alone in Athens

On to Athens

Since it was now autumn and the seas were relatively calm, Paul must have looked forward to his leisurely voyage to Athens affording him time to meditate and renew his strength and prepare for what lay ahead. His ship would have passed many renowned landmarks in Grecian history, among them the Pass of Thermopylae, the maritime sanctuary of Marathon, and the gleaming white temple of Minerva crowning the heights of Sunium. The longer he sailed the more eager he must have been to see Athens and present the gospel to her curious crowds who came together day after day for no other reason than to share the latest gossip or discuss the newest fads. Above all, he was eager to challenge the astute Athenian philosophers and entrenched religious thinkers with the claims of the risen Christ.

The Athens of Paul

If it was daylight when Paul sailed into Piraeus, Athens' harbor, he would of course have been on deck with his friends and would have seen in the distance the Acropolis rising 512 feet above the city. Here stood Greece's most celebrated temples, among them the venerable, famed Parthenon.[1] Towering over all was the

---

[1] The Parthenon (447-432 B.C.) was designed by architects Ictinus and Callicrates, but under the general supervision of the renown sculptor, Phidias. He allowed no straight lines in the Parthenon so as to make it appear straight from a distance. Even the floor is slightly convex.

At the heart of the interior was the giant, gold and ivory statue of Athena, the masterpiece of Phidias. The weight of the gold in the image is estimated to have been 400 pounds!

The Parthenon remained essentially unchanged until the fifth century, when its colossal statue was removed and the temple converted into a Christian church. In 1458, after the Turks had captured Athens, the Parthenon served as a mosque for the next nearly two hundred and thirty years before being used as an arsenal. This nearly proved the building's total undoing when in 1687 a Venetian shell struck the arsenal and storage of explosives at the center of the building, and irreparably blew up most of its interior.

noted landmark for sailors, the giant statue of Promachus helmeted in bronze and holding aloft her gold-tipped spear.

No city of the ancient world had produced more geniuses than Athens. Demosthenes, Phidias, Socrates and Plato were all her sons. Here had flowered the best in architecture, literature, philosophy and drama. When walking her streets lined with temples to Apollo, Minerva, Juno, Ceres and a host of other idols, no one would have suspected that the Athenians were other than a deeply religious people. Pliny wrote that the city in the time of Nero had well over twenty-five thousand statues and another thirty-five thousand in the Parthenon.[2] Petronius said in Athens it was easier to find a god than a man; and Xenophon declared "the whole city was an altar, a votive offering to the gods."[3] But though the city was noted for her adoration of the gods, her temples were largely deserted and the deities on Mt. Olympus were considered only heroes of fable.

The Athenians' moral fiber too had eroded; prostitution was rampant, and marriage and the home were generally no longer sacrosanct. Demosthenes candidly stated: "We have courtesans for the sake of pleasure; we have concubines for the sake of daily cohabitation; we have wives for the purpose of having children legitimately and of having a faithful guardian for all our household affairs."[4]

Thirst for knowledge and a willingness for hard work had generally given way to an insatiable desire to be entertained. The theaters and sports arenas were daily crowded to capacity with restless, unhappy throngs bent on pleasure. Life had become hollow; cynics and pessimists were everywhere. The Golden Age of Athens had expired four hundred years before Paul arrived, and her Silver Age had not yet begun. The five miles of high double walls which once connected Athens with Piraeus had long since crumbled, and much of Athens' harbor had silted up. Now with a population of about 250,000 and Rome in control, Athens was allowed only semi-independence. She was no longer a political power or center of maritime importance.

Athens' literary glory was also a thing of the past with emphasis on criticism rather than creativity, a definite sign of spiritual and intellectual decadence.[5] "Phi-

---

[2] *Paul: A Man of Grace and Grit.* Charles R. Swindoll, p. 203.
[3] *The Life and Letters of Paul the Apostle*, Lyman Abbott, p. 46.
[4] *The Letters to the Galatians and Ephesians*, William Barclay, p. 170.
[5] *St. Paul and His Mission to the Roman Empire*, Christopher N. Johnson, p. 117.

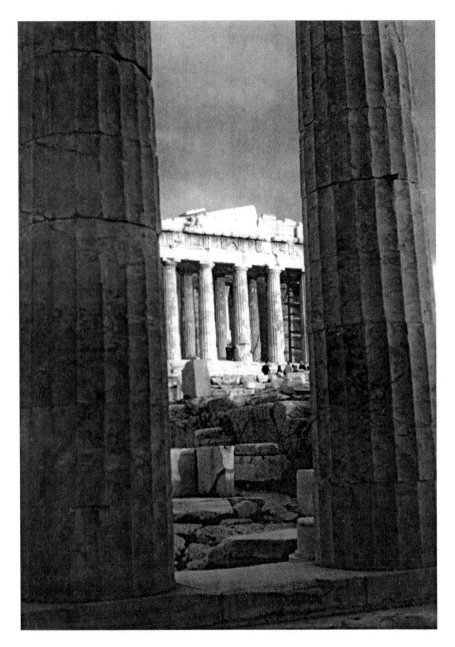

The Parthenon in Athens, Phidias's masterpiece.

The Parthenon.

losophy had degenerated into sophistry, art into dilettantism, oratory into rhetoric, poetry into verse-making."[6] Athens was "repeating with dead lips the echo of old philosophies which had never been sufficient to satisfy the yearnings of the world."[7] Though Athens still swarmed with philosophers, orators and artists, and sculptors and architects were everywhere, none of them had risen to eminence.

Paul alone

This then was the Athens visited by Paul in the year 50, and here the Bereans bade him farewell and returned to their home with Paul's instruction to send Silas

---

[6] *The Life of St. Paul*, James Stalker, p. 84.
[7] *The Life and Work of St. Paul*, Frederic W. Farrar, vol. 1, p. 530.

and Timothy back as soon as possible (Ac. 17:15). Paul had evidently sensed he would need his two strong cohorts to assist him when he began to preach the gospel to the Athenians.

In the meantime he was content to be on his own. Had he requested his Berean brethren to remain with him until Silas and Timothy arrived, they would have gladly done so; but it appears Paul wanted to be alone for a while.

Now being unknown in Athens, he could walk its streets and explore its temples and Acropolis unguarded. In the marketplace he could mingle with the throngs and learn the prevailing concerns and aspirations of the populace and listen to the oratory of roving politicians and the teachings of the philosophers. He could come to know Athens without Athens knowing him while he decided how best to reach her citizens with his powerful message of salvation.

Chapter 16

Addressing the Areopagus

Viewing Athens

As Paul walked through the crowded streets of Athens and viewed its many temples and statues erected to the gods, he would have been greatly impressed by the Athenians' genius, but far more depressed by their appalling spiritual needs. Paul's Hebrew training had taught him that man's relationship with God was much more important than what man creates and sustains. Paul's idea of true beauty lay not in art, architecture, music or drama, but in that which emanated from God and manifested itself in the spiritual life of man. A holy life was the essence of beauty—beauty personified. Other aesthetic values were not important to Paul. Athens to him was but a city filled with idols.

Paul's disregard of nature

As for Paul's awareness of the natural beauties of God's creation, practically nothing in his preaching or letters conveys this. Unlike Moses, Deborah, David, Solomon, James and Jesus, Paul seldom refers to nature. He never seems to hear the music of the birds or the whisper of the winds, or smell the fragrance of the flowers or taste the salty tang of the sea. Though he often sailed the Mediterranean and spent years traveling through the scenic valleys and awe-inspiring mountains of Greece and Asia Minor (today's Turkey), and though he viewed again and again the glories of sunrise and the brilliant hues of sunset, none of God's craftsmanship or dynamic displays of color and power seem to have inspired him.

While Jesus and the Apostle James were poetic preachers and lovers of the out-of-doors and drew many of their illustrations from nature, Paul's metaphors and similes and other figures of speech chiefly concerned the actions and emotional response of people. He writes of the pangs of childbirth and the devotion of motherhood, of the diligence of hard-working farmers and of athletes in achieving their goals. Military metaphors abound in Paul's writings. The armor and sword of the Roman soldier he labels with spiritual meaning (Eph. 6:13-17). "His world was the world of men, the world of spiritual conflicts, the world of sinning, sorrowing, struggling humanity, the world without salvation and in starving need of salvation from sin."[1]

Paul was predominantly an urban dweller. He loved people. He relished the marketplace with its throng and was ever eager to share his message with anyone who would listen. Paul was a superb communicator, outgoing, loquacious and convincing. Above all, he was a proclaimer of the Word. "I am under compulsion," he exclaimed, "for woe is me if I do not preach the gospel" (1Cor. 9:16).

In Paul's day there were two large markets in Athens, one to the north and one to the south of the Acropolis. In both of them was a great variety of goods for sale: clothing for all ages, basketry, pottery, flowers, fruits and vegetables, everything from chickens and ducks to goats and sheep. Here too were stands on which slaves were displayed—men and women born in servitude, chained and waiting to be sold.

It was at the southern market, however, that Paul most frequently came because near here were the headquarters of the Epicureans and the Stoics, the famed philosophical schools of Athens. Realizing the enormous influence these schools exerted on the religious life of the city, Paul was eager to come to know their teachers and their students.

The Epicureans

Epicureanism was a philosophical discipline founded in 306 B.C. by Epicurus, a voluminous writer (he wrote nearly 300 books) who lived and taught in Athens for thirty years. He believed that there was no god and that everything happened by chance. The universe, he declared, was simply the result of a fortuitous combination of atoms, and death was annihilation beyond which there was nothing. "Both body and soul were dissolved together and dissipated into the elements; and when this occurred, all the life of man was ended."[2] Not wanting, however, to be pronounced an atheist, which was contrary to public sentiment, Epicurus represented the gods as dwelling in perfect happiness completely apart from humanity and totally indifferent to its affairs, not even aware that the world existed.[3]

---

[1] *Paul and His Epistles*, D. A. Hayes, p. 77.

[2] *The Life and Epistles of St. Paul*, W. J. Conybeare and J. S. Howson, p. 285.

[3] *The Letters to the Hebrews*, William Barclay, pp. 39, 40.

Epicurus taught that the pursuit of happiness was man's chief aim, but warned that pleasure was not to be equated with fulfilling fleshly lust and worldly desires, but with that which produced no pain. Such happiness, Epicurus affirmed, could be achieved by striving for moral excellence.

Intent on realizing this euphoria, the Epicureans met in a walled-in garden and attempted to live aloof from all strife and heartbreak and meditate only on pleasant things. Eventually, however, with only one aim in life—experiencing pleasure—and with no real concern for others in need and no belief in a loving Creator or moral Governor, and a complete denial of an after-life or coming retribution and judgment, it is not surprising that the Epicureans grew disillusioned.

The Stoics

The Stoic school, on the other hand, was more theologically oriented. It was founded by Zeno about the same period as that of the Epicureans, with its students meeting on a porch known in Greek as the *stoa* (hence the name *Stoic*). Stoics were pantheists.

> In their view, God was merely the Spirit or Reason of the Universe. The world was itself a rational soul, producing all things out of itself, and resuming it all to itself again. Matter was inseparable from Deity. He did not create; He only organized. He merely impressed law and order on the substance, which was, in fact, Himself. The manifestation of the Universe was only a period in the development of God.[4]

The soul of man was thought by the Stoics to be corporeal and at death would be burnt and return to be absorbed in God.

> The proud ideal which was set before the disciple Zeno was, a magnanimous self-denial, an austere apathy, untouched by human passion, unmoved by change of circumstance.... Pleasure was no good. Pain was no evil. All actions conformable to Reason were equally good; all actions contrary to Reason were equally evil.[5]

Stoicism taught that everything that transpired was willed by an impersonal, unfeeling Being, and could not be altered. It must be accepted without question.

---

[4] *The Life and Epistles of St. Paul*, W. J. Conybeare and J. S. Howson, p. 285.
[5] Ibid., p. 284.

Man was to strive for virtue and listen to the voice of conscience, said to be the voice of God within.

Paul's teaching of the possibility of moral goodness among non-Jews, and a universal presence and operation of God in the human heart outside the limit of special revelation, echoed the teachings of Stoic philosophy. This was not in accord with Jewish teaching which saw no goodness or awareness of God in the heathen world.[6]

Conscience

Paul showed his appreciation for what he considered admirable in Greek philosophy in his quotations of sentences and appropriation of truths and parallelisms from Greek thought. His use of the Greek word *suneidesis* for conscience is an example of this. No writer in the New Testament had used this word as Paul used it, except for Peter who showed often in his epistles a dependence upon Pauline language and reasoning. The word came neither from the Old Testament Scriptures nor from Paul's Jewish contemporaries, but from the Stoics. Paul adopted it and introduced it into the vocabulary of the Christian church. Twenty-two times it is found in Paul's speeches and in his epistles.[7]

Stoicism taught that man was not to depend on any person or thing but to be self-reliant. He was to eliminate from his life all carnal desires. He must never show emotion, whether experiencing pleasure or pain or viewing these in others. Eventually he would come to the place where he no longer cared what happened to himself or to anyone else. Such an attitude could be realized only by a deliberate act of the will and with the firm belief that everything was controlled by inexorable laws.

Epictetus in describing this Stoic outlook explained,

> Begin with a cup or a household utensil; if it breaks, say, "I don't care." Go on to a horse or pet dog; if anything happens to it, say, "I don't care." Go on to yourself and if you are hurt or injured in any way, say, "I don't care." If you go on long enough and if you try hard enough, you will come to a stage when you can watch your nearest and dearest suffer and die, and say, "I don't care."[8]

---

[6] *A Practical Exposition of the Epistle to the Romans*, Charles Gore, p. 99.

[7] *Paul and His Epistles*, D. A. Hayes, pp. 106, 107.

[8] *The Letters to the Philippians, Colossians and Thessalonians*, William Barclay, p. 104.

Gloom and a foreboding sense of futility thus marked the world of the Stoics, and the best they could offer a father at the graveside of his child was to say, "It was a mortal you have loved and tomorrow you will die."[9]

The gospel vs. Epicureanism and Stoicism

While in agreement with some of Stoicism, Paul opposed its major tenets. Never would he have agreed it was right to live a life aloof from society, apart from the sufferings of others. The Stoic teaching of noninvolvement was totally contrary to Paul's thinking. A Christian was to be involved with humanity, always interacting with others, always willing to help in any way and wherever he could.

Never would Paul have sanctioned the rigorous monastic communities of the Essenes which later sprang up at Qumran[10]; nor would he have viewed the "Pillar Saints" as other than misguided enthusiasts.

One of these, the most fanatical, was Simon Stylites who for thirty-seven years dwelt under a tiny canopy atop a sixty-foot column. He used a rope to pull up food and water supplied to him, and thinking he was pleasing God, made sure he prostrated himself 1,224 times each day! But after some more years he felt he was overindulging his flesh and tore down his canopy and remained the rest of his life exposed to the elements![11]

Epicurus failed to realize the folly of seeking happiness as a goal. He failed to recognize that happiness comes as a by-product of serving and loving others. Though he spent his entire life as a teacher and writer on the subject of pleasure, he never gained it for himself.

Zeno, on the other hand, failed to recognize the therapeutic value of expressing pain when confronted with it and of breaking out into laughter when it was called for. The tears he held back and the overt expressions of joy he stifled eventually left him in deep depression. He needed to release his pent-up emotions, needed to be

---

[9] *A Man in Christ*, James S. Stewart, p. 64.

[10] In 1947 sacred documents of the Essenes were found, known as the Dead Sea Scrolls. They had been preserved for centuries in pottery jars hidden in caves overlooking the Dead Sea. Even more scrupulous than the Pharisees in observing the Sabbath, the Essenes on the sacred day of rest, unless absolutely necessary, would not relieve themselves lest their waste profane God's holy day! *Jesus and His Times*, Reader's Digest, p. 218.

[11] See *What's So Amazing About Grace?* Philip Yancey, p. 199.

involved in the affairs of others. Life became lonely and meaningless. Finally he and Cleanthes, the first two Stoic teachers, ended their lives in suicide.

The Areopagus

The supreme court of Athens, called the Areopagus, originally met on a small rocky elevation at the south side of the Acropolis, but in Paul's day held its sessions nearby in the marketplace in order to accommodate the crowds. The Areopagus was responsible for adjudicating legal matters and for controlling public education as well as overseeing the religious and moral life of the city.

After listening to Paul in the market, a group of Epicureans and Stoics began to dispute with him and spoke of him in private as an "idle babbler" and "proclaimer of strange deities" (Ac. 17:18). Finally, annoyed by his message and fearing he might gain too much of a hearing, they brought him to the Areopagus to explain his teachings, doubtless hoping the high court would expel him from the city. Here was Paul's great opportunity to address the judicial, academic and religious leaders of Athens as well as those in the crowd always eager to hear a new voice.

Commendation vs. condemnation

In his opening remarks Paul reminded his audience of how religious they were and how he had noticed a statue with the inscription, *agnosto theo*, "to the unknown God" (Ac. 17:23).[12] This opened the way for Paul to declare the true God. Wisely he did not denounce Athenian idolatry which would only have closed the minds of his hearers to his message. Paul was no iconoclast. He felt commendation was always better than condemnation. Provide the powerful antidote of the gospel, and in time and in its own way it would cleanse and reform society.

Paul widely read in Greek literature

Paul is the only writer in the New Testament who quotes directly from Greek literature, an example of which is found in his Athenian address where he quotes

---

[12]The altar, it appears, had been built six hundred years before Paul arrived in Athens at the time when the city was experiencing a terrible pestilence. The Cretian poet, Epimenides, claimed that the disease could be eliminated if flocks of black and white sheep were released from the Areopagus and allowed to roam the streets at will. Wherever a sheep lay down it was to be sacrificed to the nearest idol; and if there was no shrine nearby, it was to be sacrificed to the "Unknown God." According to legend, this was followed and the epidemic ceased.

Aratus, a Stoic of the third century B.C., as saying, *"We also are his offspring!"* (Ac. 17:28).[13]

Paul, having grown up in Tarsus with its predominant Greek culture, providentially had attended Gamaliel's liberal school where half of its thousand students studied Jewish law and the other half Greek wisdom. Though Paul would have thoroughly studied the Old Testament Scriptures, he would also have read widely in Greek literature. This would not have met with the approval of many of the rabbis and Pharisees of his day who were known for their narrow-mindedness and intolerance of most everything non-Jewish. The conservative rabbis taught that a study of the Jewish law was all-sufficient and that if one were determined to study Greek wisdom he must "first find an hour that is neither day nor night in which to study it."[14] Frequently the proverb was heard, "Cursed be he that eats pork, and cursed be he that teaches his son the Greek wisdom."[15]

Gamaliel, however, adverse to such prejudice, encouraged his students to include in their curriculum a careful study of Greek philosophy and the Greek masters. Paul would thus have been conversant with Greek thought, especially with the writings of Aristotle, Plato and Demosthenes. Particularly he would have been drawn to Demosthenes, the greatest of Greek orators and probably the most earnest and spiritual of them all.

A comparative study of the rhetorical forms in Paul's epistles and the writings of Demosthenes and other Greek authors clearly show how much Paul was influenced by Greek thought. Both Paul and Demosthenes used the same kind of irony and sarcasm, and Paul actually employed phrases, ideas and even entire sentences found not only in the writings of Demosthenes but in those of Aristotle and Plato.

Note the following similarities between Paul and Plato:[16]

For me to live is Christ, and die is gain. (Paul)
Now if death is like this, I say to die is gain. (Plato)

---

[13]These words conclude the close of what Aratus wrote in his Phaenomena: "Zeus fills the streets, the marts, Zeus fills the sea, the shores, the rivers! Everywhere our need is Zeus! *We also are his offspring!*"

[14]*Paul and His Epistles*, D. A. Hayes, p. 24.

[15]Ibid.

[16]*The Life and Letters of Paul The Apostle*, Lyman Abbott, pp. 20, 21.

See that none render evil for evil unto any man. (Paul)
[W]e ought not to retaliate or render evil for evil to anyone. (Plato)

For necessity is laid upon me, yea, woe is me, if I preach not the gospel! (Paul)
But necessity was laid upon me—the word of God I thought ought to be considered first. (Plato)

We also are men of like passions with you. (Paul)
I am a man, and, like other men, a creature of flesh and blood. (Plato)

We have wronged no man; we have corrupted no man; we have defrauded no man. (Paul)
I speak because I am convinced that I never intentionally wronged anyone. (Plato)

Seneca too, the most prominent contemporary spokesman of Stoicism, was well represented in Paul's address before the Areopagus as the following shows (Ac. 17:24-29):[17]

God ... does not dwell in temples made with hands.... (Paul)
Temples are not to be built to God of stones piled on high. He must be consecrated in the heart of every man. (Seneca)

[N]either is He served by human hands, as though He needed anything, since He Himself gives to all life, and breath, and all things.... (Paul)
God wants not ministers. How so? He himself ministereth to the human race. (Seneca)

He made from one, every nation of mankind to live on all the face of the earth.... (Paul)
We are members of a vast body. Nature made us kin, when she produced us from the same things and to the same ends. (Seneca)

He is not far from each one of us; for in Him we live and move, and exist.... (Paul)
God is at hand everywhere and to all men.... God is near thee; he is with thee; he is within. (Seneca)

Being then the offspring of God, we ought not to think that Divine Nature is like gold or silver or stone, an image formed by the art and thought of man. (Paul)
Thou shalt not form him of silver and gold: a true likeness of God cannot be molded of this material. (Seneca)

---

[17]See *Paul and His Epistles*, D. A. Hayes, pp. 98, 99, 102, 103, 105, 106.

Such must not, however, be seen as plagiarism on the part of Paul, but simply his use of Greek thought, sometimes rephrased, which was not adverse to his Christian message. In this way it established a common bond with his Greek listeners before sharing with them the unique concepts of the gospel.

Mockers, procrastinators and believers

Many of the Athenians at the Areopagus readily agreed with Paul's preaching up to the point where he declared that God had sent His Son, Jesus of Nazareth, into the world to be the perfect atonement for sin and that Jesus had risen from the dead and one day would judge the world. It was then that they refused to allow Paul to continue. They were willing to listen to his concepts of God as Creator and Sustainer of the universe and of man having to stand eventually before Him as Judge; but they were totally unprepared to acknowledge that Jesus had risen from the grave and one day Himself would be that Judge.

Paul's congregation soon divided into three groups: mockers, procrastinators and believers. Like the Roman soldiers at Calvary, the mockers vocally vented their contempt, while the procrastinators promised to hear Paul at a later date. That opportunity, however, never presented itself, for as far as is known Paul never addressed the Areopagus again.

Among the believers only two are mentioned by name, Dionysius, a member of the supreme court, and a woman named Damaris. Though Paul's preaching in Athens, unlike that in Thessalonica and Berea, failed to convert many, this does not mean his preaching was ineffective. Visible converts are not necessarily the measure of successful evangelism. Dionysius and Damaris and the few others whom Paul reached with the gospel in Athens may eventually have been the ones whom God used most to evangelize Athens.

Chapter 17

Corinth: Crossroads of the Roman Empire

How long Paul remained in Athens is not recorded, but it appears that Silas and Timothy eventually rejoined him there, and later Timothy was sent back to Thessalonica to bring back news of how the church there was faring. In the meantime Paul and Silas traveled to Corinth where they met Aquila and Priscilla, a Christian couple from Rome and started working and ministering with them. It was probably not long after this that Paul sent Silas to find Timothy with the welcome result that both men soon appeared in Corinth eager to labor in the gospel with him (Ac. 18:5; 1Thess. 3:6).[1]

Paul's deep love and concern for the Thessalonians is evident from the letter he wrote them from Corinth. "[W]hen we could endure it no longer ... we [Paul and Silas from Athens] sent Timothy, our brother and God's fellow worker in the gospel of Christ, to strengthen and encourage you as to your faith...." And then to re-emphasize his longing to know how the Thessalonian brethren fared, Paul repeats what he had said, only this time in the first person: "... when *I* could endure it no longer, *I* also sent to find out about your faith, for fear that the tempter might have tempted you, and our labor should be in vain" (1Thess. 3:1, 2, 5).

Corinth

Corinth, forty-five miles southwest of Athens, now became Paul's next great challenge. It had been the chief city on the Peloponnesus but was destroyed by the Romans in 146 B.C. and was not rebuilt until 46 B.C. under Julius Caesar who colonized it with veterans and freemen. It rapidly grew into a thriving metropolis until its population swelled to an estimated 700,000 people, more than half of whom were slaves. Today it lies in utter ruins.

---

[1] Silas from now on is not mentioned in any of Paul's letters or in the book of Acts. Possibly this is because he became ill and was forced to return to his home. There is no indication that he and Paul had any disagreement. Peter speaks of him as his amanuensis and "our faithful brother" (1Pet. 5:12), and it is assumed that Silas worked with him after Paul's martyrdom.

The Diolkos

Corinth, just south of the isthmus joining the Peloponnesus to Hellas proper, was situated on one of the most traveled and appreciated crossroads of the ancient world. Over this narrow section of land, four miles in length, was built a road called *Diolkos,* which connected the two harbors, Lechaeum on the Corinthian Gulf and Cenchrea on the Saronic Gulf. Cargoes from large ships coming into these harbors were regularly transported over land on the backs of slaves or in wagons to sister ships anchored in the opposite harbors. Smaller vessels, however, were able to be hauled over on rollers, thus eliminating two hundred miles of travel around the Morea, feared for its dangerous Cape Malea—the Cape of Good Hope of Antiquity. So hazardous was this voyage that it gave rise to two proverbs: "Let him who sails round Malea forget his home," and "Let him who thinks of sailing round Malea make his will."[2]

The Corinthian canal

According to legend, the Adriatic Sea was higher than the Aegean Sea and if a canal connected them it would mean the inundation of Athens. Alexander the Great, Julius Caesar, and many others scorned such folklore and attempted to cut a waterway, but since it meant excavating through solid clay, the work proved too arduous and soon was abandoned.

Then in the autumn of A.D. 66, two years before his suicide, Nero determined to create the canal at all costs and led an enormous gang of laborers to the site. Among them were six thousand young Jews captured by Vespasian in the lakeside villages of Galilee during the Jewish War which had just begun.

Upon arriving, Nero snatched a lyre and sang an ode in honor of Neptune and Amphitrite and, then, to the sound of music, ceremoniously dug up some soil and put it in a basket which he slung over his back. He then ordered the work to begin.

But, as with the earlier endeavors, Nero's attempt soon failed, and not until the year 1881 did a French engineering company with explosives and proper equipment begin excavating where Nero had left off. The enormous undertaking of cutting through the narrow four-mile slit and down seventy-five feet to the water required twelve years to complete.

Since the water is only twenty-six feet deep, small boats must use extreme care as they go through the canal. This is because of frequent turbulent currents and the

---

[2] *Ambassador for Christ*, William Barclay, p. 102.

The Corinthian canal.

The Acrocorinth towering over the Lechaeum Road leading to ancient
Corinth's western port on the Corinthian Gulf.

wash from the seas at both ends. Larger vessels squeeze through the narrow passageway with wooden bumpers tied to their sides to protect them from being marred as well as from doing damage to the sides of the canal.

The Acrocorinth

When Paul first walked into Corinth surrounded by a high wall, he would immediately have been impressed by its towering Acrocorinth, which rose 1,750 feet above the city. This mountain, which still remains much as Paul saw it, has been described as having

... the same strength, the same precipitousness, and the same bleak and uncompromising grandeur as Gibraltar.... Its massive sides are scored by corries and fret-

Ruins of Corinth from the summit of the Acrocorinth.

ted with countless pinnacles that catch the light and vary in shade from pale pink at morning to the deepest blue at sunset.[3]

From its summit in the sunlight Paul would have seen the sprawling metropolis stretched out beneath him with its many parks and marble squares and long, colonnaded avenues flanked by stately buildings all radiating from its forum. He would have grieved over the numerous temples he saw to the heathen gods—Athena, Hermes, Hera and Apollo—and would have yearned for the day they would be overthrown and Jesus as Lord would be worshipped at Corinth.

Ten miles to the south stood the shrine of Poseidon near Corinth's amphitheater (accommodating 20,000 spectators); and to the north, forty-five miles distant

---

[3] *In the Steps of St. Paul*, H. V. Morton, p. 292.

loomed the temple-crowned Acropolis of Athens, behind which stretched the snow-covered hills of Thessaly.

Far to the east and to the west sparkled the city's two busy harbors alive with an array of colorful sails. Between the two ports could be seen a variety of small vessels slowly being dragged by regimented slaves over the Diolkos to and fro. No acropolis in the ancient world offered from its summit a more exciting and meaningful view than that of the Acrocorinth.

Aquila and Priscilla

Residing in Corinth when Paul arrived were Aquila and Priscilla who, like Paul, were tentmakers. They invited Paul and Silas, and later Timothy, who soon appeared, to live with them and ply their trade. Thus began a very strong friendship between Paul and this devoted couple, a friendship which was to last for the whole of Paul's life.

Aquila was a Jew and his wife, it is thought, a Gentile, possibly from a Roman partisan family. Very probably they had been expelled from Rome in the year 50 during the Jewish persecution under Claudius. They proved dedicated Christians, greatly helping Paul in his ministry both in Corinth and Ephesus. Toward the end of Paul's life they appear to have been with him in Rome, still very active in assisting him.[4]

The Isthmian games

Corinth's famous Isthmian games held every three years were surpassed only by the Olympic games held every four years at Olympia to honor Zeus. The city during these periods was choked with visitors. They came from near and far to view the boxing, wrestling, and javelin and disc throwers, and above all to thrill to the furious driving of famed charioteers whose races displayed the greatest daring and utmost skill.

Such events provided Paul apt illustrations for living the Christian life. He sensed in the athletes their keen desire to reach their goals and noted that only through training and rigorous discipline and following the rules prescribed was this possible. Likewise, if Christians are to realize their high calling, they must submit

---

[4] Priscilla's name (Prisca) generally appears in Scripture before Aquila because she may have been the more dominant of the two.

to disciplined training and be willing to follow the way of the Cross (1Cor. 9:24, 26, 27).[5]

Asklepieion

Corinth was famous for its shrine dedicated to the deified Greek physician, Asclepius. Many plagued with illnesses of all kinds came to the Asklepieion in the hope of being healed. They generally stayed in tent encampments and often remained for weeks or even months until they recovered. Those not so blessed and finally convinced they would never be well, sorrowfully returned to their homes.

A city of unbridled lust

It was universally acknowledged that Corinth was a city of unbridled lust and the most profligate in the Roman empire. Its religious life was largely based on sensuality represented by its guardian idol, Aphrodite Pandemos, enshrined in her temple high on the Acrocorinth. In her precincts lived one thousand professional female prostitutes who regularly plied their trade on the streets of Corinth at night when not indulging in the lascivious dances and rituals connected with the pagan goddess.[6]

At the center of the city was the giant temple of Apollo, standing for the ideal of male beauty and which provided a favorite rendezvous for homosexuals. Here were found erotic nude statues of Apollo, with Sodomites, many of them boys, set apart "by the gods" to satisfy the lusts of male worshippers.

---

[5] Note in v. 27 that Paul is not saying he could lose his salvation but only could fall behind in proclaiming Christ.

[6] *Harper's Bible Dictionary* states: "Many commentators on the New Testament describe the Corinth of Paul's time as a city of unbridled sexual orgies, basing their view on certain remarks of ancient, mostly Athenian, writers, and on a passage of Strabo's geography referring to a thousand temple prostitutes of Aphrodite on the Acrocorinth. More recent scholarship has pointed out, however, both that the Athenian references were snobbish disparagements of the pre-146 city and that sacred prostitution was a Middle Eastern custom, not a Greek one at all. Corinth was probably no more or less virtuous than any other cosmopolitan port city of the Mediterranean in the first century A.D." p. 183.

Regarding the above statement, it should be noted that though Aphrodite worship with its sacred prostitution originated in the Middle East, it definitely had permeated Greece and was well entrenched in Corinth when Paul arrived there.

The temple of Apollo.

Homosexuality was widely practiced not only in Greece but throughout the Roman empire; even so respected a man as Socrates indulged in it. Fourteen of the first fifteen emperors were deviates. Nero, after a full marriage ceremony, took as his "bride" a castrated boy named Sporus; later Nero reversed his rôle and married a man named Pythagoras whom he pronounced his "husband!"[7]

Into such an amoral, sensual city swarmed the sailors from its two ports, young men out for revelry after the tedium and confinement of their voyages. Away from their families and among total strangers, they were easily exploited and tempted into vice, and at night many of them became boisterous inebriates and joined in violent brawls which often led to arrests and their being hauled into court. Alco-holics were so prevalent that theater plays usually labeled them as "Corinthians,"

---

[7] Refer to *The Letters to the Corinthians*, William Barclay, p. 60.

and a "Corinthian girl" or a "Corinthian man" was generally understood as one living an immoral life.

Paul's graphic description of ungodliness in his epistle to the Romans doubtless came from his observations while in Corinth.

> [W]omen exchanged the natural function for that which is unnatural, and in the same way also the men abandoned the natural function of the woman and burned in their desire toward one another, men with men committing indecent acts ... being filled with all unrighteousness, wickedness, greed, evil; full of envy, murder, strife, deceit, malice; they are gossips, slanderers, haters of God, insolent, arrogant, boastful, inventors of evil, disobedient to parents, without understanding, untrustworthy, unloving, unmerciful. (Rom. 1:26, 27, 29-31)

In search of wisdom

Though Corinth was never known for its centers of learning, many of its citizens were interested in acquiring wisdom and spiritual knowledge. Disillusioned with their permissive culture emphasizing the gratification of the flesh, they were ready to hear of the wisdom of God and the liberating truths of the gospel. Paul's letter to the Corinthians (1 Corinthians), written from Ephesus three years after he had left Corinth, reminds them of the power of the gospel and the humble status of most of the first believers in Corinth.

> Brothers, think of what you were when you were called. Not many of you were wise by human standards; not many were influential; not many were of noble birth. But God chose the foolish things of the world to shame the wise; God chose the weak things of the world to shame the strong. (1Cor. 1:26, 27 NIV)

Message of hope

Though Paul reminded the Christians at Corinth, as well as the Christians at Rome, Ephesus and Colossae, of their sinful past and included himself and his disciples among those who had trespassed (1Cor. 6:9-11; Rom. 6:17-22; Eph. 2:2-5; 4:22; Col. 3:5-7), he did not dwell on this. Paul's main interest lay not on his brothers' and sisters' sinful past, but rather in how they were living now, whether forgiven and set free in Christ (Rom. 6:16-18). The past is past; learn from it, but do not live in it. Hold on to the fact that a Christian is saved, not by his good works and striving to be righteous, but solely upon his repentance and faith in Christ as his sin-bearer, "who knew no sin to be sin on our behalf, that we might become the righteousness of God in Him" (2Cor. 5:21).

There was no sin, Paul declared, no matter how heinous and unpardonable in the eyes of man, which the Lord Jesus could not forgive. All sin could be washed away through His cleansing blood.[8] "For by grace you have been saved through faith; and that not of yourselves, it is the gift of God; not as a result of works, that no one should boast" (Eph. 2:8, 9). "Therefore if any man is in Christ, he is a new creature; the old things passed away; behold new things have come" (2Cor. 5:17).

"Paul was interested in salvation from the guilt of sin no whit less than in salvation from the power of sin, in justification no whit less than in the 'new creation.'"[9] Salvation according to Paul "consisted not merely in the assurance of a blessed immortality ... not merely even in the possession of a new power of holy living, but also, and everywhere, in the consciousness that the guilt of sin had been removed by the cross of Christ."[10] For the Christian to continue to bear the guilt was to disparage the work of the Savior and to discount the grace of God.

Paul turns to the Gentiles

Paul's ministry in the synagogue at Corinth was constantly opposed by rabid defenders of the Torah who viewed Paul as an enemy of Moses and a threat to Judaism. Finally, realizing the futility of remaining any longer in the synagogue after the Jews there began to blaspheme Christ, Paul shook out his garment against them and declared, "Your blood be upon your own heads! I am clean. From now on I shall go to the Gentiles" (Ac. 18:6). He then left and established his headquarters close by in the house of Titius Justus, a convert. The move proved a wise one and soon many were being won to Christ, even Crispus, the ruler of the synagogue!

Jesus' second appearance

Paul remained at Corinth for eighteen months, having been assured by the Lord that He was with him and not to be afraid, but to go on speaking. This was Jesus' second appearance to Paul (Ac. 18:9, 10).

---

[8] The unforgivable sin against the Holy Spirit of which Jesus speaks—Mt. 12:31, 32; Mk. 3:29; Lk. 12:10—refers to an incident when the Pharisees were attributing the work of the Spirit to the power of Satan. Blaspheming the Holy Spirit would connote renouncing God *in toto*, thus making it impossible for the blasphemer to be forgiven, since he would have no desire to ask for forgiveness.

[9] *The Origin of Paul's Religion*, J. Gresham Machen, p. 279.

[10] Ibid.

Cenchrea, the eastern port of ancient Corinth on the Saronic Gulf.

Accused at the Bema

After this, Gallio,[11] the older brother of Seneca, arrived as the proconsul of Achaea and sat on the judgment seat at the Bema. Immediately an angry crowd of Jews brought Paul before him with the charge that he was persuading men to worship God contrary to Roman law. Gallio, recognizing that the charges pertained only to Jewish doctrine and had nothing to do with Roman jurisprudence, forbade Paul to speak in his own defense though Paul was willing to do so. Gallio then drove the accusers from the Bema, leaving them furious over having lost their case. Promptly they seized Sosthenes,[12] the new ruler of the synagogue, and beat him in

---

[11]Gallio was known for his noble character and genteel manner. His brother Seneca said of him: "No mortal so sweet to anyone as Gallio to everyone." *St. Paul and His Mission to the Roman Empire*, Christopher N. Johnston, p. 123.

[12]Sosthenes may be the same Sosthenes mentioned in the opening of Paul's first letter to the Corinthians and, if so, like Crispus, he was won to Christ.

full view of the proconsul. They obviously felt Sosthenes had not supported them. Gallio made no effort to interfere and calmly watched the flogging.

Paul, now assured he was protected by imperial power, remained many more days in Corinth before deciding to sail with Aquila and Priscilla from Cenchrea to Ephesus and then, leaving them there to resettle, continued his voyage to Caesarea and on to Jerusalem. He had not visited the Holy City for almost three years.[13]

After arriving in Ephesus and while waiting for a ship destined for Caesarea, Paul preached in one of the synagogues. His message proved so provocative that the Jews urged him to remain and expound more of the gospel. But Paul felt constrained to continue on to Jerusalem, but promised "I will come back, if it is God's will" (Ac. 18:21).

---

[13]Acts 18:18 (NIV) reads, "Paul stayed on in Corinth for some time, Then he left the brothers and sailed for Syria, accompanied by Priscilla and Aquila. Before he sailed, he had his hair cut off at Cenchrea because of a vow he had taken."

Here it is obvious that it was Aquila, not Paul, who cut his hair at Cenchrea having taken the Nazirite vow (Nazirite from the Hebrew *nazar*, "to separate"). The vow's requirements as described below, was often taken by Jews to show publicly their appreciation to God for being delivered from serious illness or some great peril. Aquila, being a full-blooded Jew and deeply relieved that Paul had been delivered by Gallio at the Bema, and being very close to Paul, evidently wanted to take the vow to express his gratitude. He probably was planning to visit Jerusalem in the near future where the ritual of his vow could be finalized.

The Nazirite vow was threefold for both men and women in Israel, requiring abstaining from strong drink and the fruit of the vine, not cutting the hair for at least one month and not touching a cadaver (Num. 6:1-21). When the days of separation were fulfilled, the Nazirite was to come to the temple in Jerusalem and offer the prescribed sacrifice, which meant shaving the head and burning the hair in the fires of the first peace offerings.

A Jewish Nazirite candidate outside his homeland must follow the same rules and after a month cut off the hair from the head with scissors and keep it until reaching Jerusalem. There the head was to be shaved completely in the temple and the hair burned on the altar along with the hair brought in from abroad.

A distinction was made between a "Nazirite of days" and a "Nazirite for life." The former were those who took the vow for a relatively short period, but the latter applied to those who had been set apart from infancy as Nazirites, such a Samson, James the brother of Jesus, and John the Baptist.

Paul, while being grateful for Gallio's protection at the Bema, would never himself have taken the Nazirite vow in Cenchrea or, for that matter, in any other place. Not that he could not have done so as a Jew and still remained Christian, but Paul felt this would give the impression that he was still practicing Jewish rituals.

There is no evidence whatsoever that Paul shaved his head when he arrived in Jerusalem. This would have been mandatory had he taken the vow.

Chapter 18

Concerning the Second Coming

Not long after Paul arrived in Corinth he wrote his first letter to the Thessalonians, the first of his recorded thirteen epistles. Many scholars believe it was the first of the New Testament writings, while others believe the letter of James holds that place.[1]

Both 1 and 2 Thessalonians deal with a common theme, the Second Coming of Christ, though the term "Second Coming" is not mentioned in either letter or anywhere else in Scripture.

General belief in the imminent return of Christ

According to the Jew, all time was divided into two ages, the contemporary age and the age to come. The present age was considered wholly and incurably evil while the future age was seen to be the golden age of God.

Preceding this new world was the terrible Day of the Lord, which was predicted to come suddenly and without warning. A cosmic upheaval would occur, after which judgment would be meted out and a new world established with Israel restored as God's chosen people (Isa. 13:6-10; 22:5; Ezek. 30:1-3; Amos 5:18-20; Zeph. 1:14-18; Mal. 4:5).

Such apocalyptic teaching was much in vogue during Paul's ministry and on into the second century.

Many disturbing rumors were abroad and many prophesied the speedy dissolution of the then present order of things. The preaching of Paul chimed in with this general state of terrified expectation. The Christian faith confirmed the heathen auguries. New converts found that their old fears were well founded, and that the great and terrible Day of the Lord indeed was at hand. It is not strange that some

---

[1] Some, affirming the letter to the Galatians was written after Paul's first missionary journey, mark Galatians as Paul's first letter.

were swept off their feet in a tumult of religious excitement at the thought of the immediate nearness of the end.[2]

Paul along with James, Peter and John definitely believed in the imminent return of Christ, and Paul personally believed it would occur during his lifetime. James wrote, "Be patient, therefore, brethren, until the coming of the Lord ... for the coming of the Lord is at hand" (Jas. 5:7-9). Peter declared, "The end of all things is at hand ..." (1Pet. 4:7). And John, referring to Christ, wrote, "Yes, I am coming quickly" (Rev. 22:20); and again, "Children, it is the last hour; and just as you heard that antichrists have arisen; from this we know that it is the last hour" (1Jn. 2:18).

The reason for the early Christians' belief in the soon return of Jesus stemmed largely from the shocking corruption, debauchery and immorality existing all around them, as well as the persecutions and harassments they were experiencing at the hands of fanatic Judaizers and rabid Sanhedrinists. It was unthinkable to the neophyte church that a God of love and justice would allow His children to remain much longer in a world so unkind and so given to vice. Surely Jesus would come back soon and take His church with Him back into heaven! Judgment surely was on the threshold!

Evaluating apocalyptic imagery

Many of the Old Testament prophets—Isaiah, Ezekiel, Daniel, Joel and Zechariah, and the Apostle John in his account of his revelation on Patmos—clothed their preaching with apocalyptic imagery so as to make it impressive and heighten its interest. Today such rhetorical and homiletical methods are

> nothing but the drapery appropriate to that time and place ... and no longer useful but rather as hindering our perception of the things which abide. What was helpful to the Oriental of two thousand years ago may be harmful to us. No one can deny that great harm has resulted from the attempt to interpret apocalyptical symbols literally and to deduce doctrine and dates from the details of apocalyptical imagery.... Apocalypse, as such, has no place in modern literature ... no significance to modern thought. The truths it taught may abide after it has passed away.[3]

---

[2] *Paul and His Epistles*, D. A. Hayes, p. 169.
[3] *Ibid.*, pp. 177, 178.

Fear of not being ready when Christ returned

Some Christians in Thessalonica dreaded the return of Jesus, fearing their lives would not measure up to the standards Jesus had laid down, and therefore when He appeared they would be excluded from entering the Kingdom of God. In this, of course, they showed their misunderstanding of the rudiments of salvation, which stressed that a Christian is not saved by his good works but only by grace through his faith in Christ (Eph. 2:8, 9). Paul would certainly have emphasized this doctrine during his time in Thessalonica, but evidently some had not listened carefully or had become confused with conflicting instructions from pagan teachers.

Concern regarding deceased loved ones at the Second Coming

To those who were concerned for their Christian loved ones who had died and would not be on earth when Jesus returned, Paul explained that it was only the bodies of the deceased which had been interred and not their spirits, which were in heaven. When Jesus came back, the spirits of all those who were His would accompany Him and be joined with their resurrected bodies which then would be glorified and immortalized (see 1Thess. 4:14-17).[4]

This concept of the resurrection of the dead was midway between Greek and Pharisaical teaching. The Greek philosophers believed only in spiritual immortality devoid of any physical body, while the Pharisees insisted that at the resurrection man's mortal remains would be miraculously reassembled but not glorified. Paul never attempted to explain the metaphysics involved and rightly termed it a "mystery" (1Cor. 15:51).

Why work if Jesus is coming soon?

Others among the Thessalonian Christians reasoned that since Jesus was expected any moment it was senseless to continue laboring and preparing for tomorrow. This led, of course, to indolence and whiling away the hours and prompted Paul to lay down a cardinal rule of the early church: "if anyone will not work, neither let him eat" (2Thess. 3:10). The Christian is not to shirk his family responsibilities nor become insensitive to the needs of others. The time of Christ's

---

[4] Paul here was referring to the Rapture.

return should be left with God. Jesus never stated when He would return and made it crystal clear that no one but His Father knew that hour, not even the angels in heaven (Mt. 24:36).[5] The important thing is that Jesus one day will appear, and with that in mind every Christian should be ready to receive Him.

A sensible attitude toward the Second Coming

> The proper attitude to maintain in reference to the second coming of the Lord is not that of excited anticipation of an immediate catastrophe, but that of the faithful performance of daily duties and quiet waiting for the fullness of the times.... Active service and patient waiting are better than any amount of fuming and fretting and overhaste and overzeal.... The patience of Christ will wait for the appointed hour in steadfast faith and in perfect submission. It will not complain when hopes are disappointed. It will not lose heart when there are unexpected delays. It will go on in the way of faithful service, sure that in the end it will be clear that all things have been administered for the best.[6]

Paul's gospel

Though Paul personally believed in the soon return of Christ, he never overemphasized it or set a date for it. His gospel was not "Jesus *will come*," but "Jesus *has come*."

---

[5] According to William Barclay, Matthew 24 gives a composite picture of the future: Verses 1, 2 and 15-22 appear to refer to the devastating siege of Jerusalem in A.D. 70 under Titus, which left 97,000 enslaved and 1,100,000 dead! Verses 6-8 and 29-31 refer to the frightening Day of the Lord. Verses 9 and 10 point to the persecution which Christians are to experience, and verses 3, 14, 27 and 28 to the Second Coming. *The Gospel of Matthew*, vol. 2, William Barclay, pp. 334-36.

[6] *Paul and His Epistles*, D. A. Hayes, pp. 180, 181.

Chapter 19

"The Light of Asia"

Fourth Jerusalem visit

When Paul went up to Jerusalem[1] and met with the church, his welcome appears to have been disappointing. Luke records that "he greeted the church" but makes no mention of the church greeting him (Ac. 18:22). Obviously the apostles and elders were too preoccupied with their internal affairs to pay much attention to him. Finding himself thus largely ignored and with little interest shown in his ministry, Paul quickly departed and traveled north to his home church in Antioch, Syria. Here his friends received him warmly, eager to hear how God had used him abroad and keen to relate how the gospel was beginning to make inroads into Antioch's profligate society. Paul's previous energetic ministry there was beginning to bear fruit.

Third missionary journey

After some time at Antioch, Paul embarked on a third missionary journey which would doubtless have included visits to Derbe, Lystra, Iconium and Antioch and other communities in such provinces as Galatia and Phrygia where he had planted churches. Though there is no record of who accompanied him on this tour, most certainly Timothy would have been with him since his name appears twenty-four times in the account of this sojourn.

The early churches

How eager Paul would have been to be back with his converts and learn of their physical and spiritual needs as well as learn how they had grown in grace and knowledge of Christ! These converts comprised men and women from all walks of

---

[1] Jerusalem is on a tableland occupying one of the highest altitudes (2,500 feet above sea level) in central Palestine. Because of this, approaching it or leaving it is always spoken of as "going up to" or "going down from" the city. For example, "And when he [Paul] landed at Caesarea, he went up and greeted the church [in Jerusalem], and went down to Antioch [in the far north]" (Ac. 18:22).

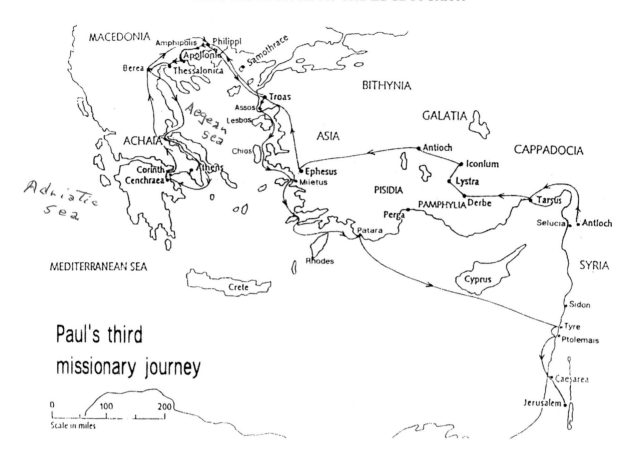

Paul's third
missionary journey

0   100   200
Scale in miles

life, some Jews and many Gentiles, some well-educated and financially secure and some leaders in society. But the majority of Paul's converts were very poor, among whom were the slaves and destitute beggars. "Brothers," Paul reminds the Corinthian believers, "think of what you were when you were called. Not many of you were wise by human standards; not many were influential; not many were of noble birth" (1Cor. 1:26 NIV). But Paul saw them all as the redeemed—male and female, master and slave, rich and indigent—it mattered not; in Paul's eyes they were his much-loved brothers and sisters in Christ, and were constantly on his mind and on his heart. "I face daily the pressure of my concern for all the churches," he exclaimed to the Corinthians" (2Cor. 11:28 NIV). "I have you in my heart," he wrote the Philippians (Phil. 1:7 NIV).

The early churches Paul founded, it must be remembered, were not structured organizations meeting in buildings built for such gatherings, but rather to be viewed as organisms—people gathered together in the name of Christ. They believed He was in their midst, as He had promised His disciples He would be when two or three had gathered together in His name (Mt. 18:20). It mattered not where they met, whether by a riverside, or under the trees, or in a home or in a barn, just as long as they could come together frequently for worship and fellowship and praise, and thereby grow in their Christian faith.

As for leadership in these early churches that Paul planted, Paul followed the example of the apostles in Jerusalem and appointed elders as the spiritual overseers of the congregations (Ac. 14:23) and doubtless also appointed deacons to care for the needy among the believers. Later, towards the close of Paul's life, elders and deacons together with pastors were elected by the congregations.

Though all of these early Christians, including Paul, anticipated the imminent return of Christ, they never set a date for His return. The emphasis was not on when Jesus would come or how He would come, but on being ready whenever He decided to come.

Baptism was not thought of as a sacrament by these early believers, but rather as an outward sign of an inward change. Any convert was at liberty to baptize another convert, and the method was always, if possible, by submersion. Affusion was not practiced generally until well into the second century. As for baptizing infants, this was unheard of in the days of Paul and not until about 180, according to Irenaeus, was infant baptism introduced into the Christian church.[2]

The Lord's Supper, as with baptism could be administered by any believer and was generally preceded by a fellowship meal known as the "Love Feast." Breaking the bread and sharing the wine reminded the Christians of the night when Jesus sat with His disciples and ate with them and then broke bread and served them

---

[2] The baptizing of infants born into a family in which one parent, at least, was a Christian, was seen as analogous to circumcision, the mark whereby a child became a member of the Chosen Race under the Old Covenant. Under the New Covenant in Christ, baptism of infants was seen as the sign and seal of the child's acceptance into the household of faith and, being brought up in the nurture and admonition of the Lord, would, when he reached the age of accountability, acknowledge the risen Christ as his Savior and Lord and unite with the church.

Paul, however, would never have been in agreement with such reasoning. Baptism to him was only meaningful as a sign of new life in Christ. Nowhere in his letters is there a hint of baptizing infants, not even in his letter to the Romans which largely discusses Christian doctrine.

The temple of Hadrian, Ephesus, built A.D. 391.

wine—the broken bread standing for His body which was soon to be broken for them, and the wine symbolizing His blood soon to be poured out on Calvary as the atonement for sin.

Women in the early church took no part in church leadership, as would be expected, considering the low view of women held by the pagan world. But women, nonetheless, maintained a very active rôle in these early church fellowships and joined with the men in worship as their spiritual brothers. Thus were the germinal principles sown which centuries later would have an enormous effect in eradicating racism and the evils accompanying it at all levels.

Ephesus

Paul had not forgotten Aquila and Priscilla in Ephesus nor his promise to the Jews there to return if it was God's will. Now with his years of experience in deal-

Marble street to the theater of Ephesus.

ing with the pagan world and his overwhelming confidence in the power of his message, he felt the time was apropos to make his way back to Ephesus and begin an all-out effort to win the city over to the Savior.

It was with this conviction that he traveled the great highway to Ephesus, and, when nearing the outskirts of the city, would have found himself deeply excited realizing he was about to re-enter the city proclaimed "The Supreme Metropolis of Asia" and the home of the celebrated temple of Artemis, goddess of the Ephesians.

Located midway between Miletus and Smyrna on a lake seven miles inland, Ephesus boasted a population of a quarter of a million. Proudly it hosted the Panionian games, vying in popularity with the Isthmian and Olympic games. Quartered compulsorily in the city were Roman troops, and governors periodically visited it to try important court cases. The city of Ephesus thus was ever conscious of Roman power and "crawled at the feet of Emperors, flattered them with abject servility and built temples to their crime or their feebleness and deified them on her inscriptions and coins."[3]

The harbor of Ephesus was fed by the short, fast-flowing river Cayster which carried an enormous amount of silt, probably the result of excessive lumbering and overgrazing on its shores. This meant the harbor had to be continually dredged to keep the waterway open. Finally, the equipment proved inadequate and the harbor was closed. The city, then deprived of its maritime trade and easy access to the west and often pillaged by its enemies, steadily declined until finally it sank into oblivion.[4]

The temple of Artemis

The original temple of Artemis[5] was burned down in 356 B.C. by Herostratus so that his name could go down in history as the arsonist. He then rebuilt it twenty-two years later with the help of Artemis cultists, including apostate Jewish women, who willingly sold their jewelry to help finance the new structure, which far outshone the original one and became one of the great architectural wonders of the world.

Ionic in style it stood on a platform about 425 feet long and 240 feet wide and was four times larger than the Parthenon, and one and a half times the size of the Cathedral of Cologne in Germany. Gold was reported to have been used between its marble blocks, and each of its 127 sixty-foot-high pillars, all monoliths of glittering Parian marble, was erected by a different king.

The cedar roof was covered with large white marble tiles supported by columns of jasper, and leading up to it was a stairway said to have been carved out of one gigantic vine from the island of Cyprus. Alexander the Great was so impressed with the magnificence of the temple that he offered all the spoils of one of his eastern campaigns to have his name inscribed on its walls. His offer, however, was refused as only the names of Ephesians were allowed this high honor.

At the center of the temple was the great altar, the work of Praxiteles, one of the most celebrated sculptors of Greece. At the rear of the altar stood the sacred image of the goddess Artemis hidden by a giant purple veil. Directly behind the idol was a

---

[3] *The Life and Work of Saint Paul*, Frederic W. Farrar, vol. 2, p. 9.

[4] The present city of Seljuk is the sixth city on the site of Ephesus.

[5] Diana is the Latin name for Artemis, the Greek tutelary goddess of the Ephesians.

large chamber wherein were stored the treasures of many potentates. It was considered the safest repository in the world and was constantly under guard.

The area extending 660 feet all around the shrine provided immunity for anyone fleeing the law, and this of course attracted the dregs of society. One could never be sure who in the crowds were hardcore criminals.

The weird figure of Artemis was believed to have fallen from Zeus (Jupiter).[6] Its lower part was swathed like an Egyptian mummy while its upper portion was studded with many protruberances said to represent the ova of bees. This indicated the idol's function as the goddess of fertility and the bee as her sacred symbol. The bee appeared on most Ephesian coins.

All the priests of Artemis were eunuchs since it was believed by many that the goddess was so virtuous she could not allow normal males near her. Others, however, maintained it was because she was so lascivious that no man could resist her charms.

Heraclitus, the "weeping philosopher," declared the morals of Artemis worse than bestial. He gave as his reason for never smiling the fact that he lived in the degraded city of Ephesus whose inhabitants, he exclaimed, were fit to be drowned.

Though Ephesus proclaimed herself "The Light of Asia," no city was so spiritually dark. Sorcery and black magic and the offering of incantations to avert or inflict evil were practiced here more than anywhere else. Talismans and silver figurines of Artemis, blessed by renown witches, were sold by the thousands to the masses of pilgrims daily flooding the city.

Paul leaves the synagogue for the school of Tyrannus

In such a city Paul now accepted the invitation offered him by the Jews and the God-fearers to teach in their synagogue. They assured him of their keen interest to learn more of Christian teaching. But Paul, after three months, found his Jewish students speaking against him and influencing others to discount his message. Finally, Paul left the synagogue and taught in a private school run by a Greek named Tyrannus and here, finding a receptive hearing, he remained for the next two years.

Paul's ministry, however, was not only in Ephesus, but reached throughout the entire province of Asia (Ac. 19:10). Many far and wide came to know Christ. On

---

[6] Among other idols believed to have fallen to the earth were Athena of the Acropolis in Athens, Aphrodite of Pathos and Tybele of Pessimus.

The partially excavated theater of Ephesus, 1962.

The completed excavation of the theater of Ephesus and the Arcadian Way
leading to the ancient harbor, silted up.

one occasion a large group of believers met in public and lit an enormous bonfire
into which they threw their books on sorcery and magical arts valued at an estimated 50,000 drachmas ($10,000), the equivalent of a yearly wage paid to a rural
laborer over a period of 138 years![7]

Ephesus in uproar

As the sales from the Artemis figurines steadily declined, even during the May
festival when Ephesus was swarming with visitors, Demetrius, a prominent crafts-

---

[7] Footnote to Ac. 19:19, *Ryrie Study Bible*.

man of the silver figurines, called an emergency meeting of his tradesmen and those in similar trades. He warned:

> Men, you know that our prosperity depends upon this business. And you see and hear that not only in Ephesus, but in almost all of Asia, this Paul has persuaded and turned away a considerable number of people, saying that gods made with hands are no gods at all. And not only is there danger that this trade of ours fall into disrepute, but also that the temple of the great goddess Artemis be regarded as worthless and that she whom all Asia and the world worship should even be dethroned from her magnificence. (Ac. 19:25-27)

Immediately the silversmiths became outraged and began broadcasting throughout the city that Artemis was under attack. So effective was their propaganda that thousands of Artemis's followers left their homes and work places and rushed into the city's amphitheater, capable of seating 24,500 spectators. There, controlled by mass hysteria, they began chanting in unison, "Great is Artemis, goddess of the Ephesians!" (Ac. 19:34). The majority were unaware of why they had come or why they were extolling their honored goddess. The frenzied cry continued for about two hours!

Since Paul was nowhere to be found, his enemies seized two of his cohorts, Gaius and Aristarchus, and dragged them into the amphitheater to face the agitated crowd. When Paul learned of this, he hurried to the theater and would have rushed in had not his brethren and some friendly city authorities restrained him. They rightly feared that the sight of Paul, who by now was well known, might easily provoke a riot, which could result not only in his death but that of many others.

The Jewish businessmen of the city, not wanting to be thought friends of the Christians realizing the damaging effect this would have on their trade, quickly presented to the crowd their spokesman, Alexander.[8] His assignment was to convince the multitude that the Jewish commercial sector of the city was in no way aligned with Christianity nor with its missionary, Paul. But the inflamed spectators, observing that Alexander was a Jew and generally believing that Christianity was a Jewish sect, refused to listen to him and continued their frenetic chanting.

The town clerk now appeared and by reason of his authority succeeded in quelling the throng. "Men of Ephesus," he shouted,

---

[8] This Alexander may well have been the one to whom Paul refers as having done him much harm (1Tim. 1:20; 2Tim. 4:14).

what man is there after all who does not know that the city of the Ephesians is guardian of the temple of the great Artemis, and of the image which fell down from heaven? Since then these are the undeniable facts, you ought to keep calm and to do nothing rash. For you have brought these men here who are neither robbers of temples or blasphemers of our goddess. (Ac. 19:35-37)

After reminding Demetrius and his craftsmen that the courts were in session and proconsuls were available to settle their disputes and after warning that if the unruly behavior continued those involved would be severely punished, he dismissed the crowd.

The fact that the town clerk recognized that Paul had not blasphemed Artemis indicates clearly that Paul, as he had in Athens, presented only the positive message of Christ. He had not come to destroy an idol but to plant a Cross. He believed that the gospel with its "expulsive power of a new affection"[9] would in its own way eventually conquer Artemis.

Paul and fetishes

Luke records that in Ephesus God performed extraordinary miracles through Paul and that handkerchiefs and aprons that had touched him were carried to the sick and laid on them and they were healed and evil spirits were cast out.[10] It should be noted that Luke was not with Paul at this time and was reporting only on what he had been told regarding the prayer cloths.

It is inconceivable that Paul would have authorized the use of any of these things, especially anything associated with himself! Charms or amulets or objects claimed to have magical powers to heal the sick or exorcise demons would never have been allowed by Paul to be associated with any Christian ministry, let alone his own. Nor would he have allowed anyone to ascribe supernatural power to himself or anyone other than the Lord Jesus. He had made this abundantly clear at Lystra when he and Barnabas tore their clothes and shouted they were not gods and forbade the priests of Jupiter to sacrifice to them (Ac. 14:11-18).

It therefore appears that in Ephesus these handkerchiefs and aprons touched him without his knowledge and were used without his consent by well-meaning, would-be faith-healers who may have considered Paul endowed with supernatural powers. Long influenced by witchcraft and the teachings of sorcery, they doubtless

---

[9] Thomas Chalmers, *The Protestant Pulpit*, Andrew Blackwood, p. 50.

10. Acts 19:11.

reasoned that any object associated with Paul, well known for his persuasive powers, would prove highly effective in exorcising demons and healing the sick.

Misusing the name of Jesus

Upon learning of the fetishes being used, Paul would promptly have pointed out the error of ascribing spiritual power to inanimate objects and the very real danger of using such objects as substitutes for faith in Christ. Paul would immediately have reminded the Ephesians of the seven sons of the Ephesian Jewish chief priest, Sceva, who had used Jesus as a shaman and in His name had tried to cast out a demon. The result was that the evil spirit caused the man in whom it resided to jump on the seven men and beat them mercilessly until they all fled from the house naked and wounded (Ac. 19:16).

The reported effectiveness of the prayer cloths or the rituals accompanying them must be discounted as having in themselves anything to do with the healings. Some, however, among the ill who believed Paul was endowed with the gift of healing, upon learning that the prayer cloths laid upon them were associated with his body, may well have been healed psychologically. But most of the healings would have resulted from a childlike faith in Jesus who of His own volition brought about the cures.

Paul prays for the Ephesians

Paul's prayer for the Ephesian Christians, many of whom had come out of witchcraft, showed how deeply concerned he was for them to know the power of Christ in their lives and the true meaning of faith. He prayed that the eyes of their hearts might be enlightened "so that you may know what is the hope of His calling, what are the riches of the glory of His inheritance in the saints, and what is the surpassing greatness of His power, toward us who believe …" (Eph. 1:18, 19) and "so that Christ may dwell in your hearts through faith … and to know … Him who is able to do exceedingly abundantly beyond all that we ask or think, according to the power that works within us …" (3:17, 19, 20).

Paul's longest ministry

Paul's three-year ministry in Ephesus, the longest in any city, was perhaps his most fruitful. Through the power of the Holy Spirit manifested in his ministry and

The marshy site of the temple of Artemis (Diana).

that of others who followed him, the notorious cult of Artemis, one of the most virulent and well-entrenched in the ancient world, was finally eliminated. Her celebrated temple was destroyed by the Goths about the year A.D. 260 and its site lost to the world until discovered in 1904.

Chapter 20

Counseling Corinthians

Silanus and his brother

After Paul had ministered two years in Ephesus, he may well have been among the many Christians who were suddenly arrested and accused by Nero of being implicated in the murders of Silanus, proconsul of Ephesus, and his brother. Unknown to the emperor, the two deaths had been instigated by his mother Agrippina, notorious for her conniving and fanatical support of her son and for her exorbitant power in the Roman court. Suspecting the brother of Silanus of intrigue, she ordered him assassinated, and then fearing that Silanus might avenge his brother's death, ordered him murdered as well. The allegations against Paul would, of course, eventually have been proven false, but in the meantime, having to be incarcerated and undergo rigorous interrogation and appear again and again in court, and wait interminably for verdicts to be handed down, would have been exasperating and incredibly hard to bear.

Disorder in the Corinthian church

Some months after the murders of Silanus and his brother, news reached Paul from the Christians in Corinth concerning many problems in the church that had developed there, among them divisions in the congregation, immorality and a disciplinary case of a man who had been censored for wrongdoing (2Cor. 2:5-11).

Promptly Paul responded by sending back a stern letter (unfortunately not preserved) and explained later that he wrote it "out of great distress and anguish of heart and with many tears, not to grieve you but to let you know the depth of my love for you."[1]

---

[1] Later Paul mentioned this case in 2Cor. 2:6-8 NIV. It evidently concerned some who wanted the offender, who had repented, given more severe punishment. "The punishment," Paul wrote, "inflicted on him by the majority is sufficient for him. Now instead, you ought to forgive and comfort him, so that he will not be overwhelmed by excessive sorrow. I urge you, therefore, to reaffirm your love for him."

It was while waiting for an answer to this letter that Paul received more disturbing news from the Christians at Corinth, informing him of four quarrelsome factions which had developed in the church, each claiming allegiance to either Paul, Apollos, Cephas (Peter) or Jesus (1Cor. 1:11, 12). But before Paul could address this matter, still another delegation arrived, this time bringing a letter from the congregation (1Cor. 7:1).[2] This was probably in answer to Paul's first letter. Paul's reply (I Corinthians) is a veritable case book of pastoral theology and shows him as masterful a counselor and arbitrator as he was a preacher and evangelist.[3]

Stressing spiritual unity

In dealing with the many divisive groups in the church, Paul shocked his readers with such questions as: "Has Christ been divided? Paul was not crucified for you, was he? Or were you baptized in the name of Paul?" (1Cor. 1:13). He then thanked God that as far as he knew he had baptized none of the Corinthians except Crispus and Gaius and the household of Stephanas, lest people be under the impression his chief aim had been to baptize. "Christ did not send me to baptize," Paul insisted, "but to preach the gospel, not in cleverness of speech, that the cross of Christ should not be made void" (v. 17).

Again and again Paul emphasized in this epistle and other of his letters the need for Christians to be united in Spirit and to avoid quarrels which produce divisions. To the Corinthians he wrote, "I exhort you, brethren, by the name of our Lord Jesus Christ, that you all agree, and that there be no divisions among you ..." (1Cor. 1:10). To the Romans, "[M]ay God ... grant you to be of the same mind with one another according to Christ Jesus" (Rom. 15:5, 6). To the Ephesians, "I ... entreat you ... to preserve the unity of the Spirit in the bond of peace" (Eph. 4:1, 3). To the Colossians, "[B]eyond all ... put on love, which is the perfect bond of unity" (Col. 3:14), and to Timothy, "[T]he Lord's bond-servant must not be quarrelsome ..." (2Tim. 2:24).

---

[2] Stephanas, Fortunatus and Achaicus, mentioned in 1Cor. 16:17, probably were the ones who brought this letter.

[3] This letter (I Corinthians) required a roll of papyrus approximately nine inches wide and nine feet in length, one third the maximum length of an ordinary Greek book. *Paul*, J. Edgar Goodspeed, p. 127.

Paul's remedy for sectarianism and disunity among Christians was, first and foremost, love for Christ. In proportion to this love would be the love of Christian believers for one another. It was the *sine qua non* for maintaining Christian fellowship.

Christians in litigation

Paul pled with the Christians at Corinth not to take their disputes before heathen courts but to settle them among themselves. "I say this to your shame," Paul exclaimed, "Is it so, that there is not among you one wise man who will be able to decide between his brethren, but brother goes to law with brother, and that before unbelievers?… Why not rather be wronged? Why not rather be defrauded?" (1 Cor. 6:5-7).

Here Paul surely was not referring to such crimes as murder, armed robbery, rape, or the spread of slander, but only to disputes which arose in the Corinthian congregation that could be solved within it.

The church, Paul would have counseled, should never become an "Artemis temple" serving as a refuge for unrepentant sinners, but as a place of prayer and reconciliation. As far as possible, if any church member was caught in a trespass, it was the responsibility of the leaders of the assembly to try and bring him to repentance and to restore him in a spirit of gentleness; each one looking to himself lest he too be tempted. "Bear one another's burdens, and thus fulfill the law of Christ" was Paul's emphasis (Gal. 6:2).

This was not, however, to mean that Christians were forbidden to take legal action when wronged in or outside the church. If a wrongdoer refused to repent and make restitution, the Christian had every right to take him to court. Laws were laid down by governments for the good and protection of all and divinely established to mete out justice for all (Rom. 13:1-7; Tit. 3:1).[4]

Concerning marriage

The Corinthians were concerned about the marriage relationship, asking Paul if it was right to be married, for widows and widowers to remarry, and, upon becoming a Christian, whether it was required to remain with one's helpmate if he or she was not a Christian. Paul's answer to all was in the strong affirmative. He instructed Christians who chose to be married to marry only Christians, pointing

---

[4] For further discussion on Paul's views of justice, see Chapter 28, "Schism in the Sanhedrin" on p. 190.

out that the marriage relationship, whether among Christians or non-Christians was indissoluble (1Cor. 7:10, 11, 39). Paul saw marriage as a holy institution ordained by God. Wives were to be subject to their husbands as unto the Lord, and husbands were to love their wives just as Christ loved the church, which Paul called His "bride" (Eph. 5:22-25).

Paul in this letter was careful to point out when he was expressing only his opinions and when they were what he believed to be commands of the Lord. This is seen in his discussion of marriage:

> … this I say by way of concession, not of command. Yet I wish that all men were even as I myself am.… But to the married I give instructions, not I, but the Lord, that the wife should not leave her husband (but if she does leave, let her remain unmarried, or else be reconciled to her husband), and that the husband should not send his wife away. (1Cor. 7:6, 7, 10, 11)

Paul's celibacy

The fact that Paul remained unmarried[5] was certainly not because he disliked women or because women disliked him. Women were devoted to him all through his ministry, and many would doubtless have rejoiced to be his wife. Even Paul's "thorn in the flesh,"[6] most probably a repulsive eye disease which disfigured his face, was not enough to cause women to shun him. Paul's overwhelming charisma and magnetic personality were more than enough to compensate for whatever he lacked in personal appearance.

While believing he had a right to be married, as was the right of the apostles and Jesus' brothers (1Cor. 9:5), Paul chose not to be married, believing that Jesus was soon to return and marriage would hinder his ministry. He explained this by pointing out that an unmarried Christian man "is concerned about the things of the Lord, how he may please the Lord; but one who is married is concerned about the things of the world, how he may please his wife, and his interests are divided …" (1Cor. 7:32-34).

But were Paul living today he would doubtless favor being married, realizing the inestimable value of having a Christian helpmate by his side. He would also not preach the imminent return of Christ, but only to be ready to receive Him whenever He comes.

---

[5] See Chapter 1, "Introducing Saul," p. 8, fn. 11.

[6] For further discussion of Paul's "thorn," see Chapter 23, "Paul's Heart Revealed" on p. 160.

Freedom vs. license

Whether Christians were allowed to buy meat that had been offered to idols was a matter on which Paul dwelt at length. He pointed out that though believers were free to eat anything they wished, they should refrain from buying such meat if doing so would cause those who observed the transaction to become idol worshippers. Paul declared, "if food causes my brother to stumble, I will never eat meat again that I might not cause my brother to stumble" (1Cor. 8:13). In stressing personal sacrifice in behalf of others in an age notorious for its greed and selfishness, Paul established the fundamental principle underlying all social reform.

The Lord's Supper

Paul urged the Corinthians to respect the Lord's Supper and not use it as an excuse for feasting and drunkenness, as was sometimes the case. The bread and wine of the Communion represented the broken body and shed blood of Christ, the perfect Lamb of God, the Atonement for sin. Those who partook of the sacred meal should first examine themselves to see that they were right with the Lord and their brethren and neighbors lest they eat the bread and drink the cup and bring judgment upon themselves (1Cor. 11:27-29).

Paul discusses the resurrection

When Paul wrote he would have been familiar with the four general concepts regarding the future life of the dead:

1. Absorption into God (Buddhism). After a succession of lives and deaths, the soul was thought to complete the spiral of its existence and come back to God and be absorbed into Him like an ocean absorbs a river.

2. Reincarnation (Hinduism). The soul was believed to pass over into another organism and live as a human being or a part of the animal kingdom.

3. The departed preserved in his or her own body (Egyptian belief). Embalming was practiced to assure life would remain until the day of resurrection.

4. Life in a disembodied state in a shadowy underworld (Greek and Roman belief).

Because of the resurrection of Jesus there appeared a fifth concept of the future life of the departed—a strong belief in the immortality of the soul and the personal resurrection of the dead. But some in the Corinthian church were confused and beginning to doubt and this prompted Paul to write his strong exposé of the Resurrection.

First it should be noted that Paul opposes the pagan belief that the body placed in the grave must rise to preserve personal immortality. He opposes also the thought that the body must find its resting place in some other body or be embalmed to preserve life, or that the soul must live in a shadowy-world without a body. Paul's teaching was unique from anything ever taught regarding the future of the dead.

The following paraphrase of what Paul writes in answer to the question, "With what body do the dead arise?" is helpful in clarifying his electrifying new message. (It also reveals Paul as a superb illustrator of truth.)

> You plant a seed in the ground. It dies. Nor will anything come from it unless it dies. But when something does come, it is not that which you put in the ground. The same life which was in the seed comes to the surface, but clad with a new body.... And so shall it be in the resurrection of the dead. That which thou sowest is a mere seed; that which rises has a new glory of its own. If there is a natural body adapted to the needs of this life, that is itself a reason for believing that there is another, a spiritual body, adapted to the needs of the other life.... If God were to bring from all the quarters of the globe all fragments of the body, it would serve no purpose; for flesh and blood can never inherit the kingdom of God, since that which is essentially corrupt cannot inherit the incorruptible, nor that which from the moment of its birth begins to die, inherit the immortal ... There must be a new organism and a new habitation for a new life. In this is Christ's supreme victory. For now we see that death is no destruction. Now we see that the end of death is not the perishing of the seed in the ground.... Death no longer conquers.... Death no longer even pricks as a sting of a wasp. Death is deprived of its sting. Death is the advent to a larger life, and God shall clothe that life with glory, as it pleaseth him.[7]

The Pharisees, in Paul's day, generally expected for the devout a resurrection from Sheol (realm of the dead) simultaneous with the advent of the Messiah. This probably was Paul's earlier view. But as the years unfolded, Paul gradually passed from his Pharisaic to his Christian view of death and resurrection, concentrating

---

[7] *The Life and Letter of Paul the Apostle*, Lyman Abbott, pp. 59, 60. Paul's mention of being baptized for the dead (1Cor. 15:29) may have referred to the practice then current of being baptized for one who had died while studying for baptism. This custom soon ceased.

less on the coming of the Messiah in the clouds of glory and more on Christ as the power and wisdom of God and the new life in Him as a continuity of spiritual life beyond the grave.[8]

Paul concludes his letter by outlining his proposed itinerary for the next few months, then give various instructions and greetings to his friends and ends with the Aramaic word *Maranatha,* which is thought to mean "the Lord is at hand." It was used as a cryptic watchword to announce that Christians were present.[9]

Corinthian visit deferred

Paul while in Ephesus had twice intended to visit Corinth by way of Macedonia (2Cor. 1:15, 16), but each time cancelled his plans, believing that the Corinthians were not spiritually ready to receive him. He felt it was better for their sake to communicate with them by letter.

Deciding now it was no longer safe to remain in Ephesus in view of the mounting opposition from the silversmiths, Paul sent Titus with a brother (probably Luke or Trophimus, and another unnamed brother) to Corinth to inform them of the situation (2Cor. 8:18, 22). He instructed Titus to return to Troas and wait for him there where it appears a significant door had opened for Paul to proclaim the gospel (2Cor. 2:12; see 2Cor. 7:6-16; 8:6, 16-18; 12:18).[10]

When Paul, however, arrived at Troas, Titus was not there, which so distressed Paul that he cancelled his preaching appointment and crossed to Macedonia in search of him. Relieved to find Titus on his way back from Corinth, he was overjoyed to learn that the Corinthians had repented of their wrongdoing and that the stern letter Paul had sent them had proved beneficial. It was now that he wrote them his third letter (2 Corinthians) and sent it back with Titus; he then departed for Illyricum (the western Balkans) where he continued to evangelize and establish more churches before returning to Corinth to spend the winter (Rom. 15:19).

---

[8] Ibid., p. 163.

[9] *The Letters to the Corinthians*, William Barclay, p. 188.

[10] Before this, Timothy had been sent to Corinth to settle the problems but evidently was unsuccessful. Paul's statement that he himself was about to come to Corinth the third time (2Cor. 12:14; 13:1), though Acts records only one previous visit, may indicate he made a brief unrecorded visit to Corinth for the purpose of exercising discipline in the church.

Chapter 21

A Highly Sensitive Issue

Speaking in tongues

Of all the sensitive issues recorded in Paul's ministry calling for wisdom and tact, nothing surpassed the phenomenon of "speaking in tongues" known as *glossolalia*, from the Greek words *glossa,* meaning "tongue," and *laeo,* meaning "speech."[1] Such was the term used for speaking in defined languages unknown to the speaker or in unknown "heavenly languages" referred to as "ecstatic utterance." To highlight the difference, Paul denoted "tongues" in the plural as known languages and "tongue" in the singular as ecstatic utterances.

Paul dealt with this phenomenon in only three chapters (1Cor. 12-14) of one of his extant letters. The matter is not mentioned in any other writings of the New Testament with the exception of the book of Acts, where it is recorded taking place at Pentecost in Jerusalem (Ac. 2:1-11), at the home of Cornelius in Caesarea (10:44-46) and in the presence of some disciples of John the Baptist in Ephesus (19:1-7).

Tongues at Jerusalem

It was while the twelve apostles were assembled in a room in Jerusalem on the day of Pentecost at nine o'clock in the morning that suddenly the sound of rushing wind was heard and cloven flames rested on each one of them. Immediately they began speaking in bona fide languages other than their own and were "filled with the Holy Spirit" (Ac. 2:1-6). The fourteen languages spoken were those of people in Jerusalem at the time who had come from Parthia, Media, Elam, Mesopotamia, Judea,[2] Cappadocia, Pontus, Phrygia, Pamphylia, Egypt, Libya, Rome, Crete and Arabia.

---

[1] The word *glossolalia* is not found in the Scriptures.

[2] The Judeans heard their dialect spoken by the apostles, all of whom were Galileans. Judas, now dead, had been the only Judean among them.

Upon hearing the loud sound of wind yet sensing no turbulence in the air, people dwelling in the vicinity of the house in which the apostles were gathered rushed to the Twelve to find out the cause of the disturbance. Upon arriving they were astounded that the apostles were able to address each one in his own vernacular. Some in the crowd ridiculed the speakers, claiming they were inebriated, but obviously these were not Jews. Had they been, they would have known that Jews, when engaged in the exercises of the synagogue on feast days, abstained from eating and drinking until 10 o'clock A.M. or until noon (2:15).[3] The majority in the crowd, however, believing the apostles were sober, were willing to listen to them.

Peter, being the spokesman, addressed the people and attested to the fact that he and his fellow apostles were witnesses to the Resurrection and that Jesus was indeed alive and the promised Messiah. Fervently Peter urged the people to repent and believe in Him.

The result was that an estimated three thousand people repented of their sins and were converted and then baptized. No mention, however, is made of any of the converts speaking in tongues or of any sound of wind or appearance of fire (2:41). The baptisms, of course, would not have taken place in Jerusalem but most probably in the river Jordan at a later date.

Tongues at Caesarea

The next occurrence of the tongues phenomenon was at Caesarea in the home of Cornelius, when Peter visited him and his associates. When the Holy Spirit fell upon the believers (Gentiles in this case) and enabled them to speak in tongues (Ac. 10:46), again there was no sound of wind or presence of fire as had occurred at Pentecost. Though the in-dwelling of the Holy Spirit always occurs at the moment of conversion, there is no indication in Scripture that speaking in tongues must follow. The ability of the Gentiles at Caesarea to speak in tongues served only as a dramatic sign to both Jews and Gentiles present that the Gentiles now had received the Holy Spirit.

Tongues at Ephesus

The third and final occurrence of tongues-speaking recorded in Acts was at Ephesus. Here Paul met with about twelve disciples of John the Baptist, men who

---

[3] See footnote concerning Ac. 2:15, *Ryrie Study Bible*.

knew only the baptism of John and nothing of the Holy Spirit (Ac. 19:1-7).[4] Immediately, after Paul had instructed them regarding the Third Person of the Trinity, they believed and were baptized and spoke in tongues. But, as with the converts at Jerusalem and those at Caesarea, there was no manifestation of wind or fire. Again, the speaking in tongues here served only as a sign, this time as a sign to John's disciples that the Age of Grace had come and fidelity to the religious cere- monies and laws of the Old Testament was inadequate to assure salvation. It was only through the atoning sacrifice of Christ and faith in Him as sin-bearer that one could be made right with God.

Just as Aquila and Priscilla had instructed Apollos (Ac. 18:24-28),[5] Paul pointed out that immediately upon conversion the Holy Spirit in-dwells the believer. This in-dwelling, as Paul later explained to the Ephesian Christians, was God's seal: "... you were sealed in Him with the Holy Spirit of promise, who is given as a pledge of our inheritance with a view to the redemption of God's own possession, to the praise of His glory" (Eph. 1:13, 14).[6] The sealing was not a subsequent work of grace nor a reward for spirituality but a confirmation of the eternal sonship of the believer with his Father (Gal. 3:26; cf. Jn. 10:27-30).

Paul insisted that once the believer is converted, his body becomes the "temple of the Holy Spirit" (1Cor. 6:19; cf. 3:16). If anyone does not have the Spirit of Christ, he does not belong to Him (Rom. 8:9). Once "born again," the convert does not require a second baptism or blessing or an emotional experience or the ability to speak a language unknown to himself. He is, however, expected to "grow in grace and knowledge" of Christ (2Pet. 3:18).

Feeling vs. fact

Always Paul cautioned against allowing one's emotions to dictate how one feels regarding his salvation. Enough to rest on the fact that God the Father, Son and

---

[4] John's message was "Repent and turn to God," while Jesus' message was "Repent for God has come to you." John excoriated those who came to him for baptism, calling them a brood of vipers fleeing from the wrath to come, and threatening them with a fiery death if they did not produce the fruits of repentance. Jesus, on the other hand, called to Himself the weary and heavy-laden, promising to give them rest (Mt. 11:28).

[5] After being warmly endorsed by the disciples at Ephesus, Apollos was sent to the church at Corinth and there became one of its strongest leaders. Nowhere is there any evidence that he ever spoke in tongues or in ecstatic utterances or ever advocated others to do so.

[6] See also Eph. 4:30 and 2Cor. 1:22. The "sealing" of the Christian is entirely the work of God.

Holy Spirit entered the believer's heart at conversion and there will continue forever. The Christian, as noted, may break the communion with his Father, but never the union; he remains forever His child. Though he may fall *on* the bridge to heaven, he can never fall *off* the bridge; and though he might feel he has lost his salvation, his salvation can never be lost (Jn. 10:27, 28).

Tongues vs. tongue

Sometime after Paul left Corinth, there developed in the church the phenomenon of uttering incoherent sounds which those who spoke them believed were heavenly languages known only to God. These "languages" were completely different from the defined languages spoken in Jerusalem at Pentecost and later in Caesarea and Ephesus. As mentioned, Paul used "tongues" in the plural to denote known languages and "tongue" in the singular to denote ecstatic utterances.

Congregation in chaos

The elders at Corinth had allowed worshippers to pray aloud whenever they felt moved, using whatever earthly language or ecstatic utterance they desired. The result was a babel of sounds—utterly confusing—with many crying out in ecstatic utterances, yet totally unaware of what they were saying. This left the startled visitors in the congregation with no choice but to conclude that the whole assembly had gone mad (1Cor. 14:23).

At one of these services, and it must have been in Corinth since Paul writes of it in his letter to the Corinthians, there was heard the shockingly blasphemous statement, "*Anathema Iesous!*" "Jesus is accursed!" Probably it was blurted out by someone who had read in Deuteronomy, "he who is hanged is accursed of God" (Deut. 21:23), and, knowing Jesus had been hanged on a cross, assumed that the statement applied to Him! Paul sharply denounced such blasphemy, declaring that "no one speaking by the Spirit of God says, 'Jesus is accursed'" (1Cor. 12:3). Such wild babblings and uncontrolled emotion were strictly forbidden by Paul who emphasized that God is not a God of confusion but of peace and that all things should be done decently and in an orderly manner (14:33, 40).

Paul's dealing with tongue-speakers

Paul was careful not to be overly critical of those in the Corinthian assembly who sincerely believed they were communicating with God when they spoke ecstatically, or of those who believed they had the "gift of interpretation" to translate what was being said. Rather he chose to deal with the tongue-speakers gently as a father would deal with his children when they erred and needed instruction.

In the Corinthian church, as previously discussed, there were many conflicting opinions regarding the flesh and the Spirit, marriage and celibacy, continence and license, the right or wrong of Christians solving their disputes before government courts, what food laws were to be observed by Christians, and whether circumcision was required for church membership. Many in the church were self-assertive and dogmatic in their opinions,[7] and this was particularly true with regard to the those who spoke in tongues or in ecstatic utterances.

Paul's masterful handling of tongues, as noted, is found only in I Corinthians, chapters 12 to 14. The twelfth and thirteenth chapters mainly emphasize the church, the Body of Christ and how all believers, whether Jew or Greek, slave or free, are by one Spirit baptized into it. Though Paul in these chapters touches on tongues and ecstatic utterances, it is not until the fourteenth chapter that he discusses in any depth these strange phenomena. His primary emphasis in these earlier chapters (12 and 13) is on love. "If I speak with tongues of men and of angels, but do not have love," he declares, "I have become a noisy gong or a clanging cymbal" (13:1). Tongues along with prophecy and knowledge would eventually cease, but faith, hope and love will abide forever and "the greatest of these is love" (13:13).[8]

Here Paul created a word for love, *agape,* unknown in the Greek language and totally different from *eros* (sexual love) or *philos* (brotherly love). It is the kind of love that reaches out to help another with no desire to possess or enjoy—a voluntary, selfless love—supremely exemplified on Calvary.

Paul's speaking in tongues and tongue

When Paul wrote to the Corinthians, "Now I wish you all spoke in tongues ..." (1Cor. 14:5), he was speaking of languages which could be understood "for the equipping of the saints [believers] for the work of service, to the building up of the body of Christ" (Eph. 4:12). The end point of preaching was to instruct, encourage and comfort those who had come to worship (1Cor. 14:3).

---

[7] See *Paul, the Man, the Missionary, and the Teacher,* Orello Cone, pp. 118, 119.
[8] See Chapter 37, "Mamertine's Message" on p. 257.

In Paul's statement, "I thank God, I speak in tongues more than you all …" (14:18), he used "tongues" in the plural which indicated he was referring *not* to ecstatic utterance, but to understandable speech, whether acquired by study or inspired by the Holy Spirit. Paul spoke at least four languages—Hebrew, Aramaic, Latin and Greek[9]—and very possibly many more. He clearly stated that in the church he would rather speak five words with his mind that he might instruct others than speak ten thousand words in a heavenly language which neither he nor anyone else could comprehend (14:19).

While there is no evidence that Paul ever spoke in tongues (specific languages which could be understood by his hearers though not known to himself), this is not to say that he did not experience this phenomenon. But as far as Paul preaching or speaking in a "heavenly language" or praying and not knowing what he was saying to God, this is so out of character with what is known of Paul as to be totally unacceptable.

An interpreter required before speaking in tongues

Paul's instruction to those in a church service who wished to speak audibly in tongues or in ecstatic utterances was that there must not be more than three and that each one should wait his turn to speak. If, however, no interpreter was present, then the tongue-speakers were to remain silent (1Cor. 14:28). By laying down this rule, Paul very tactfully limited tongue-speaking at church services since those claiming this gift could not know for sure an interpreter was present.

Man's spirit vs. God's Spirit

Paul used the word *spirit* six times in his fourteenth chapter of I Corinthians, but never used it in reference to the Holy Spirit. Correctly, *spirit* is not capitalized,[10] since Paul was referring to the spirit of man and not to the Holy Spirit.

---

[9] *Tongues!?* Spiros Zodhiates, p. 113.

[10] The words *Spirit*, beginning with a capital letter and standing for God's Spirit, and *spirit*, not capitalized, standing for man's spirit, would both initially have had all their letters capitalized as was the case with all the words of Scripture when first written. This naturally would lead to misunderstanding as to the meaning of the two words.

Paul's statements that follow clearly emphasize his insistence that Christians ought always be in control of what they say and know what they are saying.

> Unless you speak intelligible words with your tongue, how will anyone know what you are saying?... For if I pray in a tongue, my spirit prays, but my mind is unfruitful. So what shall I do? I will pray with my spirit, but I will also pray with my mind; I will sing with my spirit, but I will also sing with my mind. (1Cor. 14:9, 14, 15 NIV)

Tongue-speaking in the ancient world

The phrase "to speak in a tongue" did not originate with New Testament writers but was borrowed from Greek and Roman pagans. Ecstatic speaking often occupied an important place in their religious life, particularly in some of the temple rituals at Corinth. Among the celebrated soothsayers nearby Corinth was the drugged pythoness of the Delphic Oracle who raged over her tripod and poured forth streams of confused prophecy. She was considered divinely possessed, and if her priest was adequately paid by interested on-lookers, she was willing to allow him to interpret what she prophesied. Among other Greek cults noted for tongue-speaking were the Tracian Dionysus and the divinatory Manticism of the Delphic Phyrgia and Bacides and the Sybels.[11]

Virgil too in his *Aeneid* graphically portrayed a tongue-speaking prophetess with her arms and legs trembling and her chest heaving as she convulsively ranted and raved. Her color and face changed and her eyes stared and sparkled in fury as she foamed out her edicts and gave forth her prophecies.[12] It is therefore not surprising to find those in the Corinthian church who were not well established in Christian doctrine, subtly being influenced by such cults.

To follow the way of love (1Cor. 14:1 NIV) and maintain fervency in worship without being fanatical, and preach without being harshly dogmatic, was Paul's great desire for the church at Corinth as well as for all his churches.

Omissions of reference to tongues in Scripture

It is significant that Paul did not speak in tongues or a tongue at the time of his conversion when he was filled with the Holy Spirit. Nowhere in his writings does

---

[11]See *Tongues!?* Spiros Zodhiates, p. 104, and *Tongues and Their Interpretation*, Spiros Zodhiates, p. 301.

[12]*Aeneid* VI, 46, 98. See *New Testament Teaching on Tongues*, Merrill F. Unger, p. 164.

The Delphic Oracle at Delphi, southern Greece.

he advocate doing so or in obtaining the gift of interpretation (Eph. 5:18-21; 1Tim. 3:1-13; Tit. 1:5-9). He also omits all reference to the tongues/tongue phenomena in his list of charismatic gifts and fruit of the Spirit found in his letters to the Galatians and Romans (Gal. 5:22, 23; Rom. 12:6-8).

Furthermore, Jesus Himself never engaged in the tongues/tongue phenomena and never declared it would occur when the Holy Spirit entered the believer's heart at conversion.

When Jesus promised His disciples that they would receive power when the Holy Spirit came upon them and be His witnesses even to the remotest part of the earth, He gave no instruction that they were to engage in speaking in tongues or tongue (Ac. 1:8). Further, when He appeared to His disciples on the first night after His resurrection and breathed on them and said, "Receive the Holy Spirit" (Jn. 20:22)—meaning an empowering of the Spirit until the church was officially born at Pentecost—no speaking in tongues or ecstatic utterance is recorded. Significant too is the fact that when the Samaritans received the Holy Spirit, they too did not speak in tongues (Ac. 8:17).

Spirit in-dwelling vs. Spirit in-filling

Paul clearly distinguished between in-dwelling and in-filling of the Spirit. Baptism in the Spirit, or being in-dwelt by the Spirit, always occurs at the moment of conversion when the Father, Son and Holy Spirit enter the believer's heart with no other condition than the believer's faith in Christ. Being filled with the Spirit, on the other hand, is a continual process whereby the Holy Spirit cleanses, empowers and sanctifies the Christian, thus enabling him to grow in the grace and knowledge of Christ (see 2Pet. 3:18).

Speaking to edify

Paul concludes his discussion of tongues by stating: "Therefore, my brethren, desire earnestly to prophesy, and do not forbid to speak in tongues" (1Cor. 14:39, 40). But by saying, "do not forbid to speak in tongues," it must be remembered that Paul was referring to recognized languages understood directly or through an interpreter, and always with the proviso that whatever language was used it must edify the hearer.

Glossolalia only in Corinth's congregation and Apostolic Age

It seems evident from the above discussion that the tongue phenomenon invaded only the Corinthian congregation among all those which Paul planted. How long it continued in Corinth is conjectural, but significantly the first-century fathers, such as Clement of Rome in writing to the church at Corinth and Ignatius addressing the church at Ephesus, say nothing of tongues. Nor is there any mention of tongues in the writings of Polycarp, Papias or Barnabas, who lived in the immediate era after the apostles and represented a wide geographical area.[13] The tongues/tongue phenomena were obviously never meant to be perpetuated.[14]

Paul's apostolic authority

Paul always insisted that the Corinthians recognize his apostolic authority and even went so far as to declare that if anyone refused to acknowledge this, that person was not to be recognized (1Cor. 14:37, 38). Such an imperious command surprisingly did not alienate the Corinthians from him but rather drew them closer to him.

The edge-by-faith principle applied

Paul's diplomatic handling of the tongues/tongue phenomenon is another clear example of the way Paul used the edge-by-faith principle. He went as far as he could in counseling the Corinthians without chiding or arguing. Then he left them confidently in the hands of the Lord, knowing He would, in His own way and time, open their minds and direct them to the truth.

---

[13] *Speaking with Tongues, Historically and Psychologically Considered*, George B. Cutten, p. 32.

[14] See *New Testament Teaching on Tongues*, Merrill F. Unger, p. 151. According to many reliable evangelical textual scholars, the last twelve verses of the Gospel of Mark, as they appear today, were not a part of Mark's original gospel and were written by another author at a later date. The most trustworthy manuscripts of the New Testament do not include them though they are a part of many other manuscripts and versions of the New Testament. The ending of the original of Mark is believed to have been lost.

Because of the doubtful genuineness of verses 9-20, it is unwise to build a doctrine or base an experience on them, especially on verses 17 and 18—"And these signs will accompany those who have believed; in My name they will cast out demons, they will speak with new tongues; they will pick up serpents, and if they drink any deadly poison, it shall not hurt them; they will lay hands on the sick, and they will recover." See *The Holy Spirit*, Billy Graham, p. 252.

Chapter 22

No Other Gospel

Date of the Galatian letter

It is not known when Paul wrote to the Galatians, but it may well have been between writing 2 Corinthians and Romans. All three letters contain striking parallelisms with some sentences practically identical.

Galatians 2:7: "I had been entrusted with the task of preaching the gospel to the Gentiles...." Romans 11:13: "I am the apostle to the Gentiles...." Romans 15:15, 16: "God gave me to be a minister to the Gentiles...."

Galatians 2:16: "... know that a man is not justified by observing the law...." Romans 3:20: "... no one will be declared righteous in his sight by observing the law...."

Galatians 2:20: "I have been crucified with Christ and I no longer live, but Christ lives in me...." Romans 6:6-8: "... we know that our old self was crucified with him ... we believe we will also live with him."

Galatians 3:6: "Consider Abraham: 'He believed God, and it was credited to him as righteousness'." Romans 4:3: Abraham believed God, and it was credited to him as righteousness.

Galatians 4:6, 7: "Because you are sons, God sent the Spirit of his son into our hearts, the Spirit who calls out, '*Abba,* Father.'" Romans 8:14, 15: "... because those who are led by the Spirit of God are sons of God ... you received the Spirit of sonship. And by him we cry, '*Abba,* Father.'"

Galatians 5:14: "... the entire law is summed up in a single command: 'Love your neighbor as yourself.'" Romans 13:9: "The commandments ... are summed up in this one rule: 'Love your neighbor as yourself.'"

Galatians 3:13: "Christ redeemed us from the curse of the law by becoming a curse for us...." 2 Corinthians 5:21: "God made him [Christ] who had no sin to be sin for us, so that in him we might become the righteousness of God."

155

Galatians 6:7: "A man reaps what he sows." 2 Corinthians 9:6: "Whoever sows sparingly will reap sparingly, and whoever sows generously will also reap generously."

Galatians 6:15: "Neither circumcision nor uncircumcision means anything; what counts is a new creation." 2 Corinthians 5:17 (NIV): "… if anyone is in Christ, he is a new creation."

Both 2 Corinthians and Galatians denounce false teachers, affirm Paul's right of the apostolate and refer to his infirmities.[1] In view of this and the similarities above, it would seem that the three letters were written within a relatively close time frame.

Northern or southern Galatia?

It appears that the Galatians who received Paul's letter lived in the northern part of the Roman province of Galatia.[2] Supporting this theory is the fact that in Paul's letter to the Galatians, Paul makes no mention of Barnabas having been with him when he first brought the gospel to the Galatians. Had Paul been writing to the Galatians in the south where he and Barnabas were well known in Antioch, Iconium, Lystra and Derbe, most certainly Barnabas's name would have been mentioned.

Also supporting the northern theory is the fact that had Paul been writing to the southern Galatians he would not have stated that they had received him as "an angel of God, as Christ Jesus Himself" (Gal. 4:14)—quite to the contrary. It was at Antioch, Iconium and Lystra that he encountered some of his strongest persecution and at Lystra was actually stoned and left for dead. To say that the Galatians (meaning the southern Galatians) had received him as "an angel of God, as Christ Jesus Himself" is completely out of context.

Furthermore the pagan Lystrians became convinced that Paul and Barnabas were gods and sought to worship them as Hermes and Jupiter—not as "an angel of God or Christ Jesus Himself!"

---

[1] Cf. Gal. 1:7-9 with 2Cor. 11:4; Gal. 1:11, 12 with 1Cor. 14:37, 38, and 2Cor. 11:5; and Gal. 4:13 with 2Cor. 12:7-9.

[2] Galatia proper was north of Phrygia and Cappadocia and south of Bithynia and Pontus. From east to west it extended about two hundred miles, and its width was about one hundred miles. In the first century it was occupied by three Gallic tribes: the Trocmi, the Tolistoboli and the Tectosages. Their capitals were Tavium at the northeast and Pessinus at the southwest, with Ancyra about midway between the two.

In light of the above it seems reasonable that Paul's letter to the Galatians was addressed to the northern tribes of Galatia to whom Paul first brought the gospel on his second missionary journey. While there Paul suffered an illness which detained him for some time, but afforded him an excellent opportunity to share the gospel with many (Gal. 4:13, 14).

The Galatians receiving Paul's letter were predominantly Gauls, known also as Celts, with an intermingling of Greeks, Romans and Jews. The Celts, originating from beyond the Rhine and the outlying islands west of Europe, began their migrations eastward in the fourth century B.C. and crossed the Alps and sacked Rome in 390 B.C.

About a century later they invaded Macedonia and Greece and crossed into Asia Minor about 230 B.C., settling in its mountainous northern region. Here they remained independent until they were conquered by the Romans in 189 B.C. A succession of their own princes was allowed to govern them until about 25 B.C., after which they were made a part of the large Roman province of Galatia.[3]

The Celts seem throughout their history to have been an impulsive and mercurial race. It is not surprising then that the Christians among them became an easy prey for heretical teachers.

Reason for writing to the Galatians

During the period when Paul wrote 2 Corinthians, the Judaizers in Corinth and Galatia had made a concerted effort to disparage Paul's ministry. Their complaint was that he was not teaching the Gentile converts the Mosaic laws and traditions of the elders, but instead was preaching that faith in Christ was the sole requirement for becoming a Christian. This the Judaizers felt was inadequate. They reasoned there must be more, something that man must do to earn his salvation. Faith without works, they argued, was meaningless, and in this they felt they had the support of the Apostle James, who wrote, "faith, if it has no works, is dead, being by itself" (Jas. 2:17). But James's insistence on a show of works was not as a requirement for salvation but only as a normal response to one's faith in Christ.

While agreeing that the Levitical priesthood, the temple and its altar were no longer relevant to Christians who worshipped Jesus as the High Priest and Atonement for sin, the Judaizers still insisted that certain aspects of the law be followed.

---

[3] *Paul and His Epistles*, D. A. Hayes, p. 280.

These included Sabbath-keeping, circumcision as the mark of the believer, and adherence to Jewish dietary laws. It was upon learning that his Galatian converts were being led astray by such teaching that prompted Paul to write his impassioned letter.

Glimpsing the letter

Galatians is the most torrid of Paul's epistles. It burns with righteous indignation and concern. It is an emergency letter drafted under pressure. The gospel message is being destroyed, the dimensions of grace curtailed. Paul writes with "passionate irritation."[4] He must be heard!

The audacious paradoxes and vehement apostrophes appearing in this letter would never have been used in a calmer setting. Paul does not hesitate to say what rushes into his mind, and whether the language is crude or refined is of no matter to him. The only thing important is to refute the false teaching.

Let the false teachers who harp on circumcision go one step further and insist on castration (Gal. 5:12), but let them begin on themselves! Let anyone, man or angel, be accursed who preaches a gospel contrary to the one that was first preached to the Galatians! Again the anathema is thundered: "… let him be accursed!" (1:8, 9). "You foolish Galatians," Paul cries, "who has bewitched you?" (3:1). "I fear for you, that perhaps I have labored over you in vain" (4:11).

It is not to be wondered that this highly emotional and concerned letter to the Galatians promptly gained their attention and caused them to restudy and rethink the basics of the gospel. Soon with renewed faith and conviction they renounced the false teachers in their midst and reaffirmed the strong doctrinal teachings of Paul, their friend and mentor in Christ.

Paul's letter to the Galatians has rightly been termed "The Magna Carta of spiritual emancipation."[5] It is Paul's most lucid exposition of the doctrine of grace: salvation freely offered to all who will repent and believe in the Savior; the saved sinner set free from the bondage and guilt of sin; the promise of the in-dwelling Christ and His enabling power to live the Christian life victoriously and bring forth in abundance the fruit of the Spirit.

---

[4] *Ibid.*, p. 290.
[5] *Messages of the Books*, Frederic W. Farrar, p. 238.

Chapter 23

Paul's Heart Revealed

2 Corinthians

Paul wrote 2 Corinthians primarily to affirm his apostleship in view of the false teachers who had invaded the church at Corinth and were seeking to malign him and undermine his authority. This letter more than any other reveals Paul's heart. It was written as from a loving father to his much-loved children. "Our mouth has spoken freely to you, O Corinthians," Paul exclaimed, "our heart is opened wide … —I speak as to children—open wide to us also … Make room for us in your hearts; … you are in our hearts to die together and to live together" (2Cor. 6:11, 13; 7:2, 3).

2 Corinthians is in some respects the most personal and puzzling of all Paul's epistles. It was another urgent letter dispatched in haste and often with words omitted and constructions distressingly awkward. "No epistle needs so much of a thorough knowledge of the background of previous personal experience to explain its allusions and its phrases."[1] The language of the letter is an outpouring of anguish, grief and love, often bursting out in indignation and quivering with sarcasm.[2] "Ecstatic thanksgiving and cutting irony, self-assertion and self-abnegation, commendation, warning, and authority, paradox and apology all meet and cross and seethe, and yet out of the swirling eddies rise like rocks grand Christian principles and inspiring hopes."[3]

Sharing the Paradise experience

Only in 2 Corinthians did Paul tell of his mysterious transport to Paradise. It occurred early in his ministry and appears not to have been shared until now. Possibly Paul feared if he told of it, it would leave him suspect of being a radical visionary (12:2-4).

---

[1] *Paul and His Epistles*, D. A. Hayes, p. 257.

[2] Ibid., p. 261.

[3] Ibid.

But now with his apostleship being questioned since he had not been ordained with the Twelve, Paul may have reasoned it was time that his celestial experience be made known. This would at least point out that he was indeed a chosen vessel of the Lord and not in the least inferior to the most eminent of the apostles (11:5). It would also verify the fact that there is such a realm as heaven and encourage the Christians at Corinth to maintain their faith in a life after death.

Paul slandered

Paul's detractors claimed his speech was rude and of no account, his authority without foundation and his personal life carnal and crafty. Eyebrows were raised regarding the large offering he was collecting for the poor in Jerusalem and whether in Paul's hands it would all reach its destination.

"People who did not know Paul and who heard these things said about him, must have come to the conclusion that he was a vile impostor, branded in body, of insane mind, of impure motives, and of an utterly perverted and selfish heart."[4] Those, however, who knew Paul well would have shut their ears to such slander, knowing that none of it represented the man.

When people maligned Paul he felt it was wrong to remain silent, for to do so would injure the work of Christ to which he had been called. He therefore defended himself vigorously when wrongly accused and answered his slanderers by presenting the basics of his teaching and the record of his life. Having done this he rested his case in the spirit of the old Roman who said, "My accuser says that I have taken bribes from the enemy. I, M. Scaurus, deny it. *Utri creditus, Quirites?*—Which of the two do you believe, gentlemen?"[5]

Paul's "thorn"

Only in this letter does Paul tell of his "thorn in the flesh," which he viewed as a messenger of Satan to buffet him to keep him from exalting himself (12:7).[6] The

---

[4] Ibid., p. 250.

[5] Ibid., p. 253.

[6] The word translated as Paul's thorn in the flesh occurs only here in the New Testament. Originally the word meant a pointed stake used in defense or upon which the head of an enemy was impaled. Physical ailments are not associated with the word when used in the Old Testament (Num. 33:55; Ezek. 28:24). Some feel Paul used flesh here in the sense of physical existence and not physical ailment. Paul may have been referring to opponents or Satan tempting him to hate or covet.

"thorn" has been variously described as recurrent malaria, epilepsy, melancholia, hysteria, ophthalmia, leprosy, migraine headaches and neurasthenia. The most likely explanation seems to be ophthalmia, which was a chronic, intractable form of conjunctivitis, repulsive to behold and exceedingly common in the Palestine of Paul's day. Paul's letter to the Galatians would seem to confirm this when he reminded them that they had not abhorred him because of his illness and were willing to pluck out their eyes and give them to him.[7] Further indicative of poor eyesight are his closing handwritten remarks to the Galatians, "See with what large letters I am writing to you with my own hand" (Gal. 6:11). Paul generally used an amanuensis when writing his letters.

If, however, Paul was afflicted with epilepsy, which is the other likely explanation of his "thorn," he would be numbered with many of the most famous in history who were plagued with the same disease. The list includes Augustine, George Fox, Handel, Julius Caesar, King Alfred, Mohammed, Moliere, Napoleon Bonaparte, Pascal, Peter the Great, Petrarch, St. Bernard, St. Catherine of Siena, St. Francis, Savonarola and Socrates.

Epilepsy can occur without warning and can recur even after a lapse of many years. An epileptic seizure, which often leaves the victim unconscious and foaming at the mouth, was believed by the Jews in the first century to be a visitation of Satan, and Paul would have agreed (2Cor. 12:7). Observers of those in the throes of these seizures, according to custom, spat at them out of revulsion or with the intent of warding off demonic possession. The fact that Paul wrote the Galatians, "that which was a trial to you in my bodily condition you did not despise or loathe [literally spit out at] ..." (Gal. 4:14) may very well point to the fact that he was an epileptic.

Though Paul asked God three times to remove his "thorn," God refused to grant his request. "My grace is sufficient for you," was God's answer, "for power is perfected in weakness ..." (2Cor. 12:9a). Paul's response, "Most gladly, therefore, I

---

[7] *Ryrie Study Bible*, footnote for Gal. 4:12-15 states, "Paul is saying that he has had a good relationship with the Galatians: you have in the past been ready to 'tear out your eyes for me' (a common expression of the time for giving up everything for another, not an indication of eye trouble)." It should be noted, however, that though "tearing out one's eyes" may have been a common saying in Paul's day it does not preclude the very real possibility that Paul's "thorn" was indeed an eye malady.

will rather boast about my weaknesses, that the power of Christ may dwell in me" (v. 9b) is, without doubt, one of the most heroic statements of faith ever made.

Though Paul never hesitated to let his requests be made known to God and instructed his brethren to do likewise (Phil. 4:6), he never felt it right to demand anything of God. Paul had learned to trust the Lord in all circumstances and to be content in whatever state he found himself, whether enduring insults, distresses, persecutions or difficulties for Christ's sake. "[F]or when I am weak," he exclaimed, "then I am strong" (2Cor. 12:10).

Paul's sufferings

It is also only in 2 Corinthians that Paul elaborated on his hardships.[8] First he casually mentioned his beatings, imprisonments, tumults, labors, sleeplessness and hunger (6:5), then describes them in more detail (11:24-28). Three times Paul was beaten with rods and four times shipwrecked,[9] once spending a night and a day in the open sea. Five times he underwent scourging in the synagogues which the public was encouraged to witness. At each of these whippings he received one less lash than the forty allowed by Jewish law. This was because the ruler or *chazzan*, as the scourger was called, knew that if he exceeded the forty stripes, he himself by law would be scourged. Fearful lest he had counted wrong, he therefore refrained from delivering the last stroke.

Scourging

The procedure used in scourging was first to strip the prisoner and lay him face down with his ankles tied to a bar secured to the floor. Then the long leather thongs which bound his hands were pulled taut over a beam above and slightly ahead of him while the scourger stood close behind him with a heavy whip. This comprised six long rawhide strips to which were attached jagged bits of iron, zinc and bone.[10]

---

[8] In 1Cor. 4:11 Paul only mentions he was hungry and thirsty, poorly clothed, roughly treated and homeless.

[9] After writing 2 Corinthians, Paul experienced his fourth shipwreck. This was off the coast of Malta.

[10] Paul at other times may have been whipped while bent over and tied to a whipping post. *The Apostle: A Life of Paul*, John Pollock, p. 195.

The flogging began with thirteen lashes delivered over one shoulder so as to curl around and rip the chest and reach the navel. During the ordeal a Jewish reader intoned curses from the law:

> If you are not careful to observe all the words of this law which are written in this book, to fear this honored and awesome name, the Lord your God will bring extraordinary plagues on your descendants, even severe and lasting plagues, and miserable and chronic sicknesses. (Deut. 28:58, 59)

After the chest and stomach flagellation, the back received thirteen strokes across each shoulder blade. Such scourging has been described as "jagged wires ripping furrows in the flesh and filling them with molten lead."[11] If the prisoner became unconscious, an elder of the synagogue would order the punishment stopped. Unlike the Jewish law for scourging, under Roman law there was no set limit for the number of lashes which could be given. Often the flesh of victims was so widely ripped open that the internal organs and bones were clearly exposed.

> Presumably Paul could have claimed exemption from this discipline on the grounds of his Roman citizenship; but that would have meant in effect the denial of his Jewishness and the renunciation of his regular policy of using the synagogue as his preliminary base of operation. So long as he made a practice of visiting the synagogue as an observant Jew in each new city to which he came, he was obliged to accept its discipline, until he finally withdrew from it.[12]

Stoning

Paul mentions only once having been stoned, which occurred inside Lystra at the hands of its pagans and seems to have been done purely at the behest of the mob. It was quite unlike Jewish stonings which took place only outside the city and always in accordance with strict procedures. The Jewish method was to stand the doomed person on a nine-foot platform and, after tying him hands and feet, push him off backwards. Then the principal witness against the accused mounted the scaffold and hurled a large stone at him. If the stone missed or failed to kill him, then all the accusers standing on the ground were permitted to throw their stones until death called a halt.

---

[11] Ibid.

[12] *Paul; Apostle of the Heart Set Free*, F. F. Bruce, pp. 127, 128.

Stoning afforded the sanguinary-minded full opportunity to vent their venom, while attending a crucifixion offered only a vicarious experience. By law it was the responsibility of Roman soldiers to drive in the nails and raise the cross, and no one else was allowed to participate in the execution.

In listing his many sufferings Paul was not seeking sympathy for himself. He shared them only to let the Corinthians know that he too had experienced great hardships and that it was only by the grace of God that he had been able to endure them. "We are afflicted in every way," he exclaimed, "but not crushed; perplexed but not despairing; persecuted, but not forsaken; struck down, but not destroyed" (2Cor. 4:8, 9). Such an indomitable outlook on his afflictions could not help but encourage those who were persecuted and depressed and would have inspired them to maintain their faith and persevere in their walk with Christ.

"Yes, yes" or "no, no"

Those in the Corinthian church who accused Paul of insincerity because he had failed to keep his appointed visit with them were told by Paul that it was because of their undisciplined behavior that he had not come. He believed it would only have brought them pain. "I was not vacillating when I intended to do this, was I?" he queried.

> Or that which I purpose, do I purpose according to the flesh, that with me there should be yes, yes and no, no at the same time? But as God is faithful, our word to you is not yes and no. For the Son of God, Christ Jesus, who was preached among you by us—by me and Silvanus and Timothy—was not yes and no, but is yes in Him. (2Cor. 1:17-19)

Paul here echoed Jesus' teaching, "let your statement be, 'Yes, yes,' or 'No, no'…" (Mt. 5:37), as illustrated in His parable of the two sons who were asked by their father to work in the vineyard. The first said, "I will not," but later repented and obeyed; while the second son answered "I will, sir," but never went (Mt. 21:28-30). The second son, a "Yes, no" man, promising but not following through, was not like Paul. Paul's word was his bond; what he said he would do, he did. His answer to the one who claimed his letters were weighty and strong but his personal presence unimpressive and his speech contemptible was, "Let such a person consider this, that what we are in word by letters when absent, such persons we are also indeed when present" (2Cor. 10:11).

Concerning the offering

After spending three months in Greece (doubtless at Corinth), Paul decided to return to Jerusalem with the large offering he had been collecting for over three years for the needy in the Mother Church. Paul had not forgotten the request of James, Peter and John years earlier for him not to forget the poor (Gal. 2:9, 10).

Paul traveled with a special committee of ten representing the churches from which the offering had come. From Macedonia were Aristarchus and Secundus of Thessalonica and Sopater of Berea; from Galatia,[13] Gaius of Derbe and Timothy of Lystra; and from Asia, Trophimus of Ephesus, and Tychicus, probably of Miletus. Titus and two unnamed "brothers" were also included in carrying this large offering (2Cor. 8:17-21).[14] Since no paper currency was in existence, and not to be printed in the empire until the early ninth century, all of the collection would have been in coin and transported in bags. This accounted for the large delegation which accompanied Paul as his carriers and guards. Paul was eager to deliver the money, believing it would not only prove a blessing to those in need but would help break down Hebrew prejudice against Gentile Christians who had generously contributed to the gift.

The letter to the Romans

Paul for many years had wanted to visit Rome and would have gone there now had he not felt obliged first to return to Jerusalem (Rom. 15:22-32). After that visit, however, he planned to travel to Spain and on his way visit the capital and meet with its church (Rom. 15:28). In the meantime surrounded with friends and with some leisure afforded him, he decided to write to the Romans and include in his letter a compendium of systematic theology. The epistle, Paul's longest and requiring a scroll measuring 13 feet in length, is filled with doctrinal teaching. The governing word throughout the letter is *all*—*all* have sinned; *all* need a Savior; *all* who come to Christ will be saved; *all* believers are one in Him.

It is thought that the Roman congregation, though comprised predominantly of Gentiles, had within it a large and influential segment of Jewish believers. This accounts for Paul's heavy emphasis in his letter on the authority of the Old Testa-

---

[13]The Roman province of Galatia included Galatia proper, a part of Phrygia, Pisidia and Lycaonia.

[14]Other references to this offering and those who carried it are found in Ac. 20:4; Rom. 25-28; *15:25-28* 1Cor. 16:1-4 and 2Cor. 8:1-24.

ment Scriptures. He used more than sixty quotations from the Old Testament, more than appear in all his other epistles.

The letter to the Romans has been variously acclaimed by eminent biblical scholars as "the greatest masterpiece which the human mind had ever conceived and realized, the first logical exposition of the work of God in Christ for the salvation of the world"[15]; "unquestionably the clearest and fullest statement of the doctrine of sin and the doctrine of deliverance...."[16]

The epistle to the Romans is Christianity's constitution, setting forth all the major doctrines of the Christian faith. Here is an

> adequate discussion of anthropology and soteriology, redemption and sanctification, the wrath of God and the righteousness of God, the work of Christ and the work of the Holy Spirit, natural religion and Christian ethics, the theology of salvation and the theology of history and the theology of the Christian life. The great antinomies and paradoxes of the Christian faith are faced without flinching and discussed without dodging.[17]

The seven verses which begin the letter to the Romans have been described as

> a crystal arch spanning the gulf between the Jew of Tarsus and the Christians of Rome. Paul begins by giving his name: he rises to the dignity of his office, and then to the gospel he proclaims. From the gospel he ascends to its great subject-matter, to Him who is the Son of David and Son of God. From this summit of his arch he passes on to the apostleship again, and to the nations for whose good he received it. Among these nations he finds the Christians at Rome. He began to build by laying down his own claims; he finished by acknowledging theirs. The gulf is spanned. Across the waters of national separation Paul had flung an arch whose firmly knit segments are living truths, and whose keystone is the incarnate Son of God. Over this arch he hastens with words of greeting from his Father and their Father, from his Master and their Master....[18]

Who founded the church at Rome?

Though the church at Rome is believed by many to have been founded by the Apostle Peter, trustworthy evidence does not support this. Had Peter been in

---

[15] *Studies on the Epistles*, Frederic Godet, p. 140.

[16] *Paul and His Epistles*, D. A. Hayes, p. 314.

[17] *Ibid.*, p. 308.

[18] *St. Paul's Epistle to the Romans*, J. Agar Beet, p. 38.

Rome when Paul wrote to the Christians there, most certainly Paul would have referred to him in his letter; but he makes no mention of him. And when Paul later wrote his epistles as a prisoner in Rome, still Peter's name is not mentioned. The matter of who planted the church in Rome must remain speculative. It may have been established by Christians migrating to the capital who upon discovering fellow believers there formed a prayer fellowship from which the church emerged.

Paul's worldwide view of missions

Paul's worldwide view of missions envisioned Rome one day as his headquarters. Africa (North Africa), Hispania (Spain) and Gaul (France) were seen as ripe fields to be pioneered for Christ. Particularly was this true of Spain where Roman engineers for half a century had been constructing roads, aqueducts, temples, baths and theaters. Here Paul knew was a very large population needing to hear the gospel. Paul never wanted to build on another man's foundation (Rom. 15:20).

A sudden change in itinerary

It was while in the company of his ten carriers and probably on the eve of sailing from Cenchrea that a threat on Paul's life was uncovered. The plan presumably was to rob him of the offering when he was far out at sea, then murder him and throw his body overboard. Providentially, Paul and his guards were alerted of the plot and quickly changed their itinerary and traveled north to Philippi. Here they met Luke who had been apart from Paul for seven years.[19] Since it was at the time of the Passover in April, Paul and Luke decided to celebrate it at Philippi while the rest of Paul's company sailed with the offering to Troas to alert the church there of Paul's imminent arrival.[20]

---

[19]Since Luke did not travel with Paul on his first two missionary journeys, except when he crossed with Paul from Troas to Macedonia and was with him during Paul's time in Philippi, much of what Luke recorded about Paul thereafter until he teamed up with him again at Philippi would have been told to him by Paul or by those who had accompanied him. The book of Acts is generally thought to have been completed in Rome during Paul's house arrest.

[20]The bulky offering certainly would not have been left at Philippi for Paul and Luke to guard alone.

Chapter 24

Trauma at Troas

Voyage to Troas

When Paul and Luke left Philippi and sailed to Troas, the voyage required about five days. Seven years before, the same crossing in reverse was made in about two days, though it could have been accomplished easily in one day had not the ship stopped at Samothrace (Ac. 16:11; 20:6). Luke gives no reason for this extended period of time. It may have been rough weather which detained the ship or excessive cargo to be unloaded and taken on at Samothrace. The fact that Luke mentions the five-day crossing but gives no explanation for it is typical of the way he often wrote. Frequently he leaves his readers surmising as to what might have happened and does this perhaps purposely to stimulate their imaginations.[1]

Sunday night in the upper room

Paul and his companions arrived in Troas on a Monday and remained for one week before their ship was ready to sail for Assos. During this time Paul would have renewed old friendships and kept busy teaching and preaching and counseling many. It is not surprising his farewell Sunday service was crowded to the doors.

Eutychus

The meeting was held on a hot Sunday evening three stories above the street in a room illuminated by many oil lamps. Every window was open to let in the breeze, and in one of them sat a young boy named Eutychus. He doubtless had selected his window seat as a cool place in which to sit as well affording him a good

---

[1] Following are some examples of Luke's unanswered questions: Who was Judas on the street called "Straight"? (Ac. 9:11). Why did Mark want to join Paul again on his second missionary tour? (15:37). Who was the man in Paul's vision who called him to Macedonia? (16:9). Who was Damaris, Paul's convert in Athens? (17:34). What was the value and weight of the offering Paul brought to Jerusalem? (2Cor. 8:19).

Ruins of Troas.

view of the speaker. Paul, knowing his ship was to sail the next morning and realizing it might be his last time in Troas, paid no attention to the hour. His one desire was to preach as long as he could and answer as many questions as possible.

Over and over again he would have stressed the edge-by-faith principle, reminding his congregation that it was at Troas, after going as far as he could by faith—to the very *edge* of the Aegean Sea—that God had called him to Macedonia. Never turn back in persevering for the Lord, Paul would have strongly counseled, no matter how discouraged you become or how steep and dangerous your trail. Always forge ahead by faith trusting the Lord with all your heart and "lean not unto your own understanding. In all your ways acknowledge Him and He will direct your paths …" (Prov. 3:5, 6 NIV).

Midnight

As Paul continued talking and the night wore on, Eutychus found himself struggling to stay awake, not for want of interest in what was being said, but for want of sleep. Pinching himself and arching his back he resolved not to close his eyes, but when midnight arrived he realized he was just too exhausted and eagerly welcomed the waiting arms of Morpheus. Soon he was fast asleep. It was while in this soporific state that Eutychus gradually slumped down. Then he leaned back a little too far and suddenly plunged out the window, head first, three stories to the ground!

Someone must have noticed the empty window and sounded the alarm. Abruptly Paul stopped what he was saying and rushed with many others to the window. Then, peering down they gasped as they saw below in the moonlight the motionless body of Eutychus crumpled on the cobblestones. Frantically they fled down the stairs and over to where Eutychus lay. Luke would have been first to feel for a pulse; but there was none. The ashen pallor of death was already on the boy's face and his eyes were wide open, but fixed. Obviously the fall had proved fatal. Eutychus was dead.

Then surely would have been heard a shrill, agonizing cry of grief (perhaps from Eutychus's mother) followed by an outbreak of convulsive wailing. "Why had God permitted such a heart-breaking tragedy?" "Why had the church officers allowed the young boy to sit in the window? Why, why had Paul preached so long?" These and many other vexing questions must have surged through the minds of the mourners as they pressed in and around the body of Eutychus.

It was then that Paul suddenly noticed the boy breathing, then saw his eyes open and heard him speak! When the congregation perceived what had happened, though shocked beyond words, they began to praise God. Incredibly Eutychus was found with no broken bones, no wounds, no injuries whatsoever! Unbelievable after such a fall! It was a miracle, an absolute miracle.

Soon Paul and the congregation with Eutychus were back in the upper room which now resounded with laughter and much excited chatter. Then was heard soft singing as the Love Feast[2] began followed by the Lord's Supper. Eutychus was

---

[2] The Love Feast, as has been mentioned, p. 127, was popular among the early Christians. It represented the unity and fellowship of believers. The meal was always followed by the Lord's Supper, providing as it did, spiritual nourishment.

doubtless at the table sitting very close to Paul, who frequently gazed at him with overwhelming gratitude that God had seen fit to bring him back to life.

Paul changes his plans

In the morning, after spending all night conversing with his friends, Paul startled those who did not know his penchant for suddenly changing his plans, by announcing he had decided *not* to sail to Assos, their next port of call, but rather to walk there, thirty miles over the mountains. Calmly he instructed his companions to sail without him and wait for him at Assos.[3]

Paul's decision would have met with vehement disapproval from Luke and others in Paul's party. They would have seen it as utter folly in view of the facts that Paul was unfamiliar with the way, had had no sleep, and would be most vulnerable to attack from highwaymen.

Then too, if Paul were delayed in reaching his ship before it sailed, how difficult this would be for his comrades charged with the responsibility of guarding the very large offering. They would not think of proceeding to Jerusalem without Paul and would have had no choice but to leave the ship and wait for his arrival. In the meantime where would they stay, and if Paul did not arrive on time, then what were they to do? Where would they search for him and, if they did find him, when again would they board a ship and continue their voyage?

Admittedly Paul's abrupt decision to walk alone to Assos without having previously discussed it with his companions was most inconsiderate and uncalled for. Surely Paul would have realized later how foolhardy and wrong he had been and would have offered his sincerest apologies for his thoughtless behavior. Though no legitimate excuse can be found for his rash decision, Paul's probable reason for embarking on his solitary walk should at least be considered.

After a strenuous week of ministering in Troas and then suddenly confronted with Eutychus's fall, one of the most unnerving experiences of Paul's life, Paul wanted to be away from everyone for a while and have time to himself—a time to fellowship with his Lord and to thank Him and praise Him aloud. The thirty-mile hike to Assos he saw not as arduous, but rather as a leisurely saunter across the mountains. He had no thought of not reaching his ship on time and felt there was nothing to fear. He knew he would not be alone; he knew he would be walking with God.

---

[3] From Troas to Assos by sea was approximately forty miles.

Chapter 25

Tears in the Sand

Assos

Entering Assos at its highest point in the afternoon, Paul would have been overwhelmed by the view that greeted him. Below lay the ancient stone city on its expansive green terraces reaching down to the sea, and in the distance on the island of Lesbos rose its misty blue mountains. Scattered across the dazzling waters was a host of fishing vessels under full sail trailed and canopied by flocks of swooping seagulls, and far off on the hazy horizon, as far as one could see, stretched the slumbering, mauve hills of Greece. Few cities looked out on a more enthralling panorama.

Allegedly Assos was founded by the Aeolians in the fifth century B.C. and remained for centuries singularly Grecian with its own coinage. In its heyday two miles of double walls encircled it, the outer one sixty-five feet high with towers at sixty-foot intervals. When Paul visited the city, its walls and towers had long since crumbled though there still remained its agora, theaters, gymnasiums and baths and well-protected harbor.

Today the picturesque city of Assos that clung to its sun-drenched mountainside is but a romantic memory. Its buildings have all vanished and its harbor is no longer navigable. A tiny Turkish village called Behram now marks its site.

Assos will always be remembered not chiefly as the home of Aristotle[1] who resided there for three years, but as the only city on Paul's journeys to which he chose to walk alone. It will also be a reminder of Paul's incredible energy as well as of his unpredictable, last-minute change of plans. Though this often exasperated those with whom he worked, generally his precipitous decisions proved warranted.

Needless to say when Paul arrived on the wharf at Assos his shipmates were overjoyed to see him, though later they doubtless berated him for causing them

---

[1] Aristotle was related by marriage to Hermeas, who ruled the city at the time.

Ruins of Assos.

hours of anxiety. It was then that Paul would have sincerely apologized when he realized how stubborn and inconsiderate he had been.

Paul's next destination was Miletus, a four-day sail down the coast through the Greek archipelago past such islands as Chios and Samos, the latter being the home of Pythagoras. Purposely Paul had decided to bypass Ephesus, not wanting to delay his voyage since he hoped to be in Jerusalem on the day of Pentecost.

Miletus

Miletus in Roman times was famed for its giant theater, one of the largest in Asia Minor and erected in an open field rather than in the conclave of a hill, which was the usual site for such structures. The impressive stadium is still in remarkable

The theater at Miletus.

preservation and Paul very probably would have sat in it among its throngs. Like many of the cities familiar to Paul, Miletus now lies in ruins. The sea that once washed its shores is now six miles away. Alluvium from the Meander River long ago clogged its port.

Counseling the elders

At Miletus, Paul sent for the elders of Ephesus, thirty-six miles away, to meet him at the beach. Their prompt arrival clearly indicates how much they thought of Paul. He warned them to guard themselves and their flock against false teachers, whom he called "savage wolves" who he was convinced were lying in wait to try

The remains of the harbor of Assos.

and corrupt his teachings after his departure (Ac. 20:29).[2] For a period of three years, night and day, he reminded them, he had not ceased to admonish them with tears (v. 31) and had not shrunk from declaring to them anything that was profitable and pertained to the whole purpose of God. He had taught them publicly from house to house, urging both Jews and Greeks to repent and believe in Christ (vv. 20, 21). "I do not consider my life of any account as dear to myself," he exclaimed, "in order that I may finish my course, and the ministry which I received from the Lord Jesus, to testify solemnly of the gospel of the grace of God" (v. 24).

---

[2] After Paul was released from his first Roman imprisonment, he revisited Miletus (2Tim. 4:20) and probably also Ephesus.

Distant view of the filled-up harbor from the theater, Miletus.

Reminder of Paul's self-reliance

Paul's emphasizing to the elders his policy of remaining self-reliant is impressive. He pointed out that he had coveted no one's silver or gold or clothing.

> You yourselves know that these hands ministered to my own needs and to the men who were with me. In everything I showed you that by working hard in this manner you must help the weak and remember the words of the Lord Jesus, that He Himself said, "It is more blessed to give than to receive." (Ac. 20:34, 35)[3]

Though Paul believed with Jesus that a Christian worker has a right to expect to be supported by those to whom he ministers and thus is worthy of his wages (Mt. 10:10; cf. Lk. 10:7), and though he stressed this in his letters to the Thessalonians and Corinthians and to Timothy (2Thess. 3:7-9; 1Cor. 9:14; 1Tim. 5:17, 18), he himself refused to be dependent upon such support. He insisted rather upon earning his own living and not being beholden to anyone.

From the very first he laid down the rule to the Thessalonians, "Work with your own hands ..." (1Thess. 4:11; 2Thess. 3:8; cf. 1Cor. 4:12),[4] reminding them that he and his disciples had not eaten anyone's bread without paying for it.

> [B]ut with labor and hardship we kept working night and day so that we might not be a burden to any of you; not because we do not have a right to this, but in order to offer ourselves as a model for you, that you might follow our example. For even when we were with you, we used to give you this order: if anyone will not work, neither let him eat. (2Thess. 3:8-10; cf. 1Thess. 2:9)

Again he reinforced his belief in self-reliance when he wrote to the Corinthians, "I was not a burden to anyone ... and in everything I kept myself from being a burden to you, and will continue to do so" (2Cor. 11:9; cf. 1Cor. 9:6).

While Paul believed in shouldering his own burdens, he also believed that whenever possible it was the duty of the Christian to help other people. "Bear one another's burdens, and thus fulfill the law of Christ," he counseled (Gal. 6:2); and

> Do nothing from selfishness or empty conceit, but with humility of mind let each of you regard one another as more important than himself; do not merely look out for your own personal interests, but also for the interests of others. (Phil. 2:3, 4)

---

[3] These words of Jesus are not recorded in the four Gospels and obviously were shared orally with Paul by the apostles.

[4] See Chapter 14, "Upsetting the World," p. 91.

Farewell at Miletus

No more tender scene is recorded in the life of Paul than when he knelt down and prayed with the Ephesian elders on the beach at Miletus just before sailing. Remembering he had told them he believed they would never see his face again (Ac. 20:25, 38) broke their hearts. How they wept and kissed him and threw their arms around him as they accompanied him to the ship!

Chapter 26

"Don't Go to Jerusalem!"

Leaving Miletus

As Paul sailed out of the harbor of Miletus to begin the 210-mile voyage to Patara on the southwest coast of Asia Minor, he would surely have been at the stern of the ship waving goodbye to the sorrowing elders gathered on the shore. Though they believed with Paul they would never see each other again on earth, they were just as sure they would meet one day in heaven. It was with this comforting assurance that the elders started back to Ephesus and Paul with his brethren continued their voyage.

Colossus of Rhodes

On the route to Patara the ship touched at the island of Coz, the birthplace of Hippocrates, and then sailed for some days to the island of Rhodes. Here still protruding from the water were fragments of the bronze Colossus Apollo, which once stood at the entrance of the harbor.[1] The giant nude statue, with its halo of sunrays and its right hand holding aloft a blazing torch, had stood one hundred and twelve feet above the water. The Statue of Liberty in New York's harbor only surpasses it in height by about forty feet.

Inside the Colossus was a spiral staircase that lead to its head, in the eyes of which, according to tradition, large nightly fires were kept burning to serve as beacons. The gargantuan image stood for fifty-six years from 280 B.C. to 224 B.C. and was regarded as one of the chief wonders of the ancient world. Then one day a violent earthquake toppled it into the harbor where it lay for four-hundred and forty-eight years.

Pliny, who visited Rhodes in the same century as Paul, wrote of the mass of bronze lying at the entrance of the harbor. "Even as it lies," he exclaimed, "it excites

---

[1] The medieval tradition is fallacious that the giant figure had straddled the entrance of the harbor and that ships sailed between its legs.

our wonder and imagination. Few men can clasp the thumb in their arms, and the fingers are larger than most statues. Where the limbs are broken asunder, vast caverns are seen yawning in the interior. Within, too, are to be seen large masses of rocks, by aid of which the artist steadied it while erecting it."[2]

As Paul gazed at the shattered image sprawled out in its watery grave and mused over the fact it had been dedicated to the sun god, he would surely have rejoiced in its destruction. The very thought of deifying man-made objects or anything to do with idolatry, as has been stressed, was anathema to him. The more he moved through the empire steeped in gross paganism, the more intense became his resolve to present the electrifying good news of the risen Christ.

The removal of Rhodes' Colossus occurred in A.D. 672 when the Saracens conquered Rhodes and sold the statute as scrap metal to an enterprising Jew. It required nine hundred camel loads to haul off the mountain of bronze, estimated to weigh nine hundred tons![3]

Tyre

When the ship at last reached Patara, Paul and his company transferred to another vessel destined for Tyre four hundred miles across the sea. The voyage would have been slow and tedious requiring many days, and all would have rejoiced when at last the ship dropped anchor. Here at Tyre it remained for one week engaged in its mercantile trade while Paul and his men, with their impressive offering, were warmly received by a large group of Christians residing there.

When Paul announced his plan to visit Jerusalem during the Feast of Pentecost, all his new friends were greatly alarmed. Promptly they pointed out that the city would be filled with Jews from Asia who would certainly know Paul and view him as a traitor to Judaism, calling for his execution. Paul's life, they insisted, would be in grave danger if he entered Jerusalem. Paul, however, was not to be dissuaded though day after day he was pressured to alter his plans.

When the ship was again ready to sail, whole families accompanied him to the beach to bid him farewell and, like the elders of Ephesus, fell on their knees and prayed with him. But the deep love for Paul, so apparent on the beach of Miletus,

---

[2] *In the Steps of St. Paul*, H. V. Morton, pp. 342, 343.

[3] Ibid, p. 343. It was at Rhodes that Herod the Great built at his own expense a beautiful temple to Apollo. A Jew erecting a temple to an idol!

seems lacking on the beach at Tyre. No mention is made of anyone weeping in Paul's behalf and no one it appears kissed him goodbye. Perhaps the initial concern for him had waned through the week because of his refusal to heed advice and cancel his voyage to Jerusalem.

Ptolemais

At Ptolemais (the old Canaanite city of Acre) Paul's ship dropped anchor for only one day but long enough for Paul to meet with another group of believers. Nothing, however, is said of anyone trying to persuade him to change his plans or of anyone showing anxiety over his entering Jerusalem. Paul doubtless at the outset made it clear that he was in charge of a large love gift for the Mother Church and nothing must prevent him from delivering it.

Caesarea

When finally the great walls of the harbor of Caesarea appeared on the horizon and Paul knew he would soon be on his way to Jerusalem, his joy knew no bounds. At last his goal of entering the Holy City was about to be realized.

Caesarea was the capital of the Roman province Judea, and next to Jerusalem had no rival in the province. It was named after Caesar Augustus and built by Herod the Great beginning in 25 B.C. and required twelve years to complete.

Its harbor was protected by an enormous sea mole, two hundred feet wide comprised of stone blocks some measuring fifty feet in length by nine feet by eighteen feet in girth. Comparable in size to the harbor of Athens, it served as Jerusalem's main port.

Philip the evangelist

Living in Caesarea at this time was Philip the evangelist who would have had no way of knowing the date and time of Paul's arrival (if he expected him at all.) Paul's abrupt change of plans at Cenchrea from which he had anticipated sailing to Caesarea had required much additional travel by land, not to mention endless delays and hundreds of miles of extra sailing. The ships of his day were of course all dependent upon the caprice of the winds and with no means of communication, other than by letter, the times of departure and arrival of sea-going vessels was always conjectural.

Agabus

Philip, doubtless well acquainted with Paul during his *first visit to* Caesarea, gladly entertained Paul and his companions in his home and invited many to come and fellowship with them. Present at one of these gatherings was Agabus the prophet who seems to have been the same prophet Paul knew in Antioch, Syria, years before. If so, it was he who had predicted the world famine which occurred in the days of Claudius Caesar (Ac. 11:27, 28).

When it came time for Agabus to speak, he surprised everyone by suddenly approaching Paul and removing the tasseled cord from his waist. Then squatting on the floor and tying the cord around his own hands and feet, Agabus declared, "This is what the Holy Spirit says: 'In this way the Jews at Jerusalem will bind the man who owns this belt and deliver him into the hands of the Gentiles'" (21:11).

Upon hearing this ominous prediction and seeing the bound hands and feet of the prophet, the guests and those traveling with Paul broke out into loud crying. Earnestly they implored Paul not to continue his journey, but Paul was not to be shaken. "What are you doing, weeping and breaking my heart?" he exclaimed. "For I am ready not only to be bound, but even to die at Jerusalem for the name of the Lord Jesus" (v. 13). Seeing that Paul's mind was made up, everyone stopped crying and "fell silent, remarking, 'The will of the Lord be done!'" (v. 14).

Luke's mention that he was one of those who wept, indicates how much he loved Paul and how greatly concerned he was for his life. Aware of the many attempts that had been made to destroy Paul and now hearing the prophecy of Agabus, Luke found it impossible to hold back the tears and not sob with the rest.

Mnason

On the night before entering Jerusalem, Paul and his company lodged with Mnason, a Cypriot well known to the Christian community and who may have been won to Christ by Paul on his first missionary journey. He doubtless would have known Mark and Barnabas when they had ministered in Cyprus, but nothing is said of his opinion of them.

Chapter 27

Furious Opposition

Fifth and final visit to Jerusalem

As soon as Paul and his delegation arrived in Jerusalem, it is presumed they delivered to the church council the large offering they had brought for the poor. The council could not help but have been impressed with the many bags of coins. But what surely impressed the council most was the fact that much of the offering had come from Gentile converts. Luke, however, strangely enough, does not mention this in his chronicle, but only records, "the brothers received us warmly" (Ac. 21:17 NIV). Perhaps this was because Luke was reluctant to draw attention to himself and his Gentile brethren in view of their generous part in the gift.

Paul's report

The following day Paul met with James and all the elders and shared with them how God had blessed his labors among the Jews and Gentiles over the last four years. During this period Paul had traveled about four thousand miles and had planted churches in the provinces of Phrygia and Asia and north and south Galatia, as well as in areas of Macedonia and Illyricum. His ministry had proven particularly fruitful in the city of Ephesus and its environs.

Paul was well aware of the Pharisaic faction within the Jerusalem church and how this deeply concerned James, the president of the council, and many of the elders. Great caution had been taken not to offend needlessly those in the state of transition from Judaism to Christianity, lest, feeling criticized and misunderstood for their prejudices, the young converts would renounce their new faith. Paul too, not wanting to agitate the Jewish proponents, was careful when he spoke to emphasize that Jews as well as Gentiles were among his converts.

When he finished his report, the elders spontaneously broke out praising God for what had been accomplished through Paul. No one could doubt that God had called him to minister to the Gentiles as well as to the Jews.

But the praise was short-lived as the elders began exclaiming,

You see, brother, how many thousands there are among the Jews of those who have believed, and they are all zealous for the Law; and they have been told about you, that you are teaching all the Jews who are among the Gentiles to forsake Moses, telling them not to circumcise their children nor to walk according to the customs. What, then, is to be done? They will certainly hear that you have come. (Ac. 21:20-22)

Such misinformation would have infuriated Paul and taxed his patience to the limit. He knew there were not "many thousands" of Jewish converts who were zealous for the law but only a relatively small number. He knew also he had never urged the Jews to forsake Moses and had only concentrated on preaching the gospel. This he had confirmed in his letter to the Corinthians when he wrote "I determined to know nothing among you except Jesus Christ, and Him crucified" (1 Cor. 2:2).

Circumcision vs. faith

As for forbidding circumcision, Paul had been explicit in his teaching that "neither is circumcision anything, nor uncircumcision, but a new creation" (Gal. 6:15). He had circumcised Timothy, who was half Jewish and half Greek, only so as not to offend the Jews to whom he was to minister. But he had refused to circumcise Titus who was a pure Gentile (Gal. 2:3-5). Paul, as he wrote to the Romans, never claimed one must be circumcised to become a Christian.

[H]e is not a Jew who is one outwardly; neither is circumcision that which is outward in the flesh. But he is a Jew who is one inwardly; and circumcision is that which is of the heart, by the Spirit, not by the letter.... (Rom. 2:28, 29)

Where, then, is boasting? It is excluded. On what principle? On that of observing the law? No, but on that of faith. For we maintain that a man is justified by faith apart from observing the law. Is God the God of Jews only? Is he not the God of Gentiles too? Yes, of Gentiles too, since there is only one God, who will justify the circumcised by faith and the uncircumcised through that same faith. (Rom. 3:27-30 NIV)

The elders' proposal

The elders, eager to prove to the Judaizers that Paul was not bent on destroying the Mosaic law, proposed that he join four men taking the Nazirite vow,[1] in a spe-

---

[1] See Chapter 17, p. 120, fn. 13.

cial chamber set apart in the temple and to remain with them until they had completed the required week of purification. In addition, Paul was asked to pay all the required expenses which comprised buying sixteen sacrificial animals for the meat and peace offerings. He was expected to stand with the Nazirites when the priest sacrificed the animals and to watch the men's heads shaved and their hair burned under the boiling cauldron of the peace offering.

Such a request one would have expected Paul to reject, since agreeing to it would have made it appear he was still involved with Jewish rituals and possibly even was coming back under the law. But surprisingly, Paul acquiesced to the wishes of the council and on the very next day entered the temple with the four initiates as the week of purification commenced.

Compromise of Christian witness?

Paul affiliating with the Nazirites in their ceremony has been severely criticized by some who see it as having damaged Paul's Christian witness. They maintain he should have immediately turned down the council's proposal and reprimanded the elders for suggesting it. But Paul obviously did not agree and felt that by complying with the elders' request was "to preserve the unity of the Spirit in the bond of peace" (Eph. 4:3).

His thinking on the matter of preserving unity is clearly explained in I Corinthians where he states,

> Though I am free and belong to no man, I make myself a slave to everyone, to win as many as possible. To the Jews I became like a Jew, to win the Jews; to those under the law I became like one under the law (though I myself am not under the law), so as to win those under the law. To those not having the law I became like one not having the law (though I am not free from God's law but am under Christ's law), so as to win those not having the law. (1Cor. 9:19, 21 NIV. Refer to 1Cor. 8 and Rom. 14)

Since Paul was a recognized missionary leader of the church and therefore linked with the council, it was important to the church leaders that they not be thought to be in agreement with Paul's purported teaching that the Jews must forsake the law. It was mainly this concern that prompted the council to request Paul to be with the Nazirite initiates—not so much for the welfare of Paul as for the welfare of the council. Very probably many councilmen were uneasy in having Paul back in Jerusalem and looked forward to the day when he returned to the mission field. They feared his vigorous preaching might cause more divisions in the church and knew Paul was not one to be easily silenced.

As far as Paul's decision to remain with the Nazirites in the Jewish court until their week of purification had finished, this, as will be seen, was undoubtedly the *worst* decision Paul ever made.

Within the Jewish court

The Jewish court of the temple was surrounded by a high wall containing four massive gates which required twenty men to open or close one of them. Gentiles were warned by many signs clearly posted in Greek and Latin that trespassing within this court would result in immediate death.

It was here after about six days in the company of the four Nazirite initiates that Paul was seen by some Asiatic Jews. Having observed him in the streets with his Gentile copartner, Trophimus, they hastily concluded, without evidence, that Paul had brought him into the Jewish precinct. Irate that Paul would dare desecrate this area by bringing in a Gentile, they went wild with rage and screamed out, "Men of Israel, come to our aid! This is the man who preaches to all men everywhere against our people, and the law, and this place; and besides he has even brought Greeks into the temple and has defiled this holy place" (Ac. 21:28). Hearing this, the Jews swarmed around Paul and without giving him opportunity to explain, dragged him into the court of the Gentiles and there began beating him.

Claudius Lysias to the rescue

Nearby in Fort Antonia were garrisoned more than one thousand soldiers on the alert to put down any sign of rebellion, especially at festival seasons. When Claudius Lysias, commander of the Roman troops stationed in Jerusalem, observed from Antonia's 75-foot tower the milling crowd around Paul, he promptly rushed his troops down to quell the disturbance. He remembered that in the previous year it was in the Jewish court that Jonathan the high priest had been murdered by the Sicarii (also known as "Dagger Bearers" or "Assassins.") Also in that year an Egyptian false prophet arose and led four thousand members of the Sicarii out of the city to the Mount of Olives, from where he claimed he could cause the walls of the city to crumble. He escaped, however, before soldiers could apprehend him.

Suspecting now that Paul might be this rebel, Lysias ordered him bound with two chains and then questioned the Jews as to who he was and what he had done to offend them. But finding the agitated Jews in no mood for interrogations, Lysias commanded Paul placed under full guard and brought back to the fort. Furious that Paul had been rescued, the rowdy Jews crowded in behind the contingent and followed it all the way to the tower. There they attempted to seize Paul and would have succeeded, had not Lysias instructed that Paul be lifted onto the shoulders of the guards and carried up the stairs. When Paul reached the landing, though humiliated at the way he had been treated, he managed to compose himself enough to speak to the commander. Speaking in Greek and with the air of an ambassador, he requested Lysias to allow him to address the angry throng. Completely taken aback to find Paul able to converse in Greek and realizing he was not the suspected Egyptian prophet, Lysias granted Paul's request.

Paul addresses the raucous mob

The restless mob became more raucous than ever when Paul appeared at the railing and looked down. Though he raised his hand for silence, the roar increased until suddenly they heard Paul speak in the Hebrew dialect. Pleased to hear this and now eager to know what he had to say, the mob promptly stopped shouting and quieted down.

Paul began by giving his background—born a Jew in the city of Tarsus, educated under Gamaliel, strictly brought up under the Mosaic law and as zealous in keeping it as anyone listening to him below. He declared he had been the foremost persecutor of Christians, hunting them far and wide and often responsible for throwing them into prison and putting them to death.

He then went on to describe his conversion in Damascus, and how later Jesus appeared to him in the temple and told him the Jews would not accept his Christian testimony, and therefore to preach to the Gentiles.

Up to this point the crowd was content to remain silent and listen to Paul, but when they heard him speak in favor of the Gentiles, pandemonium broke out. "Away with such a fellow from the earth," they screamed, "for he should not be allowed to live!" (Ac. 22:22). Throwing off their cloaks and hurling dust into the air, they rushed with one accord to the stairs and would have climbed them and captured Paul had not the soldiers locked their shields and blocked the way. Lysias now commanded his men to disperse the crowd and quickly withdrew Paul into the barracks. Determined to discover who Paul really was and convinced whipping him would reveal the answer, he ordered him prepared for flogging.

Paul prepared for scourging

As Paul was stretched out with thongs and the scourging was about to begin (Ac. 22:25),[2] he feared that in his weakened condition and with his back lacerated he might not be able to endure another flogging. Convinced that God yet had much work for him to do, he accosted the scourger standing nearby and asked, "Is it lawful for you to scourge a man who is a Roman and uncondemned?" (v. 25). Startled by the question, the officer quickly alerted the commander, who rushed to Paul. Upon learning from his lips that he claimed indeed to be a free-born Roman citizen[3] and believing he was telling the truth, for to make such a claim falsely was a capital offense, the commander promptly released him.

Shuddering over what he had done by putting Paul, a Roman citizen, in chains and then nearly having had him flogged, Lysias carefully reconsidered Paul's case and came to the conclusion it had nothing to do with Roman law but only the religious affairs of the Jews. In this belief he ordered the priests and all the council to assemble the next day to examine Paul, and promised personally to bring him before them.

---

[2] See Chapter 23, "Paul's Heart Revealed" on p. 162.

[3] Paul probably verified his status by producing his certificate of Roman citizenship. Lysias, not having been born a Roman, was required to pay heavily for his citizenship (Ac. 22:28).

Chapter 28

Schism in the Sanhedrin

The Sanhedrin

Close to Fort Antonia was the hall named Gazith, where the Sanhedrin met. It was strictly off limits to non-Jews, and it was only because Paul was in the custody of Lysias that Lysias and his soldiers were allowed to enter.

The Sanhedrin met every day except on the Sabbath or during religious festivals. But in view of the fact that Paul, a free-born Roman citizen, had been brutally assaulted inside the Jewish court of the temple and subsequently harassed outside the military headquarters, Lysias ordered a special meeting of the Sanhedrin, even though it was in the midst of the Feast of Pentecost. The Sanhedrin, eager to interrogate Paul and hoping to find enough evidence against him to try him, willingly consented to the meeting.

Presiding over the Sanhedrin at the time was Ananias, Israel's eighty-third high priest and rated by historians as one of the worst. The Talmud describes him as a rapacious tyrant who reduced the inferior priests almost to starvation by defrauding them of their rightful tithes. He even went so far as to bludgeon some of them on the threshing floors and then took their food by force.

Paul had not been before the Sanhedrin for over twenty-four years, the last time being when he had gained its permission to arrest Jewish Christian converts in the synagogues of Damascus and bring them back to the Sanhedrin to be tried (Ac. 9:2; 22:5; 26:10). Undoubtedly there would have been a few of the Sanhedrinists who would have remembered Paul as the outstanding protagonist of Judaism in his early days and, though now regarding him as an enemy of Moses and disobedient to the law, would still have held him in high respect as a born leader and recognized scholar. But the majority of the Sanhedrin were strangers to Paul and knew him only as an outcast of Israel.

Paul's address before the Sanhedrin

Paul's opening statement was utterly shocking to the high court! "I have lived my life with a perfectly good conscience," he declared, "before God up to this day"

(Ac. 23:1). By exclaiming this, Paul, of course, was not claiming to be without sin but only stating his position in Christ. Paul knew that he had acknowledged and repented of his sins and knew that he had been totally forgiven. In the eyes of God therefore he was confident he was seen righteous through the atoning blood of His Son.

But the high priest interpreted Paul's statement as blasphemous and without warning ordered him struck on the mouth. Not realizing that it was the high priest who had given the harsh order,[1] Paul lashed back at him, "God is going to strike you, you whitewashed wall! And do you sit to try me according to the law, and in violation of the law order me to be struck?" (v. 3).[2] But upon being informed by some bystanders that it was the high priest who had excoriated him, and remembering the injunction in Exodus not to curse a ruler of Israel (Ex. 22:28), Paul immediately apologized.

Paul's prediction that God would one day strike Ananias literally came true in the eleventh year of his reign as high priest. Alerted of an imminent plot on his life by the Sicarii, he fled and hid in a sewer, but soon was discovered and dragged out and stabbed to death. Few high priests were more despised than Ananias and at his burial few, if any, mourned him.[3]

"Turning the other cheek"

Paul's angry retort over being slapped on the mouth was wrong from a Christian standpoint—not because of exercising indignation when struck, but wrong because of not first affording the high priest an opportunity to apologize and make restitution. When slapped, Christians were to follow Jesus' instruction and turn the other cheek (Mt. 5:39). But once was enough. If offenders refused to repent and continued their attack, then it was only right to bring them to justice.

Though Jesus instructed His disciples to forgive their enemies when they asked to be forgiven, and if need be, to forgive them seventy-seven times seven (Mt. 18:22; Lk. 17:4), He never meant that Christians when wronged were to keep turning their cheeks for more abuse. They were not doormats for the world to wipe

---

[1] Some attribute this to Paul's poor eyesight.
[2] "Whitewashed" is understood to mean "hypocrite."
[3] *The Life and Work of Saint Paul*, Frederic W. Farrar, vol. 2, pp. 312, 322.

its feet on. They were the children of God, the children of the King, and as such they were to be "loyal to the royal" within them.

Denouncing evil

Paul violently reacted against those who practiced evil, especially hypocrites and charlatans.[4] Sometimes, however, his righteous indignation turned into caustic denunciation, as it was seen when he pronounced Elymas the sorcerer "full of all deceit and fraud," and then labeled him "the son of the devil and enemy of all righteousness ..." (Ac. 13:10); and when he called the Judaizers "dogs" (Phil. 3:2); and roared out at the Corinthians, "If anyone does not love the Lord, let him be accursed ..." (1Cor. 16:22); and twice repeated the same imprecation to the Galatians (Gal. 1:8, 9). Such harsh pronouncements of course were totally unbecoming a Christian, and Paul, in retrospect, would have admitted this and asked for God's forgiveness.

But Paul insisted that if anger is displayed when addressing wrong, it must never develop into hatred or into a vendetta. "Never pay back evil for evil to anyone" (Rom. 12:17; cf. 1Thess. 5:15).

> Be angry, and yet do not sin; do not let the sun go down on your anger ... Let all bitterness and wrath and anger and clamor and slander be put away from you, along with all malice. And be kind to one another, tender-hearted, forgiving each other, just as God in Christ also has forgiven you. (Eph. 4:26, 31, 32)

Between Pharisees and Sadducees

Paul, now aware that he stood before a hostile and highly prejudiced Sanhedrin, knew he would never receive a fair hearing, and therefore decided the best way to extricate himself from the situation was to turn its two factions against each other. With this in mind he shouted out, "Brethren, I am a Pharisee, the son of a Pharisee; I am on trial for the hope of the resurrection of the dead!" (Ac. 23:6). Such a declaration promptly drew the Pharisees to his side but riled the Sadducees who, unlike the Pharisees, denied the resurrection of the dead as well as the existence of angels and spirits.

Soon, to Paul's great satisfaction, the elders were on their feet arguing over doctrine. Surprisingly, some of the Pharisees supported Paul, affirming he had done no

---

[4] Regarding Jesus' fiery preaching, refer to Mt. 23:13-33.

wrong, and that it did not matter if an angel or spirit might have spoken to him. This infuriated the rest of the assembly, most of whom had nothing good to say about Paul.

As the arguing continued, the Pharisees and Sadducees moved closer and closer to each other with Paul standing in the midst. Angrily, while shouting at each other, they grasped hold of Paul and started ripping off his clothes and violently pulling him to and fro. This left Paul in imminent danger of literally being torn apart.

Lysias, observing what was happening and remembering what Paul had suffered at the hands of the furious mob in the temple, quickly again ordered his soldiers to the rescue. Forcefully they dragged Paul away from the wrought-up councilors and hurried him outside into the narrow lane leading to the tower. There Paul, badly shaken and with his hair wildly disheveled and his clothes bloodied and torn, was examined for serious injuries and then rapidly escorted back to the barracks.

Chapter 29

Governor Felix Trembles

Back in Fort Antonia's cell

When Paul arrived at the fortress and was locked up in his cell, he would have gone to his bed exhausted. His turbulent encounter with the Sanhedrin would have left him black and blue and his arms and back wracked with pain. His head too would have ached severely as he thought of how close he had come to being torn apart.

Regretting that he had been so foolish as to follow the dictates of the council and realizing now its requests were all self-centered, Paul must have berated himself for being so naïve. Never should he have been involved with the Nazirites while they were completing their vow and never should he have entered the temple during the crowded Pentecost festival.

He had been warned again and again that many fanatical Jews would be in the city at this time, and were they to cross his path could do him great harm. Nonetheless he had been determined to hold to his schedule and meet the church council and deliver the large offering.

Who now would defend him against the accusation that he had desecrated the temple and was denigrating the law and speaking evil of Moses and the Prophets? How could he notify his friends regarding what had happened and about his imprisonment, and even if they did know his whereabouts, what could they do to extricate him? What possible good could come out of this miserable predicament and what was the purpose of it all?

These and many other vexing questions must have flooded Paul's mind as he lay on his bed and stared into the night. Though he had no answers at the moment, still he clung to his firm belief that God had not forsaken him. He would wait for Him to reveal His will in His own way and in His own time; he would wait prayerfully and expectantly on the edge by faith.

Jesus' third and final appearance

It was while Paul slept that Jesus appeared to him for the third time and stood beside him. It was but for a moment but long enough to declare, "Take courage, for as you have solemnly witnessed to My cause at Jerusalem, so you must witness at Rome also" (Ac. 23:11).

Startled at the vision of Jesus and thrilled with His announcement, Paul knew without a doubt he was destined to see Rome. How he would reach there, Paul had no idea, but upon the authority of Jesus he knew he would arrive.

The next morning when the noisy iron gate of Paul's cell was opened, there to his great surprise stood his young nephew, the son of his sister. Their home, it is thought, was in Jerusalem, and it may well have been here that Paul had resided before entering the temple with the Nazirites.

Though Luke says nothing of his relatives' names or anything about where they lived or how the boy had gained entrance into the fortress, he does make plain why the boy had come. It was to warn Paul of an imminent, serious plot on his life.

Forty men, probably all from the Sanhedrin, and probably including the high priest, had taken a blood oath not to eat or drink anything until Paul lay dead at their feet! Their plan was to request Lysias to return Paul to the Sanhedrin and on his way to ambush and murder him.[1] The dastardly plot was not to be taken lightly; it prompted Paul without delay to request a centurion to take his nephew to Commander Lysias, and share with him all he had told Paul.

When the boy arrived before Lysias, and upon hearing his story, the commander was now firmly convinced that it was virtually impossible to guarantee Paul's safety while he remained in Jerusalem. Dismissing Paul's nephew with the stern command to say nothing to anyone of the threat on his uncle's life, he immediately made plans to evacuate Paul that very night 68 miles to Caesarea to appear before Governor Felix. In the meantime he wrote the governor why he was sending Paul and instructed that the letter be delivered upon Paul's arrival.

---

[1] Paul's nephew, according to some translations of the New Testament, is said to have overheard the conspirators forming the plot to murder Paul. Obviously this was not known to the assassins.

The evacuation

Remembering that Paul was a freeborn Roman citizen and one of the most hated and controversial figures in the Jewish orthodox world and, wanting to be certain he reached the capital safely, Lysias assigned one of the largest contingents ever to guard one man. It totalled 470 men—200 soldiers, 200 spearmen and 70 cavalrymen. Paul was supplied with two horses, one to ride initially and the other to serve as a replacement when needed. All preparations were made in strictest secrecy, and the evacuation was scheduled to take place at nine o'clock that evening. But the departure proved anything but quiet with the clattering hooves of so many horses and the clanking armor of 400 soldiers and spearmen marching through the streets.

The 42-mile route from Jerusalem to Antipatris was mountainous and inhabited mostly by Jews, while the remaining 26 miles to Caesarea were relatively flat and in the possession of Gentiles primarily. Since this latter stretch of the journey was relatively safe for Paul to travel, the commander in charge, upon arriving at Antipatris, ordered the soldiers and spearmen to return to Jerusalem, leaving only the cavalry to continue with Paul the rest of the way to the coast.

The next morning, back in Jerusalem, Ananias the high priest greeted the day confident that Paul would be returned to the Sanhedrin, and the murderous plot would be accomplished. Imagine his rage when he learned that Paul had been escorted out of the city during the night and was on his way to Caesarea. Determined that Paul would yet meet his death, he summoned his attorney, Tertullus, and others, and ordered them immediately to start preparing charges against Paul to be presented before the governor at Caesarea. This required about five days before Tertullus and his men were on their way to the capital to present their case before the governor.

Felix

Governor Felix and his brother Pallas had previously been slaves in Rome and were brought up in the imperial household, but eventually were emancipated, probably at the hand of Anatonia, the mother of Emperor Claudius. Pallas steadily rose to a position of great influence, and finally in the year 52 gained for Felix his appointment as governor of Palestine. He was Pontius Pilate's successor and the first slave ever to govern a Roman province.

After some years in office, according to Jewish and Roman historians, he proved to be a highly corrupt and much-despised administrator, known for his notorious greed and cruelty and very low morals. It was he who was primarily responsible for the assassination of Jonathan the high priest in the temple, and for provoking widespread bloody insurrections.

When the day came for Paul's trial, Paul and his accusers assembled before Felix. Tertullus, the prosecutor, eager to win the governor's favor, commenced by flattering him as an able reformer and the one responsible for the peace prevailing in the province. He then presented his accusations against Paul, whom he averred had become a pest and a troublemaker and had stirred up riots all over the Jewish world. As the ringleader of the Nazarenes, he had even tried to desecrate the temple. Tertullus then pointed out that Commander Lysias had sent Paul to Caesarea to be tried, insinuating that Paul had seriously broken Roman law and defied Caesar.

But Felix, well acquainted with the teachings of the Way, was not to be impressed with the validity of the accusations. He knew that Paul, as a devout Christian leader, would be adverse to stirring up riots and basically was a peace-loving citizen.

After hearing the barrage of complaints against Paul and after listening carefully to his defense, Felix decided to adjourn the case until Lysias arrived and could brief him further.[2] In the meantime Paul was kept in Caesarea under house arrest, much to the great annoyance and anger of his accusers who had no choice but to return to Jerusalem and wait for the trial to resume.

Witnessing before Felix and Drusilla

Though Felix was well informed of the Way, he wanted to hear more of its doctrines and soon called Paul before him again. This time accompanying him was his third wife, Drusilla,[3] whom he had married three years earlier when she was seven-

---

[2] Lysias it seems never appeared before Felix, probably with Felix's approval.

[3] Felix's two previous wives were likewise princesses. One of them, also named Drusilla, was the daughter of Juba, king of Mauretania, and the granddaughter of Egypt's Antony and Cleopatra. Felix's son Agrippa, by his third wife, Drusilla, perished in Pompeii the night Vesuvius erupted. *The Life and Work of Saint Paul*, Frederic W. Farrar, vol. 2, p. 345.

teen years of age. She was of the royal line of the Herods and renowned for her beauty.[4]

Paul's message of righteousness, temperance and judgment appears to have made no impression upon Drusilla, who probably dismissed Paul's preaching as mere rantings of a fanatic. But it did deeply trouble Felix as it probed his heart and tortured his conscience and caused him to tremble violently. Yet, despite this emotional and physical response to Paul's preaching, he still was curious to hear more about Jesus and often would summon Paul to share the message of the gospel. In the meantime Felix hoped Paul would offer him money to be set free, but Paul was not one to offer bribes or to accept them. He firmly believed he would be released when God willed it. He was still willing to wait at the edge by faith.

Two years passed with Paul's case still not heard. Then a fierce dispute broke out in Caesarea over whether the capital should be governed by Jews or Greeks. Felix sided with the Greeks and attacked the Jewish rioters. Twenty thousand Jews were slaughtered in the Jewish quarter, and many of its wealthiest homes were looted and gutted. The priests in Jerusalem, long annoyed with Felix for his refusal to return Paul to them and now angry over the way he had mistreated the Jews, swiftly reported him to Caesar. Soon Felix was recalled and made to surrender most of his ill-gotten wealth. He would have been banished, if not executed, had it not been for the intercession of his brother Pallas, who still enjoyed high favor with the emperor.

---

[4] Drusilla's father, Herod Agrippa I, beheaded James, the brother of John, the first of the apostles to be martyred (Ac. 12:2). He then incarcerated Peter, doubtless intending to execute him after the Passover. Peter, however, was miraculously released before Herod could behead him (vv. 3-19).

It was while Herod I was in Caesarea that he died. "He had been quarreling with the people of Tyre and Sidon; they now joined together and sought an audience with him. Having secured the support of Blastus, a trusted personal servant of the king, they asked for peace, because they depended on the king's country for their food supply.

"On the appointed day Herod, wearing his royal robes, sat on his throne and delivered a public address to the people. They shouted, 'This is the voice of a god, not of a man.' Immediately, because Herod did not give praise to God, an angel of the Lord struck him down, and he was eaten by worms and died" (Ac. 12:20-23 NIV).

Chapter 30

Before Festus and Agrippa

Porcius Festus

The moment the new governor of Judea, Porcius Festus, arrived in Caesarea, he would have sensed the hostility of the Jews. The misadministration of Felix and the bloody riots which had ensued were still remembered bitterly. More and more the hated yoke of Rome was resented, and whispers of revolution were heard everywhere. The Jews had had enough of Gentile rule, enough of bribery and corruption and plundering of their land, enough of interference in their religious festivals and temple worship.

Both the Zealots, the extreme wing of the Pharisees, and the Galileans were continually disrupting the peace. From the Galilean rebellions had sprung the dreaded Sicarii, the secret society of bandits and murderers. These fanatical assassins, armed with poniards (*sica,* hence their name) concealed under their garments, mingled with the crowds in Jerusalem at festival times and inflicted mortal wounds on those whom they adjudged enemies of God and His people. Often they were at open war with Roman authority.

It was in this angry, unhappy province of Palestine seething with discontent that Festus with great trepidation began his governorship. Obviously it was imperative as soon as possible to win the Jews to his side and establish himself in their eyes as a just and forthright administrator. With this in mind, after spending only three days in the capital, Festus hurried up to Jerusalem to confer with the religious leaders.

Among the many complaints they brought to him was the fact that Paul for two years had been confined in Caesarea and still no date had been set for hearing his case. The elders insisted that he now be returned to Jerusalem to answer before the Sanhedrin the serious charges against him. Secretly they retained their original plan to murder him on the way.

Though Festus undoubtedly had been well briefed regarding his noted prisoner and knew of the previous assassination plots on his life, he was much more concerned in placating the Jews than in protecting Paul. Since Paul was in Caesarea, Festus promised the Jerusalem leaders that upon return to the capital in about a week and a half he would immediately hear Paul's case. Pleased by this announcement, though annoyed that Paul was not to be tried by the Sanhedrin, the elders once again prepared to go to Caesarea, this time confident that Paul would be found guilty of their charges against him.

But the outcome of the proceedings proved for them devastatingly disappointing, as there was insufficient evidence against Paul to warrant a government trial. Not wanting, however, to appear biased in favor of Paul, Festus offered to bring him back with him to Jerusalem and there to hear the case again. Festus's plan was to hand Paul over to the Sanhedrin as soon as he had established the fact that Paul's case concerned only Jewish matters and had nothing to do with Roman jurisprudence.

Paul, of course, refused to return, remembering the blood oath two years previously to assassinate him. Knowing that the high court of the Jews had already condemned him, he therefore decided the time had come to exercise his Roman prerogative and declare, *"Caesaro appello!"* (I appeal to Caesar!) Recognizing Paul's right as a Roman citizen to demand to be tried in Rome, Festus had no choice but to grant his request. The priests, outraged that Paul had escaped them again, but still bent on hunting him down, begrudgingly returned to Jerusalem to prepare to follow him to Rome.

Before King Agrippa and Queen Bernice

It was soon after this that King Herod Agrippa II, who ruled a small realm on the slope of Ante-Lebanon, came to Caesarea to pay his respects to the new governor. Agrippa was the last of the Herods, and though addressed "king," was only a vassal under Rome. Educated in Rome in the palace of the emperor, he became renowned as a scholar and especially known for his wide knowledge of Jewish customs and laws. Though he had long supported the Jews and was believed to be a devout Hebrew, he quickly renounced his Jewish allegiance in A.D. 70, the moment the armies of Titus sacked Jerusalem and the Jewish nation fell and its inhabitants were exiled all over the world. From then on he aligned himself with Rome.[1]

---

[1] *The Great Physician*, G. Campbell Morgan, p. 376.

Mt. Hermon's snowcapped peak.

Accompanying the king on this state visit was Agrippa's sister, Bernice, serving as queen and living with him in an incestuous relationship. She was well known for her promiscuity as well as for her striking beauty which rivaled even that of her sister Drusilla. Initially Bernice had been married to her uncle, Herod of Chalcis, but after a brief period left him and consorted with Agrippa. Then she united with Polemo of Sicily, but this too was short-lived and she returned to her brother. Later Bernice went to Rome where she continued her immoral living, becoming the mistress of Emperor Vespasian and then of his son Titus. This latter union so infuriated the public that Titus was forced to annul the marriage and dismiss her.

After spending many days with Festus and learning from him that Paul had been held in Caesarea for two years waiting to be tried, Agrippa requested that Paul be brought before him. Pleased that the king showed interest in his detainee, Festus

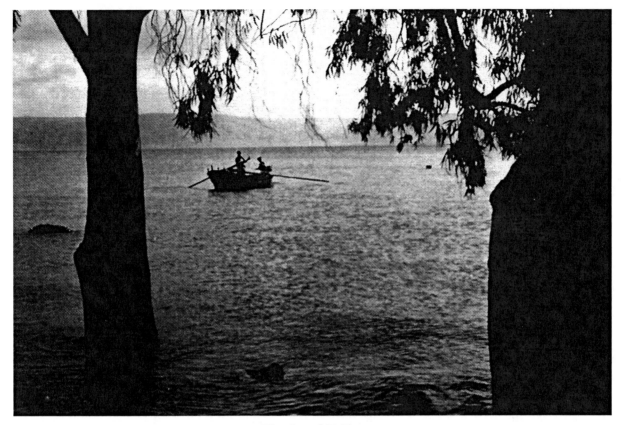

The Sea of Galilee.

assured him that he would meet Paul the very next day at a prearranged reception for Agrippa and Bernice to which many officials of the city had been invited.

When the king and queen arrived in dazzling attire accompanied by an impressive entourage, all eyes were upon them until Paul, chained to a guard, was led in. Then the focus was upon him. Pleased over the high interest Paul's unexpected appearance evoked, Festus publicly proceeded to review for Agrippa and his officials the salient facts of Paul's charges and how he had appealed to be tried before Caesar. He stressed that Paul's Jewish enemies at Jerusalem and again at Caesarea had vehemently advocated his death, yet had not been able to present credible evidence to support their allegations against him. Since there was no proof that Paul had committed any crime, let alone one that called for his execution, Festus complained he was at a loss as to what to write Caesar, and therefore had brought Paul before Agrippa for him to interview and then advise what should be done (Ac. 25:26, 27). The king, now highly curious to hear what Paul would say, granted him permission to speak.

Up to this point Paul had stood before four governors: Sergius Paulus in Cyprus, Gallio in Corinth, and Felix and Festus in Caesarea. Now was his first time to stand before one known as "king."

Stretching forth his hand from which a chain may have hung, he declared, "I consider myself fortunate, King Agrippa, that I am about to make my defense before you today; especially because you are expert in all customs and questions among the Jews; therefore, I beg you to listen to me patiently" (Ac. 26:2, 3). Then, after stressing how ardently he had lived as a Pharisee and how brutal had been his persecution of the Christians, he related in detail his Damascus experience.

> [A]t midday, O King, I saw on the way a light from heaven, brighter than the sun, shining all around me and those who were journeying with me. And when we had all fallen to the ground, I heard a voice saying to me in the Hebrew dialect, "Saul, Saul, why are you persecuting Me? It is hard for you to kick against the goads." And I said, "Who art Thou, Lord?" And the Lord said, "I am Jesus whom you are persecuting. But arise, and stand on your feet; for this purpose I have appeared to you, to appoint you a minister and a witness not only to the things which you have seen, but also to the things in which I will appear to you; delivering you from the Jewish people and from the Gentiles, to whom I am sending you, to open their eyes so that they may turn from darkness to light and from the dominion of Satan to God, in order that they may receive forgiveness of sins and an inheritance among those who have been sanctified by faith in Me." (vv. 13-18)

It was apparent as Paul spoke that his two years of confinement in Caesarea had in no way dampened his zeal or dulled his ability to present the gospel. He remained the same fiery, convincing evangelist he had always been, still pressing on to the edge by faith, still intent on saving souls.

Festus, uneasy that Paul was gaining too much attention, and perhaps secretly regretting that he had brought Paul publicly before Agrippa, suddenly shouted out, "Paul, you are out of your mind! Your great learning is driving you mad" (v. 24). But Paul, not to be deterred, quickly retorted, "I am not out of my mind, most excellent Festus, but I utter words of sober truth. For the King knows about these matters, and I speak to him also with confidence, since I am persuaded that none of these things escape his notice; for this has not been done in a corner" (vv. 25,

26). Then, turning to the king and blazing with emotion and yearning to win the young monarch to the Savior, Paul looked straight into his eyes and asked, "King Agrippa, do you believe the Prophets?" But before the king could answer, Paul exclaimed, "I know that you do" (v. 27).

Stunned at such an interrogation and the bold pronouncements of Paul, Agrippa replied, "In a short time you will persuade me to become a Christian" (v. 28). Immediately Paul responded, "I would to God, that whether in a short time or long time, not only you, but also all who hear me this day, might become such as I am, except for these chains" (v. 29).

It was then that the king and queen with the governor and dignitaries rose and left the hall. Undoubtedly the king was humiliated at being caught off guard and wanted no more of Paul. When alone with the others, Agrippa admitted that nothing Paul had done was worthy of imprisonment, let alone death, and that if Paul had only not appealed to Caesar he could have been set free (v. 32).[2]

Some believe Agrippa's reply, "In a short time you will persuade me to become a Christian,"[3] was said with a sneer, while others believe it indicated that the king was very near to being converted. Both views may be correct. Agrippa may very well have spoken with a contemptuous air to mask his troubled heart, a heart most probably deeply moved and not far from acknowledging Christ as its Savior.

Agrippa ruled for the next forty years but never embraced Christianity. He died at the age of seventy-three. Festus too remained an unbeliever but, unlike Agrippa, lived for only two more years.[4]

---

[2] One wonders what Festus must have written to Caesar regarding Paul, since there was no valid charge against him.

[3] The NIV places a question mark after Agrippa's statement.

[4] When King Agrippa at Jerusalem built a dining room in his palace overlooking the court of the temple, priests protested and built a wall to block his view. But since the wall prevented the Roman guards from keeping a vigilant eye on the inner court where uprisings often occurred, Festus ordered the wall demolished. The command, however, was never executed as the religious leaders loudly complained to Nero who, wanting to avoid any possible uprising, allowed the wall to remain.

Chapter 31

The Euraquilo

Commencing the voyage to Rome

Paul, having exercised his right of appeal to Caesar, was now required by law to be taken to Rome without delay. Since it was September and the seas would soon be unnavigable until March, it was important that Paul and others in Caesarea, marked for court hearings in Rome, were on their way soon.

The centurion appointed to be in charge of them was named Julius, and the route chosen was via Myra on the southern coast of Lycia in Asia Minor. Here grain ships from Alexandria, Egypt, regularly stopped on their way to Rome and on to one of these Paul and the other prisoners were transferred.

Significantly, Luke and Aristarchus[1] sailed with Paul serving as his slaves, since two slaves were allowed to accompany each Roman citizen on his way to Rome to appear before Caesar.[2] The ship probably left Caesarea at night and Paul's presence on board was kept secret. No one is mentioned as bidding him farewell.

The Ancients' view of the sea

Sailing in Paul's day was never preferred over traveling by land. Horace felt that only greed or poverty could induce anyone to take a voyage, and Cicero always felt uneasy when land was out of sight. Ovid declared that safety ended at the beach, and Lucretius saw in the driftwood strewn on the shore ominous warnings of the wilds of the deep.[3]

It is not difficult to understand the Ancients' aversion to the sea after learning of their ships and the means by which they were navigated. All vessels were con-

---

[1] Aristarchus was with Paul in Ephesus during the upheaval in the amphitheater (Ac. 19:29) and later with Paul in Rome when he wrote to the Colossians and Philemon (Col. 4:10; Philem. 24).

[2] *The Letters to Timothy*, William Barclay. p. 248; *The Letters to the Corinthians*, William Barclay, p. 256.

[3] See *In the Steps of St. Paul*, H. V. Morton, p. 372.

Paul's journey to Rome

structed of timber which, when under excessive strain, often developed serious leaks. The vessels were steered by two rope-controlled paddle-rudders, rather than by a single rudder which was not used for large ships until late in the Middle Ages.

Rising from the center of ships in Paul's day was a giant tall mast from which hung a huge sail made of linen or stitched hides. In heavy gales the leverage of these masts exerted tremendous pressure on the ships' timbers and often caused them to start.

The seas were all uncharted and the shores unlighted, and the compass, quadrant and sextant were unknown. Navigation thus depended solely on the sun, moon, and stars, and when these were obliterated in heavy storm, ships found themselves in great peril of running aground. Even in broad daylight this frequently occurred on unmarked reefs.

Stopover at Sidon

Thanks to favorable winds, the 67-mile voyage to Sidon was accomplished in one day. Upon arrival Julius allowed Paul to go ashore and meet with his Christian friends and "receive care" (Ac. 27:3). Paul may well have become seasick during the blustery voyage and would have greatly appreciated this kindness. How shocked his friends must have been to find him in chains and how solicitous they would have been in ministering to him!

When the time came for Paul to depart, those accompanying him to the wharf would have had no reason to remain waving goodbye, for Paul would not have been able to see them, as he would have been taken immediately below and chained with the other prisoners.

On to Myra

The voyage to Patara at first proved relatively calm, but soon strong winds from the northwest forced the ship to change course and sail to Cape Padelium on the southeastern promontory of Cyprus. Hugging the shore under the lee of the island as far as Cape Dinaretum, the ship then crossed to Asia Minor and continued west to Myra.[4] Here Paul, Luke, Aristarchus, and the rest destined for Rome were transferred to a large Alexandrian grain ship. It was probably the last of the imperial fleet subsidized by the government to sail before winter set in.

Rome depended heavily on imported wheat to feed her population of about two million, and any delay in the arrival of grain ships[5] could cause riots, as occurred during the reign of Claudius. In Nero's time some two hundred thousand citizens were on the corn dole and received six or seven bushels of corn monthly.

After smooth sailing for one hundred and thirty miles, the ship ran into heavy seas. The winds increased so alarmingly that the captain, afraid to continue further, decided to anchor at the small, nearby island of Cnidus, but northeasterly gales prevented him. This left him with no option but to veer south and sail to the island

---

[4] Buried at Myra is the body of St. Nicholas who through folklore has become known as "Saint Nick" (Santa Claus).

[5] Rome annually imported from Egypt 135,000 tons of grain to feed her population. Some ships in the Egyptian fleet measured approximately 180 feet in length with a beam of about 45 feet and a draft of 33 feet. Each could accommodate in its hold about 13,000 tons of grain. *Jesus and His Times*, Readers Digest Association, Inc., Pleasantville, N.Y., p. 181.

of Crete.[6] Once there he planned to reach the harbor of Fair Havens[7] on its southern coast.

Fair Havens

The ensuing 200-mile voyage to Crete was exceedingly tempestuous with winds often reaching hurricane velocity. Often all hope must have been lost of ever seeing land again as the ship plunged in and out of the monstrous waves.

Finally after many days and nights of agonizing sailing, there rose on the near horizon the stately blue mountains of Crete. No sight was ever more welcome; not long and they would be out of the storm!

The captain, as he approached the island, cautiously sailed east around Cape Salmone and then proceeded west another seventy miles until he was outside the coveted harbor of Fair Havens. Skillfully tacking with the fierce winds he approached the entrance of the little harbor. Then amid the jubilant cheers of all on board, he sailed into the port and dropped anchor.

The passengers, prisoners and crew, 276 in all, wearily made their way down the gangplank, all enormously relieved to be on *terra firma* again. All were resolved never to sail the high seas again until winter had passed and spring had arrived.

But soon they discovered Fair Havens not the fair haven they had imagined, but only a drab, uninteresting small port. The thought of being cooped up in such a place for many months was abhorrent. Then they learned of the booming port city of Phoenix only about forty miles west on the coast. Here were all the amenities needed for the long layover. Oh, that they could winter there!

Excited over this possibility, they approached the captain and asked him if he thought there was any possibility of harboring in Phoenix, providing of course the weather permitted. To their great joy they found the captain amenable to the idea and only too happy to be in a larger port, if and when the weather became favorable.

But Paul adamantly opposed leaving Fair Havens. He knew only too well the capricious winds at this time of year, having experienced three shipwrecks and a day and a night in the open sea (2Cor. 11:25). "Beware of the lure of siren zephyrs and glassy seas," he warned. "They can turn ferocious in a moment's time. Be wise;

---

[6] Crete is 160 miles in length and 35 miles wide.

[7] Also known as "Safe Harbors."

remain in Fair Havens until spring." But Paul's words fell on deaf ears; all had opted for Phoenix. With the city so near and with good winds, they were confident they would have no trouble in easily reaching it.

Then came the day when the sun burned through the thick, heavy clouds and clear sunny skies once again appeared. Gone were the savage winds and threatening storms. The waters were now tranquil and crystal blue. The day surely had arrived to set sail for the coveted nearby port of Phoenix.

The captain, eager to take advantage of the welcomed change in the weather, promptly ordered all passengers on board. Then, after giving orders to weigh anchor and hoist the great sail, he piloted his crowded vessel, with everyone thronging the rails, slowly out into the placid sea. As the harbor faded on the horizon, no one but Paul wanted to go back. "Farewell, Fair Havens, you dismal little port!" was the cry that must have gone up from the minds of everyone on board (except Paul.) "Farewell, you miserable little harbor. We never want to see you again!"

The Euraquilo

For the first few miles the sailing went well with everything under control. The passengers lounged on the decks basking in the sunshine and rejoicing in the fact that they were on their way. Soon they were sure they would be sailing into the exciting harbor of Phoenix, the harbor of their choice, and there they would remain content and secure until winter had passed.

Then, suddenly there appeared on the far-off horizon ominous clouds rapidly filling the sky. Terrified, the passengers watched the sun disappear and Mt. Ida, rising seven thousand feet and normally clearly visible far out at sea, vanish from sight. The gentle breeze now stiffened and the waves began to mount as furious gales swept down on the helpless vessel. The dreaded Euraquilo, alas, had arrived! There was no turning back. The demons of the sea were now back in control.

The ship was rapidly blown twenty-three miles south off the southern coast of the tiny island of Cauda, now known as Gozzo,[8] whose only harbor, Cnossus, was on its northern shore. This, however, was impossible to reach because of the velocity of the winds. Unable thus to find refuge and knowing his vessel would soon be

---

[8] The island is known for its unusually large jackasses.

driven back into the open sea, the captain released the prisoners under guard and commanded them to join in an all-out effort to save the ship.

First the lifeboat towed in the wake of the vessel was hauled on board and lashed down at the bow. This called for the arduous work of many. Then great hawsers were passed under and over the hull and tightened by means of a windlass, a process known as *frapping*. This was to help prevent the vessel from breaking apart in heavy seas. Fearing now that the ship might be driven into the Libyan bay of the Greater Syrtis,[9] notorious for its treacherous quicksands, the captain commanded the massive sail lowered and the storm sail set.

The next day, with the vessel beginning to leak badly, the sailors remained at the pumps to empty the bilge while others threw overboard all nonessentials to lighten the ship. On the third day the main yard, now a useless encumbrance, was heaved into the sea. Only the valuable wheat was retained with the hope that it might yet be delivered to Rome.

---

[9] The Goodwin Sands.

Chapter 32

"I Told You So!"

Vessel appeared doomed

For nearly two weeks the battered vessel floundered in a sea gone mad, with never a glimpse of the sun, moon or stars. When it slid under the waves there was always the horror of striking some unknown reef or being sucked into quicksands from which no ship ever emerged. Though the pumps were manned incessantly, the ship continued to fill, and it was obvious to the crew that the vessel was doomed. But Paul, clinging to the edge by faith, refused to believe the ship would go down; God would somehow intervene.

Angel appears

It was at night when Paul was alone, perhaps praying, that an angel appeared and stood before him (Ac. 27:23).[1] "Do not be afraid,[2] Paul," the angel declared, you must stand before Caesar; and behold God has granted you all those who are sailing with you" (v. 24). Then he announced that the ship would run aground on an unidentified island, and having said this, disappeared.

Confident that a heavenly messenger had indeed spoken to him, the next morning Paul summoned the crew around him and announced he had good news to share with them. Here, if ever, were dejected men, exhausted from their long ordeal. They had not bathed nor eaten for many days and their eyes were bleary from lack of sleep. With the ship now far below its water line and the storm showing no signs of abating, all were indeed convinced it was only a matter of a few hours before the vessel would sink. What good news could Paul possibly have for them? What could he say of any consolation?

---

[1] This is the first recorded time Paul saw an angel, but doubtless he would have seen many when transported to the third heaven, sixteen years earlier.

[2] The phrase, "Do not be afraid," occurs 366 times in the Bible.

Paul's opening outburst, "Men, you ought to have followed my advice and not to have set sail from Crete, and incurred this damage and loss" (Ac. 27:21), would have dropped like burning acid in their ears. It was totally unexpected and of course deeply resented. The sailors all knew they had made a drastic mistake to leave Fair Havens. But now was no time to be reminded, and certainly no time to be reprimanded. The mistake had been made, there was nothing they could do about it. Why then discuss it? "Give us the promised good news or leave us alone." This would doubtless have been the attitude of the sailors.

Paul here succumbed to the very human and *delicious* temptation of saying, "I told you so." Up to this point it appears he had remained silent about the folly of leaving Fair Havens and had worked diligently side-by-side with the crew to try and save the ship. But now, with the heavenly guarantee that no one on board would perish and all would escape safely to land, he could not refrain from blurting out and saying in essence, "I told you so." The fact that Luke records this incident reveals once again how candid he was. He was not writing to praise or criticize Paul, only to portray him as he was.

When Paul related to the seamen what the angel had said, they doubtless, not believing in angels, scoffed at him. Their religion had taught them that Neptune and Poseidon, the Roman and Greek gods of the sea were the only ones in control of the waters. It was obvious to them that the wrath of the gods was being poured out upon them and there was nothing, absolutely nothing, they could do but accept their fate.

It thus came as a shocking surprise to the sailors to hear on the fourteenth day about midnight, the sound of breakers crashing on an unknown shore. Immediately they dropped the lead and found the water a hundred and twenty feet deep, but then after a short time plumbed it again and found it only ninety feet deep. Alarmed that the ship was fast approaching shoals, they flung four anchors from the stern in an all-out attempt to restrain the vessel until dawn. It was hoped then they would see a place where the ship could be run aground.

Attempted escape

Though most of the sailors longed for the day, some wanted prolonged darkness, planning to abscond in the vessel's only dinghy. Already they had unleashed it from the bow and lowered it to the water's edge. If discovered they were prepared to explain they were merely in the process of ferrying out more anchors to steady the ship.

But Paul came upon them just as they were ready to descend to the boat and immediately warned the centurion and the soldiers: "Unless these men remain in the ship, you yourselves cannot be saved" (Ac. 27:31). Such a caveat prompted the soldiers to slash the ropes and let the boat float out of sight.

Paul now again assured his shipmates of the truth of the angel's message and urged them to take some food. He then broke bread and thanked God in the presence of them all and began eating. Impressed with the confidence of Paul that all would be well, the seamen finally decided to trust him and do as he instructed.

Wheat jettisoned

The captain, as well as the owner of the vessel, now convinced they could no longer retain the wheat, and desperate to lighten the ship before it was blown ashore, ordered the precious cargo all thrown into the sea. Prisoners and slaves, and probably Luke and Aristarchus would have been assigned this arduous task, being as they were connected with Paul. But Paul, though a prisoner, would probably have been excused, considering his age and citizenship status. Julius would never have forced him into such backbreaking labor.

As the stormy night dragged on with the ceaseless ululation of the winds and the sound of violent breakers exploding on the unseen shore, the atmosphere on board grew tense with foreboding. What would the morning reveal?

Finally in the early light of the dawn, there appeared, shockingly near, the shadowy features of an unknown shore with high forbidding cliffs and a rock-strewn beach. Then a sandy cove was spotted where it was hoped the ship might be beached.

Orders were now given to sever the hawsers to the four anchors and leave them in the sea and at the same time to untie the ropes to the two rudders that had been lashed to the deck. This was to steer the ship, if possible, onto the beach.

Shipwreck

All now crowded the decks as the foresail was raised into the wind, leaving the stricken vessel at the mercy of the waves, a "weltering plaything for the gale."[3] Rap-

---

[3] *The Life and Work of Saint Paul*, Frederic W. Farrar, p. 570.

idly it was raised on the swelling tide, then, reaching the crest of the last giant wave, it was suddenly blown over and crashed, not onto the sandy beach as was hoped, but onto an unseen, jagged reef. Here it remained immovable with its bow driven deep into the mud and its stern almost perpendicularly raised high above the waves.

The soldiers' decision

The captain now ordered all who could swim to make out for the shore and the rest to follow, clinging to whatever they could find. The soldiers, however, remained on board with their prisoners, fearful to let them swim to land lest they escape. If this occurred, the soldiers knew by Roman law they would be held responsible and face the death penalty. Realizing thus the enormous risk of allowing the prisoners off the vessel, the brutal decision was made to slaughter them. Their deaths could be logged as "casualties of shipwreck" and who would be the wiser?

But the brutal plan was aborted when Centurian Julius suddenly appeared. Alarmed to see the upraised swords and sensing the soldiers' intent, he promptly ordered the weapons sheathed and all the soldiers *and* the prisoners to strike out for shore. He did this primarily to save Paul, whom he highly respected and held as his secret friend.

What if the plot had succeeded?

Of the thirteen recorded epistles of Paul, seven would never have been written if the soldiers' murderous plot had succeeded. These comprise the four prison epistles (Ephesians, Philippians, Colossians and Philemon) as well as the pastoral epistles (1 and 2 Timothy and Titus). What an immeasurable loss to countless millions who through the centuries have found in these inspiring letters direction for their lives and overwhelming encouragement! Then too, without these epistles many valuable insights into the character and life of Paul would never have been known.

Chapter 33

Winter in Malta, Spring in Rome

Melita

The little island on which Paul was shipwrecked was known in his day as Melita[1]; the name was changed later to Malta. It is located in the center of the Mediterranean and is seventeen miles long and eight miles wide. Successively governed by Phoenicians, Greeks and Carthaginians, it was under Roman rule when Paul arrived.

The Greeks called the Maltese "barbarians," the term they used for all those who could not speak Greek; but this was not to say they considered them wild savages. Indeed the Maltese were highly civilized and known for their friendliness and compassion as indicated by Luke's statement, "the natives showed us extraordinary kindness; for because of the rain that had set in and because of the cold, they kindled a fire and received us all" (Ac. 28:2).

The "fire" would have comprised many fires around which the 276 survivors would have gathered. Such fires, probably built in large caves nearby, would have required enormous quantities of firewood to keep them burning. Paul, though as exhausted and chilled as his shipmates, was among the volunteers to bring in the wood. He was never one to shirk his duties. For him to remain inside while others searched for firewood in the icy rain was unthinkable; it would never have occurred to him!

The fire, the fuel, and the viper

It was while Paul was placing a bundle of dripping brushwood on the fire that a viper hidden in the sticks coiled on his hand and bit him. Instantly, Paul flung the writhing creature into the flames and continued gathering sticks.[2] When the

---

[1] *Melita* was a Canaanite word meaning "escape" or "refuge" and coined originally by Phoenician sailors. Doubtless, this was because the island often served as a haven in stormy weather.

[2] Doubtless, Paul would have done his best to remove the poison.

St. Paul's Bay, Malta, the traditional site of the Apostle's shipwreck.

natives spied the viper strike, they immediately concluded Paul must be a murderer, and though he had escaped the sea the snake had brought him finally to justice. But Paul showed no signs of being poisoned and continued collecting firewood. After a long time of observing him and astounded that he had not swollen up and fallen dead, the natives changed their minds and concluded he must be a god.

First they pronounced Paul the worst thing they could think of, a murderer, then the best they could imagine, a god. They were as capricious as the pagans of Lystra who first gathered flowers to worship Paul, then gathered stones to destroy him.

Paul was never one to nurse his wounds or to question his afflictions. When working with people he expected at times to be hurt, sometimes emotionally,

215

sometimes physically. Recognizing this he learned to be content in whatever circumstance he found himself, "both of having abundance and suffering need" (Phil. 4:11, 12).

Paul and healing

The chief official on the island was a warmhearted man named Publius, who for the next three days provided food and lodging for the shipwrecked crowd, while seeking out better accommodations. It was hoped when spring arrived, Paul and the rest could board another ship destined for Rome.

Learning that Publius's father lay ill with recurrent fever and dysentery, Paul prayed for him and laid hands on him, and his health was restored. Hearing of this healing, many others with infirmities were brought to Paul and they too were healed.[3]

Though Luke says nothing of medicines being used in these healings and writes only of the results of Paul's prayers and the laying on of his hands, this must not be construed to mean that medicines were not used.

Neither Paul nor Luke claimed to be "faith healers" and would strongly have protested being labeled as such. Though both believed in the power of prayer and that faith can move mountains (Mt. 17:20) and can restore the sick (Jas. 5:15), they also believed with Jesus that the sick have need of a physician (Mt. 9:12).[4]

When ministering to the ill, both physician and pastor should work together, always bearing in mind that in the last analysis it is the Lord who heals, whether through medicines, which He creates and empowers, or through earnest prayers which He graciously answers.

Resuming the voyage to Rome

In the spring, after spending three months in Malta, Paul and the passengers and crew were taken aboard another Alexandrian grain ship which had wintered in Valletta on the south coast of the island. This vessel, destined for Rome, was one of

---

[3] The Greek word here for healing is the same word as for receiving medical attention. Here is the first biblical reference to Christian medical missionary work.

[4] Paul's instruction to Timothy, "No longer drink water exclusively, but use a little wine for the sake of your stomach and your frequent ailments" (1 Tim. 5:23), would indicate that Paul was not adverse to using other means beside prayer for healing.

the largest in the Egyptian fleet and entitled to have on its prow the well-known figureheads of Castor and Pollux, the twin sons of Zeus.

Its captain of course would have commiserated with Paul's captain over the loss of his ship and would have invited him to the bridge. From here he could watch the swarms of people coming and going and hear the familiar sounds of port life: the welter of languages and shouts of vendors calling out their wares; the rumbling arrival of ox carts and horse-drawn wagons piled high with cargo, all to be unloaded by waiting slaves frequently prodded on by the whips of their masters.

The atmosphere was emotionally charged especially among families who had come with their children to bid farewell to their loved ones standing at the rails of the crowded ships. Everywhere could be heard the cacophonous cries of seagulls flying over the crowds and darting in and out of the rigging of the great variety of vessels tied up at the wharf. Such scenes would have brought back to the captain of Paul's ill-fated ship burning memories of Alexandria. Six months before he had sailed out of her harbor on his way to Rome, never dreaming it would be his ship's last voyage.

Syracuse

The first port of call on the way to Rome was Syracuse, founded in 8 B.C., and described by Cicero as the greatest and most beautiful of the Greek metropolises. It was the birthplace of the famous "dreamer-mathematician" Archimedes, who during the Roman invasion of the city was so intent on working out his formulas in his laboratory that he failed to realize his city had fallen. When a soldier approached and ordered him to report to Gen. Marcellus, Archimedes, not wanting to be disturbed, summarily waved him off. This so enraged the soldier that he drew out his sword and thrust him through. Thus died the genius who perhaps is best known for having laid down the principle of water displacement according to the bodies it contains.[5]

Paul's ship remained at Syracuse for three days, then continued past the smoking cone of Mt. Etna, Paul's first view of an active volcano, and on to Rhegium near the mouth of the Straits of Messina. Here, encountering a strong north wind, which frequently blows through the narrow pass, the captain anchored for a day until the winds reversed. Then he continued fifteen miles up the straits, flanked by

---

[5] *How They Blazed the Way*, J. Walker Spaden, pp. 41, 42.

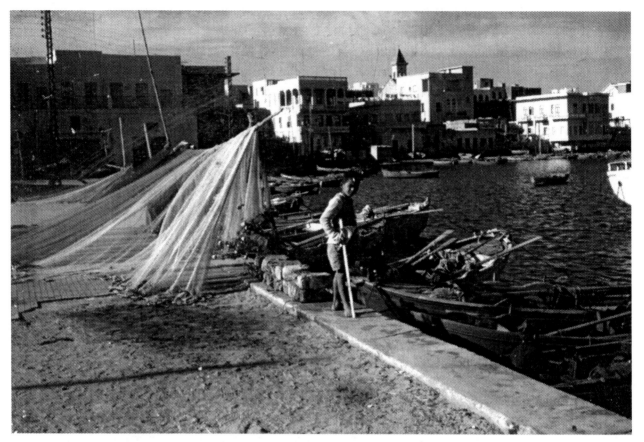

The harbor of Puteoli (modern-day Pozzuoli).

high, rocky cliffs, and sailed out at the northern end where was believed to be the abode of Homer's legendary monsters, Scylla and Charybdis.

Scylla was the behemoth with six long-necked heads that growled at every passing vessel, while Charybdis, near the Sicilian coast, was the creature that lurked in its whirlpool eager to suck in whatever ventured too close.[6]

Puteoli and Naples

Continuing for another 167 miles, past the active volcano of Stromboli with its impressive display of fireworks, the ship at last sailed into the port of Puteoli (Poz-

---

[6] *The Life and Epistles of Saint Paul*, Thomas Lewin, vol. 2, 4th ed., pp. 217, 218.

zuoli) in the Bay of Naples.[7] Puteoli was used by Alexandrian grain ships since Ostia, Rome's main port, was not deep enough to accommodate them.

Seneca owned a villa here and would have thrilled at the arrival of the massive grain ships from Egypt on which Rome depended so heavily for her wheat. The government, to show its gratitude for these life-saving vessels, exempted them from having to lower their topsails as they slowly moved into the harbor of Puteoli. Multitudes crowded the wharves to greet these special vessels, especially the first to arrive in the spring. No ships were more welcome.

Pompeii and Herculaneum

Overlooking Puteoli was Mt. Vesuvius, covered with villas and vineyards, and at its base were the famous resort towns, Pompeii and Herculaneum. When Paul arrived, no one suspected that innocent-looking Vesuvius was an active volcano, which, in less than twenty years, on a warm August evening, would suddenly erupt and bury the two towns beneath it.

Pompeii was covered with seven to eight feet of pumice-stone, followed by vast deposits of ashes and water. Though the majority of its twenty thousand residents escaped, an estimated two thousand perished in the eruption.

Herculaneum's destruction, however, differed from that of Pompeii's in that it was destroyed by a swift-moving river of hot lava which flowed five miles down Vesuvius's side and buried it and its immediate neighborhood to a depth of sixty-five feet. So completely was Herculaneum covered, as well as Pompeii, that the towns remained forgotten throughout the Middle Ages, not to be discovered until the eighteenth and nineteenth centuries. Today Pompeii is largely unearthed; but Herculaneum remains still locked in its lava.

Enthusiastic crowds were, as usual, waiting to greet Paul's ship, the first in the year to bring grain to Italy. About fifty years before, another grain ship from Alexandria had sailed into this same harbor where at the time the royal barge was anchored. On her deck lay the dying Emperor Augustus whom the world had begun to worship as a god. Being informed that the old emperor was on board, the Egyptian sailors, eager to see him, crowded the yards. Then in awe they gathered

---

[7] See *In the Steps of St. Paul*, H. V. Morton, pp. 383, 384.

Mt. Vesuvius overlooking Pompeii.

Mt. Vesuvius overlooking Pompeii.

flowers and reverently scattered them on his deck and burned incense to his name. How incongruous that they were worshipping a dying "god"![8]

Remaining one week at Puteoli

At Puteoli the Christians requested Julius to allow Paul, Luke and Aristarchus to remain with them for one week before they were taken the 120 miles to Rome. Why Julius would have consented to this, let alone stay with them, is another of Luke's intriguing, unexplained sidelights. One would think that Julius would have wanted to reach the capital without further delay and be discharged of his responsibility for his detainees.

---

[8] See *Story of Saint Paul's Life and Letters*, H. J. Patterson Smyth, p. 193.

A plausible explanation for this is that Julius may have become a Christian under the influence of Paul. He therefore would have wanted to meet more Christians and fellowship with them as well as spend more time with Paul, his spiritual mentor. Julius, it must be remembered, greatly admired Paul and was the one who prevented the soldiers from slaying him and his fellow prisoners at the time of the shipwreck off the coast of Malta.

The Market of Appius

Seventy-seven miles along the Appian Way towards Rome was the despised little village of the Market of Appius. It was at the end of a canal and noted for its drunken bargemen and knavish innkeepers. It proved, however, a most welcome rendezvous for Paul, for it was here that he was met by a group of Christians, probably mostly Gentiles from Rome.

Upon learning of his arrival at Puteoli but not finding him among the other detainees who reached the capital, they had decided to travel to Puteoli to find out what had befallen him. How excited and overjoyed the group would have been to meet the great apostle at the Market of Appius! They had only known him through his long letter to them, and since it proved a compendium of Christian doctrine, they were eager now to know its author. When Paul saw these brethren, Luke notes, Paul thanked God and "took courage" (Ac. 28:15),[9] which would indicate his apprehension of what lay ahead. But his spirits revived upon meeting these friends and he was more than eager to press on.

Paul reaches Rome

Paul's first sight of Rome was after he had passed the Albanian Lake and reached the wide plain of the Campagna, across which stretched the forty-mile aqueduct of Claudia, with arches 110 feet high, and over which water was conducted to the capital.[10] On both sides of the Appian Way were the memorials and tombs of former conquerors and other distinguished men who had raised Rome

---

[9] Why Luke should have mentioned the Market of Appius (forty-three miles from the capital) as the distance the delegation traveled, and then mentions Three Inns (thirty-three miles from Rome) is not clear. Perhaps it was an afterthought to indicate the route that the Roman party had taken.

[10] Rome at this period had eight aqueducts.

The Appian Way outside Rome.

from an obscure Italian town to a city "with a halo of martial glory, unexcelled by any other metropolis" in the world.[11]

Paul granted observatio

In Rome Julius handed Paul over to Afranius Burrus, known as an upright and humane officer. Receiving good reports from Julius concerning Paul and expecting more such reports from the Judean procurators and Commander Lysias, Burrus granted Paul *observatio*. This kind of *custodia militaris* allowed a prisoner, awaiting

---

[11]*Archeology of the New Testament*, Merrill F. Unger, p. 316.

trial, to meet with his friends, providing he remained chained by his right hand to a soldier's left.[12]

To be constantly fettered to a heathen guard with whom at first Paul had nothing in common, especially from a Jewish or Christian standpoint, would have been exceedingly vexatious. But Paul used it as an opportunity to win his guards to Christ, and although alluding to his chains in all his prison epistles (Eph. 6:20; Phil. 1:7, 13; Col. 4:18; Philem. 10, 13; 2Tim. 1:16), he never once complained of them.

Paul saw in the armor of the soldier to whom he was chained spiritual meaning. The belt represented "truth," the breastplate "righteousness" and the shoes the walk of "peace." The shield stood for "faith" and the helmet for "salvation" offered freely to all, while the sword was the "sword of the Spirit" (Eph. 6:14-17).

Paul recognized that Christians were in constant spiritual warfare: "our struggle is not against flesh and blood, but against the rulers, against the powers, against the world forces of this darkness, against the spiritual forces of wickedness in the heavenly places" (Eph. 6:12) Satan Paul saw as the Christian's ceaseless adversary, often disguised as an angel of light (2Cor. 11:14), sometimes responsible for unfulfilled ambitions (1Thess. 2:18), sometimes causing bodily afflictions (2Cor. 12:7). But Paul firmly believed in the triumph of righteousness and that nothing could separate the Christian from the love of Christ, whether tribulation, distress, persecution, famine, nakedness, peril, or sword—nothing, not even death itself (Rom. 8:35, 38, 39).

---

[12]"When an accusation was brought against a Roman citizen, the magistrate, who had criminal jurisdiction in the case, appointed the time for hearing the case, and detained the accused in custody during the interval. He was not bound to fix any definite time for the trial, but might defer it at his own arbitrary pleasure; and he might also commit the prisoner at his discretion to any of the several kinds of custody recognised by the Roman law." *The Life and Epistles of St. Paul*, W. J. Conybeare and J. S. Howson, p. 612.

There were three kinds of custody: first, confinement in a public jail (*custodia publica*) which was the most severe. Jails throughout the empire were notorious for their filthy conditions where prisoners were chained and often bound in torturous positions; second, free custody (*custodia libera*) where prisoners were placed in the care of a magistrate or senator whose obligation was to assure that their detainee appeared in court on the day and hour of their trial. This species of detention was granted only to men of high rank; third, military custody (*custodia militaris*) as discussed.

Paul's quarters in Rome

It is thought that Paul's private quarters were not in the Jewish ghetto, a crowded part of the city, which would have caused great inconvenience to the soldiers commissioned to guard him. More likely he was housed in close range of the praetorium camp, away from the congested parts of the city and where the rent was lower. Payment for Paul's dwelling, aside from what he could afford himself, may have come from offerings sent to him from his churches, principally from the one at Philippi.[13] Aquila and Priscilla, who now had returned to Rome, would also have helped him greatly.

Witnessing to the Jews

Three days after Paul's arrival in Rome, he called together the leading Jews of the city and set a date when he could meet with them to explain why he had been brought to the capital. It is believed during this period the Jews in Rome numbered between forty to sixty thousand, yet surprisingly the city had only seven synagogues.

Relieved that no one had come to Rome to press charges against him, Paul anticipated being released by default. But when? He had waited in vain for two years in Caesarea for two governors to hear his case. And now before Caesar, how much more time would he have to wait before his case was adjudicated?

The called meeting with the Jews was well attended with many eager to meet Paul and hear more of the Christian faith. From morning until night Paul expounded the Scriptures and did his best to win his brethren to Christ. Though some indeed were beginning to believe, the majority remained opposed to his message.

Finally, out of exasperation, Paul quoted Isaiah declaring that the heart of Israel had become dull and though her people would keep on hearing and seeing, they would not understand or return to the Lord (Isa. 6:9, 10). Highly offended by such a quotation (and certainly Paul was unwise to use it) and feeling the quotation was aimed at them, Paul's visitors sprang to their feet and left the room in high dudgeon. This would not have surprised Paul in the least for he had never really been successful in evangelizing the Jews.

---

[13]Epaphroditus had been sent to Rome by the Philippian congregation with a gift of money for Paul (Phil. 2:25; 4:10).

For the next two years Paul concentrated on reaching the Gentiles, and in this he was eminently successful, so much so that he wrote the Philippians:

> … the cause of Christ is well known throughout the whole praetorian guard and to everyone else, and that most of the brethren, trusting in the Lord because of my imprisonment, have far more courage to speak the word of God without fear. (Phil. 1:13, 14)[14]

---

[14]The praetorian guard (palace guard) in Rome was about nine thousand strong and distinct from the army or Roman police.

Chapter 34

Rome's Glitter and Gore

Rome at this time had a population of approximately two million people. It was the seat of a vast empire of about 220,000,000, which stretched from the Atlantic Ocean to the borders of Persia (Parthia) and the Caspian Sea, and as far north as the tip of Britain (Britannia) and south five hundred miles down the Nile. The whole north coast of Africa, all of Spain (Hispania), France (Gaul) and Germany (Germania), up to the Rhine, were under Roman control, as well as the Balkans (Illyricum), Greece (Achaea), Turkey (Asia Minor), the Black Sea, and Armenia. The entire Mediterranean was thus an imperial sea which Rome proudly called *mare nostrum,* "our sea." No armies or armada could conquer the Roman empire.

Roman law

Perhaps the most impressive thing about Roman government was its judiciary. Law and order were strictly maintained throughout the empire by well-trained police, and military and district courts. Generally magistrates were of a high caliber and known for their fairness and legal knowledge. Roman citizens appearing before them could usually be assured a just verdict.

Frequently Paul owed his very life and safety to Roman jurisdiction, as was evident in Philippi when the magistrates realized they had beaten him unlawfully, and in Corinth when Gallio drove the Jews from the Bema upon finding the accusations against Paul spurious. Twice in Jerusalem in the midst of angry factions Roman soldiers came to Paul's rescue and again in Jerusalem it was Roman law which saved him from flagellation and assassination.

In Caesarea for two years while in house arrest waiting for his case to be heard, and again in house arrest at Rome waiting perhaps even longer to come before the court, always Paul remained under the protection of Roman law.

When at last it was proven there was no evidence to support the accusations of the Jews that Paul was opposed to Caesar, he was set free. Always Rome insisted that a man is innocent until proven guilty: no evidence, no conviction.

Rome's Forum.

Rome's élite

At the top level of Roman society were the wealthy patricians living in unparalleled luxury. The extravagance of their lifestyle is evident from the food they served at their banquets, such as brains of pheasants and peacocks, tongues of flamingos and nightingales, livers of pike and milk of lampreys.

Nero once ordered for a feast Egyptian roses at a cost of $70,000; and Vetellus, who was emperor for less than a year, spent $14 million on food! It was an extraordinary age of gluttony, with emetics generally taken during meals so the diners could continue eating and enjoying new courses.

Petronius described a banquet given by Trimolchio: one course represented the twelve signs of the zodiac while another dish comprised a large roasted boar with baskets of sweetmeats hanging from its tusks. During the course of the feast a huge bearded hunter appeared with a knife and slashed the animal's side from which issued a flight of thrushes. The guests sat enthralled as they watched the birds fly wildly about the room then one by one skillfully captured in nets.

Toward the end of the meal the banqueters were again startled by strange sounds above the ceiling which suddenly opened to allow a great circular tray to descend. In the center of it was a figure of Priapus, and to the delight of all the tray bore a great variety of fruits and bon-bons.[1]

In one day Caligula squandered the revenues of three provinces amounting to $200,000, and in a single year scattered to the winds $40 million! Once he actually sprinkled the floor of the circus arena with gold dust instead of sawdust![2]

Silver was highly prized and found on everything from dishes, fruit baskets and bathtubs to the hilts of swords, ankle chains and frames for mirrors. Poppius Paullinus carried with him on his campaigns silver dishes weighing twelve thousand pounds.[3] Even the hooves of mules were covered with the costly metal!

Precious stones and pearls also were in constant demand and served not only as jewelry but in decorating clothing. Pliny reported seeing a Roman bride whose gorgeous gown was bedecked with jewels estimated at over $2 million.[4] Caligula built galleys with sterns elaborately studded with pearls and followed the custom in vogue of drinking pearls dissolved in vinegar. Horace told of Valerius Maximus giving a feast and setting before every guest a pearl to drink. He himself, after gaining permission from Mettala, one of the honored guests at the banquet, selected a pearl from one of her fabulously expensive earrings and dissolved it in wine and then swallowed it so as to be able to say he had swallowed a million sesterces at a gulp![5]

Such was the inordinate lifestyle of Rome's pampered élite in the days of Paul. Most of her wealthy lived to eat and drink, and most gave vent to their unbridled lust. It mattered not how or with whom the sexual act was performed; pleasure was all that mattered. To be moral was to be mocked in such an amoral society.

---

[1] *The Revelation of John*, William Barclay, vol. 2, pp. 203, 204.

[2] *The Letter to the Romans*, William Barclay, p. 24.

[3] *The Revelation of John*, William Barclay, vol. 2, p. 36.

[4] *Letters to the Seven Churches*, William Barclay, p. 36.

[5] *The Revelation of John*, William Barclay, vol. 2, p. 203.

Slaves

At the lowest end of the social scale were the slaves, numbering two out of every three persons in Rome—more than sixty-five million throughout the empire. They were responsible for performing practically all the work, and it was not unusual for well-to-do masters to own four hundred slaves or more.

Aside from being manual laborers, torch-bearers, sedan chair carriers, and street sweepers, some slaves were well educated and served as highly trained secretaries, shorthand writers and research scholars. Occasionally among the emancipated were those who obtained high government positions, as was the case of Governor Felix.

All bona fide slaves were deprived of legal assistance and whenever they did appear in court it was only to be prosecuted, never defended. They were at the mercy of their masters who considered them their lawful property to do with as they wished.

For example, a slave owner could wipe his soiled hands on his slave's hair and box his ears and beat him at will. Augustus once crucified a slave for killing a quail; and another master branded his slave for life for having lost two towels!

Mistresses too, when disgruntled with their slaves frequently tore out their cheeks and uprooted their hair. Slaves were never allowed to marry, and if a slave woman did give birth, her child automatically became the property of her master. Old slaves, no longer able to work, were generally dismissed and left to starve.

Juvenal pictures a master who rejoiced in hearing clanking chains and delighted "in the sound of cruel flogging, deeming it sweeter than any siren's song."[6] If a slave raised his hand against his owner, the slave's whole family, however innocent, could be put to death.[7]

Aristotle held that it was "the nature of things that certain men should be slaves, hewers of wood and drawers of water, to serve the higher classes of men."[8] "[A] slave," he declared, "is a living tool, just as a tool is an inanimate slave."[9] "Whatever a master does to a slave," wrote a Roman author, "undeservedly, in

---

[6] *The Letters to Timothy, Titus and Philemon*, William Barclay, p. 310.

[7] This law was put into force by the Senate in the year A.D. 61, after Pedanmius Secundus, the prefect of the city, had been murdered by one of his slaves. *The Life and Work of St. Paul*, Frederic W. Farrar, vol. 2, p. 403, fn. 1.

[8] *The Letters to Timothy, Titus and Philemon*, William Barclay, p. 311.

[9] *The Letters to the Galatians and Ephesians*, William Barclay, p. 179.

anger, willingly, unwillingly, in forgetfulness, after careful thought, knowingly, unknowingly, is judgment, justice and law."[10]

Clearly illustrating the inhumane treatment of slaves in Paul's day is the story of Vedius Pollio[11] whose slave accidentally broke a crystal goblet while serving him in his courtyard. Angrily Vedius ordered him thrown into his fish pond filled with lampreys.[12] Happily the slave managed to escape.

Paul's views on slavery

Though Paul would have been totally opposed to slavery, including the Old Testament law allowing Jews to buy slaves from other nations and bequeath them to their children (Lev. 25:44-46), there is no record of his speaking out publicly against slavery or in any way attempting to foment a revolution to overthrow it. The institution was sanctioned by law and was an integral part of the ethos of the upper classes who believed it had been ordained for their benefit by the gods. Without slaves who would provide the work force?

To become a Spartacus and try to free the slaves, Paul realized, would create not only more misery for the slaves but could lead to his own arrest on the charge of treason. Paul therefore chose to continue following the edge-by-faith principle, going as far as he could in stressing Christian moral and social behavior, then leaving the matter with God. Paul knew that only through the acceptance of the gospel would slavery ever be eliminated. In view of this, Paul's main emphasis was on love, the *agape* love exemplified in the life and teachings of Christ and finally dramatically displayed on His cross (Gal. 5:14; cf. Mt. 22:39). It was an all-embracing, outreaching love inspired by the Savior's love. "We love, because He first loved us" (1Jn. 4:19). Paul urged Christian masters to show this kind of love to their slaves; and both master and slave were reminded that their Master in heaven showed no partiality (Eph. 6:9; cf. Gal. 3:28; Col. 3:11).

Christian slaves too were counseled "to be subject to their own masters in everything, to be well-pleasing, not argumentative, not pilfering" (Tit. 2:9, 10), "not by way of eyeservice, as men-pleasers, but as slaves of Christ, doing the will of

---

[10]Ibid., p. 180.

[11]Seneca, *On Mercy*, Book 1, Section 18, Book 8, Section 1.200-1.236.

[12]Lampreys: fish with a funnel-shaped sucking mouth surrounded with rasping teeth with which it bores into the flesh of other fish to suck their blood.

God from the heart" (Eph. 6:6; cf. Col. 3:22), and doing whatever they did "heartily, as for the Lord rather than for men" (Col. 3:23). Paul further urged the slaves to regard their masters as worthy of all honor and if their masters were believers, to serve them all the more because they were brethren (1Tim. 6:1, 2).

Social conditions in Rome

The Rome Paul knew, while celebrated for its wealth and luxurious suburbs, was also notorious for its poverty and deplorable living conditions for its poor. The streets were for the most part too narrow to accommodate horse-drawn vehicles, and the general populace took to their feet. The wealthy, however, when visiting the inner city left their carriages at the gates and rode in on horseback or were carried by slaves in comfortable sedan chairs.

Because many streets were unlighted, those who ventured out at night were usually accompanied by torchbearers as were Londoners of the eighteenth century by "linkboys."[13] There was always the danger of being struck by loosened tiles from dilapidated roofs or attacked by roving bands of thieves.

Juvenal records a poor man's description of Rome as he found it in the first century.

> I am a poor man. I cannot stop in Rome any more. An honest man cannot make a living here. The city is full of Greeks who lie and cheat. They can do anything they like. If you tell a Greek to go to hell, he'll get there. You ought to pity us Romans. We are the ones who are suffering. Everyone laughs at me, my cloak is torn, my toga is dirty, and I've got holes in my shoes. Some people don't know how expensive it is to live in Rome. A poor man can only afford to rent a room in the attic of a great block of flats. And what happens when there is a fire? The poor man in his attic is the last to know. If a rich man's great house is burnt down, all his friends come with presents to help him start again. That doesn't happen to the poor. Life is so unfair.

> I cannot get to sleep at night. I have to live in the noisiest parts of Rome where traffic all night long keeps me awake. When I get up in the morning to visit a wealthy friend for a loan of some money or a little food, life is so difficult. I try to dash through the streets to get there before anyone else, but the streets are all crowded. Someone digs me with his elbow, someone hits me on the head with a great pole he is carrying. The soldiers tread on my toes and my legs get filthy with

---

[13]See New American Standard, Master Study Bible, p. 2138, "Rome in Paul's Day."

the mud from the streets. If I go out at night, some bully who is drunk attacks me and beats me.

It is just not worth living in the city of Rome—if you are poor. I am emigrating—to a nice little Greek city in the south of Italy.[14]

Seneca called Rome, "a cesspool of iniquity," and Juvenal spoke of it as "the filthy sewer into which flowed the abominable dregs of every Syrian and Achaean stream."[15] The streets swarmed with young men and women, jaded and depraved from indulgence in vice before they were out of their teens. Followers of oriental religions performed their wild orgies of prostitution openly in the temples with priests being hired to invoke the gods. Even Agrippina, the empress, often served at night in a brothel to satisfy her insatiable lust.

The plebeians

Between the very rich and the very poor were found the greatest number of Roman citizens. These were the plebeians, the lower middle class who concurred with the belief that work was only for slaves. Usually these indolent citizens became clients of patrician patrons who enjoyed boasting about how many people they were supporting. In the morning the plebeians would appear at the doors of their patrons to pay their respects and receive their doles, then spend the rest of the day in the city squares whiling away the hours.

Gladiatorial combats

Primarily to amuse this lethargic middle class, gladiatorial combats and other carnivals of blood were inaugurated and held in Rome's giant Circus Maximus,[16] accommodating 350,000 spectators. Daily it was crowded with screaming multitudes of men and women, frequently accompanied by their children. Prisoners, many of whom were Christians and often imported from afar, were brought into the arena to face ravenous lions, tigers and other ferocious beasts. Among the thou-

---

[14] *Great Civilizations; Rome*, Clarence Grieg, Ladybird Books, Ltd., p. 34.

[15] *The Gospel of Mark*, William Barclay, p. 12.

[16] Rome's Colosseum was not in existence at the time of Paul. After Nero's death it was begun by Vespasian on the site of Nero's lake and inaugurated by Titus in the year 80. It held 50,000 spectators and was four stories high, constructed largely by slaves. The amphitheater, able to be canopied and flooded for naval battles, was one of the most popular centers for gladiatorial combats.

sands made to fight to the death were dwarves pitted against dwarves and women against women. Frequently crocodiles and other deadly reptiles were introduced to afford an extra thrill for the sanguinary crowds. Gladiators were sometimes armed with swords to defend themselves while others had only nets and tridents. Again and again the excited hordes thronging the stadium would rise from their seats and lay wagers on who would be next to go down in blood.

During the inauguration of the great amphitheater of Titus (79-81) as many as five thousand wild animals and four thousand tame ones were killed.[17] And in the reign of Emperor Trajan (98-117) in a period of 123 consecutive days ten thousand gladiators and eleven thousand animals were slaughtered.[18] This insatiable hunger for violent and dehumanizing entertainment continued late into the fourth century.

Telemachus

One day in the reign of Emperor Honorius (384-423) an old monk named Telemachus arrived in Rome determined to put an end to gladiatorial combats. Entering the stadium, where eighty thousand spectators were viewing the conflicts, he was so shocked and grieved to see such brutality and wanton destruction of human life that he scaled the barricade and rushed into the arena. There he pled with the gladiators to stop fighting. The combatants, impressed with his courage and fervor, stopped to hear what he had to say, which so infuriated the crowd, who resented the combats being interrupted, that it roared out in unison: "Kill him! Kill him!" The commander in charge, fearing that the angry spectators might break out into a riot, and perceiving that Telemachus had no intention of vacating the arena, callously ordered the old monk struck dead. As his body fell to the ground and lay motionless on the blood-soaked sand, silence fell across the stadium. No one moved, stunned and repulsed over what they had seen. Then one by one rose and left the stadium, no longer interested in viewing more carnage. According to history, from that day onward gladiatorial combats ceased in Rome.[19]

---

[17] *Everyday Life in New Testament Times*, A. C. Bouquet, p. 183.

[18] *Great Civilizations; Rome*, Clarence Grief, Ladybird Books, Ltd., p. 34.

[19] *The Gospel of Mark*, William Barclay, pp. 204, 205. Though Emperor Constantine after 313 had officially abolished gladiatorial combats as incompatible with Christianity, they continued until near the end of the century.

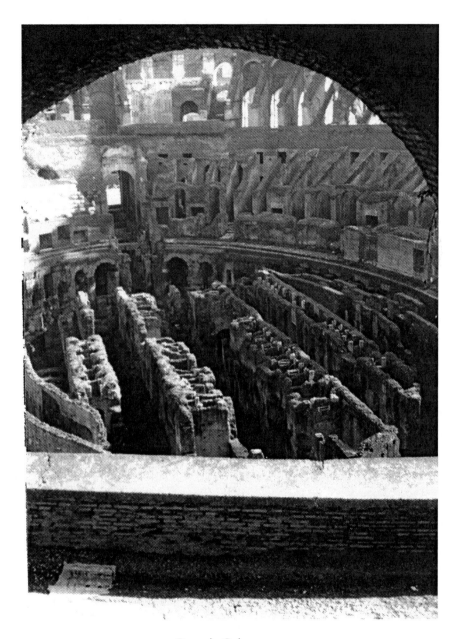

Rome's Colosseum.

Chapter 35

Released by Default—
Finally Convicted

Paul's prison epistles

During Paul's house arrest in Rome, which may have extended as long as two years or more, Paul doubtless would have written many letters of which regrettably only four are extant: Ephesians, Philippians, Colossians and Philemon. Known as the "prison epistles," these are among Paul's most inspiring and have rallied the faith of millions down through the centuries.

Many of their spiritual insights are reflected in the writings of such notables as Ann Askew, Savonarola, Ridley and Latimer, all martyred for their faith, and in the triumphant hymns of Madame Guyon and James Montgomery, as well as the works of John Bunyan, William Tyndale, Samuel Rutherford and George Withers, all incarcerated for long periods.

Though Paul was chained, his spirit was free. He knew the One who "is able to do exceeding abundantly beyond all that we ask or think …" (Eph. 3:20). He was confident that his citizenship was secure in heaven (Phil. 3:20). He was at peace.

> Be anxious for nothing, but in everything by prayer and supplication with thanksgiving let your requests be made known to God, and the peace of God, which surpasses all comprehension, shall guard your hearts and your minds in Christ Jesus. (Phil. 4:6, 7)

Letter to Philemon

Paul's brief letter to Philemon, his shortest, should never be viewed as of little importance in evaluating the life and thought of Paul. The letter is immensely valuable in revealing many aspects of Paul's character as well as shedding light on his complex personality.

Onesimus, a runaway slave of Philemon in Colossae, some one thousand miles away, suddenly appears unannounced at Paul's dwelling in Rome where Paul is confined in house arrest continually chained to a soldier. He waits to answer in court the unfounded charges that he is an enemy of Caesar.

The fact that Onesimus located Paul in the sprawling city of Rome is readily understood when remembered that Philemon was Paul's convert who must often have shared with the church at Colossae, as well as with his own household, stories of Paul's exciting missionary life and how Paul had won him to Christ. Onesimus would certainly have listened to these stories and would have learned that Paul was now imprisoned in Rome awaiting his trial. Therefore, upon arrival in the capital, Onesimus would have approached the Roman authorities and requested to visit Paul who by law was permitted to receive visitors.

Paul, having never visited Colossae, would not have met Onesimus and therefore would not have suspected he was one of Philemon's slaves. Nor would Paul have guessed that Onesimus had stolen from his master unless Onesimus had been willing to share this information.

Paul was not one to dig into people's past to see where they had erred before associating with them. He generally took people at face value and trusted them implicitly, though sometimes his trust was misplaced, as proved true of Demas, Hermogenes, Phygelus, Philetus and others, who he believed were his loyal friends and true to the gospel, only to find he had misjudged them.

When Onesimus had revealed to Paul that he was a thief and a fugitive slave of Philemon, and after Paul subsequently won him to Christ, Paul had to make a decision—retain Onesimus in Rome to assist him, or send him back to his Christian master to confess his wrong and face the consequences. The fact that Paul persuaded Onesimus to go back, but not without Paul's letter in hand urging Philemon to forgive him and regard him not only as his spiritual brother, but as Paul's very heart, re-emphasizes Paul's immense love and loyalty for his converts.

Paul, whenever possible, was an advocate of the fallen, always willing to take a personal part in the process of reconciliation. His brief but powerful letter to Philemon makes this abundantly clear. Paul pleads with Philemon to take Onesimus back

> no longer as a slave, but better than a slave, a dear brother. He is very dear to me but even dearer to you, both as a man and as a brother in the Lord.

So if you consider me a partner, welcome him as you would welcome me. If he has done you any wrong or owes you anything, charge it to me. I, Paul, am writing this with my own hand. I will pay it back … (Philem. 16-19 NIV)

The fact that Paul was willing to pay *whatever* Onesimus owed Philemon shows how deeply sincere he was in what he wrote. Then, almost as an afterthought, Paul adds another compelling reason for Philemon to forgive Onesimus, "not to mention that you owe me your very life" (v. 19).

Finally Paul's request of Philemon to ready a guest room for him, "because I hope to be restored to you in answer to your prayers" (v. 22), is perhaps the most persuasive of all the arguments in Paul's letter regarding Philemon being reconciled with Onesimus. For Philemon to realize that his spiritual father might soon be facing him *personally* would surely have prompted him to put away all thoughts of not receiving Onesimus back. Being Paul's convert he knew Onesimus had now become his brother in Christ.

In conclusion, let it be said that though the letter to Philemon (Paul's most personal) is exceedingly brief, it is not in any way shallow. Of all the letters Paul wrote none reveals more succinctly the essence of Paul's character and the kind of a man he really was.

Released by default

Sometime during this period, a large ship on its way to the capital was reported by Josephus to have sunk. Many Jews perished and among them very probably were Paul's accusers. This may have accounted for the fact that eventually Paul was released by default, since no one arrived in Rome to testify against him.

Further missionary travels

Undaunted by his long years of imprisonment (two years in Caesarea and probably two years or more in Rome), Paul enthusiastically resumed his missionary travels. Presumably these included a return to Ephesus (1 Tim. 3:14; 4:13 NIV) with a stopover at Philippi (Phil. 2:24), then into the Lycus River Valley to Laodicea,

Hieropolis and to Colossae to see Philemon and his congregation, which also Paul had never met (Philem. 22).[1]

Gnosticism

While visiting the churches at Ephesus and Colossae, Paul found to his distress the heretical teachings of Gnosticism[2] being taught, against which he had vigorously written from Rome. Gnosticism was much more adverse to Christian doctrine than anything spread by the Judaizers. It attempted to syncretize Jewish legalism, Greek philosophic speculation and oriental mysticism into a sort of "higher thought." God, it declared, had nothing to do with creation and was completely out of contact with the world, which was said to be totally evil. Since all matter was defiled, this meant of course that Jesus, whom the Gnostics worshipped as the Son of God, could not have had a flesh and blood body; His resurrection was only that of His spirit.

Another branch of Gnosticism was even more radical. It particularly appealed to the libertarians and taught that man was free to do as he wished and would not

---

[1] The three cities, Laodicea, Hieropolis and Colossae formed a triangle; Laodicea and Hieropolis, six miles apart, faced each other across the Lycus River, and Colossae, twenty miles east, straddled the Lycus. Today Laodicea and Hieropolis lie in ruins while the exact site of Colossae is unknown.

The river Lycus and its tributaries are impregnated with chalk which is fatal to vegetation and chokes up river beds. Its white incrustations form grottoes and gleaming glacier-like cascades. When Paul visited Hieropolis with its many springs and hot vapors, it was a popular spa to which thousands flocked to bathe.

Laodicea was also famous for its manufacture of fine garments, using its chalky waters in the process of dying its cloth. The city was further noted for a popular eye salve it produced.

Colossae, a small, insignificant community, was the home of Philemon. Here probably Paul would have met Onesimus, now emancipated from slavery after Philemon had received Paul's letter.

Onesimus most likely remained in Colossae and became a leader of the church there. Later, according to Ignatius, he was appointed a bishop of the church at Ephesus and served there with great distinction. (See Introduction to Philemon, *Ryrie Study Bible;* see also Col. 4:7-9.)

Paul instructed the Colossians that, after reading his letter, they were to send it to the Laodiceans and likewise he sent a letter to the Laodiceans asking it to be sent to the Colossians (Col. 4:16). It is believed, however, that this letter was not actually addressed to the Laodiceans but was the Ephesian encyclical letter meant to be read by both the Laodiceans and Colossians as well as by the Ephesians to whom it was addressed. (See *Paul and His Epistles*, D. A. Hayes, pp. 381-84.)

[2] From the Greek word *gnosis,* meaning knowledge.

Laodicea's ruined stadium.

be complete until he had experienced all aspects of good and evil. He must scale the heights of every virtue and plumb the depths of all iniquity before he could savor life to its fullest.[3] Such a heresy obviously threatened to destroy the moral fabric of the church.

Christianity vs. Gnosticism

Paul, of course, emphatically opposed such teachings, as clearly seen in his letters to the Philippians and Colossians which aver Paul's belief in the deity of Christ while declaring at the same time that Jesus was made in the likeness of man (Phil. 2:7, 8), in whom "all the fullness of Deity dwells in bodily form ..." (Col. 2:9).

---

[3] *The Letters to the Philippians, Colossians and Thessalonians*, William Barclay, p. 85.

Crystalized falls at Hieropolis.

The resurrection of Jesus was not to be seen as only a spiritual awakening from the grave, but as the return of a flesh and blood human being—man very man, God very God.

The virgin birth

Though there is no mention of the virgin birth in any of Paul's extant letters, this is not to say he did not consider it an essential part of Christian teaching as recorded by Matthew and Luke (Mt. 1:18; Lk. 1:26-31).[4] Jesus, born of a virgin and conceived by the Holy Spirit, to Paul, was the only logical way to explain the fact of His atonement. Had Jesus been born with a sinful nature, He could not

---

[4] Paul's acceptance of the virgin birth of Jesus is clearly implied in Gal. 4:4.

have been "the Lamb of God, who takes away the sin of the world" (Jn. 1:29). His empty Cross would then remain but a symbol of grievous suffering and offer no hope for the penitent sinner.

Though Paul strongly disagreed with the Gnostics that man's flesh is corrupt, he would have concurred with them that man's nature is depraved: "all have sinned and fall short of the glory of God" (Rom. 3:23).

From the beginning of creation, Paul believed all men have been given freedom of choice and therefore will be held responsible for whatever they decide. But Paul also believed that all men are potentially redeemable and that God desires all to be saved and come to the knowledge of the truth (1Tim. 2:4; cf. 2Pet. 3:9). If a sinner, no matter how evil, truly repents of his wrongdoing and genuinely surrenders his life to Christ as his sin-bearer, he will automatically be saved (Rom. 10:9-13). This diametrically opposed the teaching of the Gnostics who declared that man was incurably evil.

Paul's further travels

Shortly after Paul's release,[5] he spent the winter at Nicopolis and then sailed with Titus to Crete, leaving him there in charge of the Christians (Tit. 1:5)[6] and later traveling with Trophimus to Miletus where he left him ill (2Tim. 4:20).[7] After revisiting Miletus, he then traveled to Spain, probably not via Rome, as originally planned, but by sea (Rom. 15:23, 24, 28).[8]

Neronian persecutions were then at their height, and Paul would not have ventured near the capital. It appears Paul remained in Spain, perhaps for two years,

---

[5] Paul, it is thought, was released in the year 62.

[6] Titus is not mentioned in the book of Acts. He was a Gentile convert of Paul, referred to as his "true child" (Tit. 1:4) and one of his most trusted evangelists. When Timothy had failed in quelling the troubled, quarreling congregation at Corinth, Titus was dispatched to handle the situation and carried with him Paul's second letter (I Corinthians). The mission proved highly successful, and subsequently Titus delivered Paul's third letter (2 Corinthians) to the Corinthians.
Again Titus showed his ability to motivate people by inspiring the Corinthians to pledge an offering for the poor in the church at Jerusalem. Corinth was the first of Paul's churches to offer help, but the last to fulfill its promise, and had not Titus tactfully reminded the Corinthians of their pledge, the promise might never have been kept.

[7] Since Trophimus is not mentioned again it may be assumed he did not recover.

[8] Eusebius, Chrysostom and Jerome all attest to the fact that Paul visited Spain.

widely evangelizing the country, then returned to Ephesus where he found much false teaching had crept in and many had fallen away or backslidden.

Paul arrested in Troas

After leaving Ephesus, Paul traveled north to Troas and there resided with Carpus and continued his ministry. It was while preaching publicly at Troas that Paul was suddenly arrested and informed he had broken Nero's mandate forbidding all preaching of the Christian faith in public upon pain of death. Though Paul knew what he had done, he felt he had had no choice but to continue proclaiming the Word. "I am under compulsion;" he explained, for woe is me if I do not preach the gospel (1Cor. 9:16).

Leaving his books and valued manuscripts with Carpus (2Tim. 4:13), and bidding him and his family goodbye forever, he was then put under guard and, very likely, in the company of Luke, taken back to Rome. This time he had no intention of defending himself. He had made his decision to continue preaching Christ; he was now ready to pay the price.

Chapter 36

"A Mixture of Blood and Mud"

Ahenobarbus

Nero, before whom Paul may have been personally arraigned, was the son of Cnaeus Domitius Ahenobarbus and Agrippina. Upon being congratulated for fathering a son, Ahenobarbus cynically replied that any son born to Agrippina and himself could not prove other than a public danger and a universal detestation.[1]

Ahenobarbus was notoriously wicked. He killed a freedman simply because he refused to drink more wine and deliberately ran over a child while riding in his chariot on the Appian Way. He finally died of dropsy brought on by his debauchery.

Agrippina

When Nero was three years old, Agrippina was banished by Emperor Caligula. Later she was recalled from exile by her uncle Claudius who succeeded Caligula and whom she persuaded to marry her. When Nero reached eleven, Agrippina was determined to make him emperor even though she was warned by oracles that if she achieved her goal one day he would murder her. "Let him kill me," was her nonchalant reply, "so long as he reigns Emperor."[2]

In order to achieve her aim and make sure that Claudius's fourteen-year-old son, Britannicus, did not inherit the position of his father, Agrippina in the year 52 arranged for the betrothal of Nero at thirteen to Octavia, Claudius's teenage daughter. After two years they were married.

Soon after this, Claudius, while eating his favorite mushrooms, abruptly sank into a coma. It was believed his food had been poisoned by Agrippina who, to hasten his death, took a lethally medicated feather and thrust it down his throat.

---

[1] *Ambassador for Christ*, William Barclay, p. 137.
[2] Ibid., pp. 137, 138.

The "Golden Age"

For the first five years of Nero's reign, the empire was governed by Seneca, the wise philosopher, and by Afranius Burrus, the experienced general. It was the period known as the "Golden Age." Then followed a radical change in government as Nero assumed control and began his course of madness and savagery.

Agrippina's cruise

Though aware that his mother was responsible for his being made emperor, Nero never really trusted her and sought repeatedly without success to have her killed. Finally, he concocted what he thought was a foolproof murder plan which was carried out in the year Paul arrived in Rome.

Nero arranged a reception in Agrippina's honor on the shore of Lake Baiae, and after the guests had retired persuaded his mother to take a short cruise on the scenic lake. Unknown to her the vessel on which she sailed was fitted with disguised trap doors, which, when opened, would cause the ship to sink rapidly.

Claiming he had another urgent appointment, he saw his mother on board, then watched until her ship was far out on the lake and suddenly disappeared. Assuming his mother had drowned, he returned to Rome, confident he would never see her alive again.

But Nero had overlooked the fact that Agrippina was an excellent swimmer and had succeeded in swimming back to shore. When Nero discovered she had returned to her villa, his rage knew no bounds. Promptly he dispatched his trusted guard, Anicetus, with orders to assassinate her.

When he arrived at Agrippina's villa, immediately Agrippina surmised why he had come and brazenly tore open her robe. "Strike my womb;" she commanded, "it bore a Nero!"[3] Anicetus then drew his sword and thrust her through.

Nero continued his ruthless killings which included many of his loyal officers and faithful friends. Seneca, his former tutor and intimate adviser in the affairs of state,[4] and Gallio, Seneca's highly respected brother, both committed suicide upon discovering that Nero had marked them for execution.

---

[3] Ibid., p. 138.

[4] Seneca chose to die by bleeding to death in a warm bath.

Nero kicked his wife Octavia to death and then had her head packaged and sent as a gift to Poppaea Sabina, his beautiful but vain mistress![5] Following this, he offered his stepbrother, Britannicus, a steaming beverage, after it had been sipped by a taster to prove it was not poisoned. Britannicus, however, complained that the drink was uncomfortably hot and requested water to cool it. After the water was added, he took a swallow; but before he could take another one, dropped dead. Nero had poisoned the water!

Rome burns

On July 1, 64, a fire broke out in Rome which lasted six days and seven nights and devastated over two-thirds of the metropolis. Many of the most sacred shrines and famous structures went up in flames. Included were great blocks of wooden tenements near the Circus Maximus. Nero's strategy for rebuilding his capital included the demolishing of these tightly-packed slum quarters, and it surprised no one that it was here that the fire broke out while Nero was away from the city.

It was reported upon his return that Nero watched the conflagration from the tower of Maecenas while playing his violin and exclaiming over what he termed "the flower and loveliness of the flames." It was also reported that when the fires began to die, Nero's servants were seen gathering wood and rekindling the flames.[6] This substantiated more than ever the persistent rumor that it was Nero who had masterminded the inferno.

Eager to be absolved of the arsonist allegation, Nero promptly accused the Christians of being responsible for setting the fires. Great numbers of them were arrested and among them may have been Paul. If so, as a Roman citizen, he would have been carefully examined and when found he was not involved, would soon have been released.

But others without citizenship credentials were doomed to suffer inhumane tortures. Some were sewed up in animal skins and mauled to death by ravenous dogs, while others were rolled in flammable materials and nailed to crosses in the Circus Maximus. At night they were then set aflame to illuminate the race course

---

[5] Nero was Poppaea's third husband. She was said to have kept three thousand she-asses so as to bathe in their milk to preserve her superb complexion.

[6] *The Letters to Timothy, Titus and Philemon*, William Barclay, p. 191.

for Nero as he rode around naked in his chariot, loudly singing and gloating over his dying victims.

The catacombs

Catacombs, or subterranean labyrinths, usually three or four feet wide and often not high enough in which to stand, are found all over the Mediterranean world (Tunisia, Sicily, Syracuse, Malta and Egypt) as well as at ancient Sidon, under the city of Paris, and in many parts of Italy, including Naples and Erutria. But the early Roman and Christian catacombs around Rome are the most extensive and best known of all.

It has been estimated there are sixty sprawling catacomb complexes just around Rome alone, some so deep as to have created as many as twelve tiers of long horizontal recesses in which the dead were laid. These recesses were cut into the walls on both sides of the passageways and, if joined, it has been estimated their length would stretch at least sixty miles. No one knows how many thousands upon thousands of skeletons are entombed in these expansive underground cemeteries.

It was into these darkened tunnels that the early Christians often fled in times of severe persecution. Here they had frequently buried their dead and worshipped in small groups. Scratched on the stones are the symbols of their faith—the cross, chalice, rose, anchor, dove and fish, the fish being the only one to have a cryptic meaning. The Christians saw in the letters of the Greek word *ichthus,* meaning "fish," the acrostic, *Jesus Christ, God's Son, Savior.*

But the widespread belief that Christians continued to the third and forth centuries worshipping in the catacombs is fallacious. By the third century A.D. it is believed that there were more than 50,000 Christians in Rome. To have held their worship services in the winding, narrow corridors of the catacombs would have been unthinkable. Even one of the largest rooms in the catacomb complex, the Chapel of the Popes in the catacomb of Calixtus, barely accommodates forty people. The interment in the catacombs by A.D. 350 had become rare and ceased altogether after the sack of Rome by Alaric in 410.[7]

---

[7] *Encyclopædia Britannica*, vol. 5, 1964. pp. 55, 56.

The Mamertine dungeon

According to tradition, Paul was incarcerated near the Roman Forum in the notorious Mamertine dungeon, a foul, dank underground cell into which prisoners awaiting execution were lowered through its roof. Here in chains, as a condemned criminal, Paul spent the last months of his life (possibly as long as two years). Luke, it appears, was the only one who remained near him to the very end (2Tim. 4:11).

The fact that no one came to Paul's defense is not surprising, since the evidence against him was overwhelming. He had without question disobeyed Nero's orders not to preach the gospel upon pain of death and knew that no court would exonerate him. Paul, therefore, wanted no one criticized for not standing up for him and this he made abundantly plain in his final words to Timothy: "no one supported me, but all deserted me; may it not be counted against them" (v. 16).

Paul's statement, "I was delivered out of the lion's mouth" (v. 17), may have referred to a change of orders at the last moment not to throw him to the lions. Paul, of course, would have viewed this as providential.

It is not known if Paul in his final trial was brought before Nero himself, but if so he would have appeared before the most powerful potentate of all time as well as the undisputed autocrat of paganism. Nero, on the other hand, would have appeared before Paul, who more than any other was responsible for bringing the world the dynamic, timeless message of the gospel which in less then three centuries was to conquer the whole empire.

Nero visits Greece

It was in the midst of nationwide growing discontent with his leadership that Nero embarked on a frivolous concert tour of Greece. He had billed himself as an noted singer-composer as well as a fine violinist. Only because he was emperor did anyone come to hear his cracked voice and listen to his inane doggerel.[8] He was the height of conceit and anything but an accomplished musician.

Upon returning to Rome, Nero discovered to his alarm that the revolt by an insurgent named Galba had grown out of hand. Spain and the legions in Germany were demanding a republic and every day brought fresh reports of desertion. At last the palace guards abandoned their posts.

---

[8] *The Life and Work of St. Paul*, Frederic W. Farrar, p. 553.

Upon learning that the Senate had voted Galba to replace him, Nero disguised himself and fled for his life some four miles to a freedman's villa. Here he hoped to remain hidden until he could escape from the country, but his whereabouts were soon discovered and the militia was dispatched to bring him before the Roman tribunal.

The death of Nero

Knowing that his death sentence was inevitable, Nero decided to commit suicide by plunging a dagger into his throat. But he found that he lacked the courage. After several unsuccessful attempts, he heard soldiers approaching. Dreading the thought of capture, he handed his dagger to his slave who upon Nero's command thrust it in. When the militia arrived they found him gasping and lying in a pool of blood, but it was too late to save him.

Nero had ruled for fourteen years and died when he was only thirty-two. He was the worst of the Caesars. Those who knew him best labeled him "a mixture of blood and mud."[9]

---

[9] Ibid., p. 554. The mysterious number of the beast, 666, in Rev. 13:18 may well have stood for Nero. In Hebrew and other ancient languages, the letters of the alphabet were used as numbers, and therefore every letter had a numerical value. "Nero Caesar" when written in Hebrew totals 666 and when written in Latin is 616, a variant of 666, and also found in some Greek manuscripts of Revelation.

Chapter 37

Mamertine's Message

The pastoral epistles[1]

Paul's letter to Titus and his two to Timothy (the last one having been written in the Mamertine dungeon in Rome) are well called the "pastoral epistles." They contain much practical counsel for pastors and church leaders, especially for widows and young people and slave owners and their slaves. The emphasis throughout these rambling epistles is on Christian deportment more than on Christian doctrine. Such letters would have been welcomed by Timothy and Titus now serving in their own pastorates—Timothy ministering in Ephesus and Titus in Crete.

Paul's initial encounter with Jesus was dramatically different from that of the apostles who first came to know Him as the Son of Man, then came to worship

---

[1] "Some have questioned whether Paul himself wrote these letters on the ground that (1) Paul's travels described in the Pastorals do not fit anywhere into the historical account of the book of Acts, (2) the church organization described in them is that of the second century, and (3) the vocabulary and style are significantly different from that of the other Pauline letters. Those who hold to the Pauline authorship reply: (1) there is no compelling reason to believe that Acts contains the complete history of Paul. Since his death is not recorded in Acts, he was apparently released from his first imprisonment in Rome, traveled over the empire for several years (perhaps even to Spain), was rearrested, imprisoned a second time in Rome, and martyred under Nero; (2) nothing in the church organization reflected in the Pastorals requires a later date (see Acts 14:23; Phil. 1:1); and (3) the question of authorship cannot be decided solely on the basis of vocabulary without considering how subject matter affects a writer's choice of words. Vocabulary used to describe church organization, for instance, would be expected to be different from that used to teach the doctrine of the Holy Spirit. There is no argument against Pauline authorship that does not have a reasonable answer. And, of course, the letters themselves claim to have been written by Paul." (1 Timothy, Introduction, Authorship, NIV, *Ryrie Study Bible.*)

Him as the Son of God. Paul, however, first met Jesus as the Son of God,[2] then years later came to revere Him as the Son of Man.[3]

The arrangement of Paul's letters

As one studies the thirteen letters of Paul and traces the development of his thought, it is regrettable that his epistles are not arranged chronologically instead of, as they are, by length. As it is now, his first letters, 1 and 2 Thessalonians, and his last, 1 and 2 Timothy, are side by side, while Romans, his longest letter, heads the list, and Philemon, his shortest letter, concludes it.[4]

Paul's special mark

Most of Paul's letters were dictated, and to prevent them from being forged, as evidently happened in some cases, and lest Paul's name be used by unscrupulous Judaizers to verify their false doctrines, Paul signed his letters with a special mark. This he pointed out to the Thessalonians, "I, Paul, write this greeting with my own hand, and this is a distinguishing mark in every letter; this is the way I write" (2Thess. 3:17). In four other of Paul's letters, 1 Corinthians, Galatians, Colossians, and Philemon, Paul also mentions writing with "my own hand" (1Cor. 16:11, Gal. 6:11, Col. 4:18, Philem. 19).

Jesus' promise of inspiration

Jesus promised His apostles that His Father would send them the Holy Spirit who would "teach you all things, and bring to your remembrance all that I said to you" (Jn. 14:26).

---

[2] There is no indication that Paul ever met Jesus in the flesh, though he may have witnessed His crucifixion. When the reports reached him of Jesus' resurrection, immediately he would have dismissed them as fallacious—incredible nonsense! Doubtless it was the work of men bribed to overpower the guards and make off with the body or by some other means the body had been removed. Jesus, in the eyes of Paul, before he became a Christian, was nothing more than a man claiming to be the Messiah—a false prophet who deserved to be crucified.

[3] *Spiritual Development of St. Paul*, George Matheson, p. 321.

[4] See Appendix V, "Probable Dates and Chronology of New Testament Writings" on page 295.

Then on the night before His crucifixion, Jesus told His apostles, "I have many more things to say to you, but you cannot bear them now. But when He, the Spirit of truth, comes, He will guide you into all truth; for He will disclose to you what is to come" (Jn. 16:12, 13).

It thus appears that Jesus "was indicating that during the corporate lifetime of the apostles who had been with Him during His three-year ministry, all of the additional truth He wanted the church to have would be delivered to them by the Spirit."[5]

Ratifying the New Testament as inspired

The New Testament, including all the letters of Paul who considered himself "not in the least inferior to the most eminent apostles" (2Cor. 11:5), were considered by the early church divinely inspired in view of the fact that its writers, with the exception of Mark, Luke, Jude (the brother of James, leader of the Jerusalem church and half brother of Jesus), and the unknown writer of Hebrews, were all apostles of Christ. Mark and Luke, before writing their Gospels, would have gained, of course, as much information as possible from the apostles regarding Jesus' way of life and teaching as well as the experiences they had encountered while living with Him.

As for Jude, his blood brother relationship with James and being the half brother of Jesus qualified him in the eyes of the early church as an inspired writer of the New Testament. The writer of Hebrews, on the other hand, was always considered writing under divine inspiration though incredibly his name is not known today.

It is therefore not surprising that the Third Council of Carthage in 397 pronounced the present twenty-seven books of the New Testament divinely inspired. Since then no serious attempt has ever been made to alter this pronouncement.

Qualifications for church leaders

Paul's qualifications for church leaders in I Timothy and Titus call for men not only of sterling character but

---

[5] *Israel My Glory*, April/May 1997, p. 30.

the husband of one wife, temperate, prudent, respectable, hospitable, able to teach, not addicted to wine or pugnacious, but gentle, uncontentious, free from the love of money. He must be one who manages his own household well, keeping his children under control with all dignity (but if a man does not know how to manage his own household, how will he take care of the church of God?); and not a new convert, lest he become conceited and fall into the condemnation incurred by the devil. And he must have a good reputation with those outside the church, so that he may not fall into reproach and the snare of the devil. Deacons likewise must be men of dignity, not double-tongued, or addicted to much wine or fond of sordid gain, but holding to the mystery of the faith with a clear conscience. And let these also first be tested; then let them serve as deacons if they are beyond reproach. (1 Tim. 3:2-10; see also Tit. 1:5-9)

Men and women were both admonished. "Older men are to be temperate, dignified, sensible, sound in faith, in love, in perseverance" (Tit. 2:2); and

Older women likewise are to be reverent in their behavior, not malicious gossips, not enslaved to much wine, teaching what is good, that they may encourage the young women to love their husbands, to love their children, to be sensible, pure, workers at home, kind, being subject to their own husbands, that the Word of God may not be dishonored. (vv. 3-5)

Likewise the young men are

... to be sensible; in all things show yourself to be an example of good deeds, with purity in doctrine, dignified, sound in speech which is beyond reproach.... (vv. 2-6)[6]

Let no one look down on your youthfulness [Timothy,] but rather in speech, conduct, love, faith and purity, show yourself an example of those who believe. (1 Tim. 4:12)[7]

All Christians are

... to be subject to rulers, to authorities, to be obedient, to be ready for every good deed, to malign no one, to be uncontentious, gentle, showing every consideration for all men. (Tit. 3:1-2)

---

[6] Men, women and young people are all urged to be "sensible."

[7] Fifteen years had passed since Timothy became Paul's helper. The word Paul uses for youth (*ncotes*) included anyone up to the age of forty-six. Timothy at the time was about thirty-five.

First-century Jewish, Greek and Roman women

Jewish women in the first century occupied a very low position in society and were classed with children and slaves. Under the Jewish law a husband could divorce his wife for any reason; but his wife could not divorce her husband for any cause. Women, as has been noted, had no part in the synagogue service and sat in a gallery behind a perforated screen through which they could see and hear but not be seen. They were not allowed to teach anyone, not even their own children.

A woman's work was to tend the home and send the children to the synagogue and to leave her husband free to study in the schools. Jewish men thanked God every morning that they had not been born a Gentile, slave or woman; and a strict rabbi would never greet a woman on the street, even though she was his wife or daughter or mother or sister![8]

Greek women as well enjoyed few rights and could be divorced at any time at the behest of their husbands. Women's dowries, however, by law, had to be returned to them. They were largely confined to their own apartments and were never allowed on the streets alone or with men at meals or at public functions. A woman, according to Xenophon, was to "see as little as possible, hear as little as possible, and ask as little as possible."[9]

In Rome too the marriage bond was generally no longer sacrosanct. During the first 520 years of the republic, divorce had been unheard of, but in the first century A.D. it had become commonplace. To have a family was generally considered a misfortune. Seneca records that women were married to be divorced and divorced to be remarried.[10]

Jerome tells of a woman who was married to her twenty-third husband and she herself was his twenty-first wife![11] According to Cato, if a man's wife committed adultery, he could kill her with impunity, without court judgment; but if her husband proved unfaithful, it was unlawful for her to speak out against him.

---

[8] *The Letters to Timothy, Titus and Philemon*, William Barclay, p. 76.

[9] Ibid., p. 77.

[10] *The Letters to the Galatians and Ephesians*, William Barclay, p. 170.

[11] *New Testament Survey*, Merrill C. Tenney, p. 58.

Unwanted children were regularly, after nightfall, abandoned in the city squares of Rome. Hilarion's letter to his pregnant wife, Alis, reveals the calloused outlook prevailing. "Should you bear a child," he wrote, "if it is a boy, let it live; if a girl, expose it."[12]

Wealthy first-century women among the Greeks and Romans spent long hours selecting costly jewelry and adorning themselves in luxurious attire. The finest coiffeurs were hired, and hair was arranged in the latest fashions which often included elaborate styles of braiding. The proponents of the Greek mystery religions, shocked over this inordinate love of dress and adornment, stipulated: "A consecrated woman shall not have gold ornaments, nor rouge, nor face-whitening, nor a head-band, nor braided hair, or shoes except those made of felt or of the skins of sacrificed animals."[13]

In light of the mores of the first century and the attitude toward women, it is understandable why Paul instructed Christian women to be modest in their attire and not braid their hair or adorn themselves with costly jewelry or teach or exercise authority over men (1Tim. 2:9, 12). To have done so would only have denigrated women and brought shame to the Christian community.

Paul's apostolic authority

2 Timothy opens, as do all of Paul's epistles, except those to the Thessalonians, Philippians and Philemon, with the affirmation of his apostleship. Always Paul maintained that Christ had set him apart from his mother's womb and had personally appeared to him and ordained him as His envoy to the Gentiles (Gal. 1:15, 16; 2:8, 9; Rom. 11:13; 15:15, 16; Eph. 3:8; 1Tim. 2:7). As a representative of the Savior, he saw himself and his fellow workers as envoys of God: "we are ambassadors for Christ," he explained, "as though God were entreating through us ..." (2Cor. 5:20). When he urged the Christians at Thessalonica, Corinth and Philippi to model their lives on his life and those of his copartners (2Thess. 3:9; 1Cor. 4:16, 11:1; Phil. 3:17, 4:9),[14] it was always, of course, with the proviso that he and his evangelists were practicing what they preached.

---

[12]*Ambassador for Christ*, William Barclay, p. 30.

[13]*The Letters to the Galatians and Ephesians*, William Barclay, p. 171.

[14]See *Epistles of Paul to the Philippians*, Charles Erdman, p. 114.

Since Paul believed himself called of God to preach to the Gentiles, he felt not in the least inferior to the most eminent of the apostles (2Cor. 11:5). Though he could not qualify for an apostle according to the apostolic rule which stipulated that to be an apostle one had to have accompanied Jesus during the whole of His ministry, beginning with the baptism of John, and had to have witnessed Jesus' resurrection (Ac. 1:21, 22), Paul yet insisted that his apostleship was as genuine as that of the Twelve since Christ had commissioned him as His ambassador.

Paul considered much of what he preached and wrote regarding spiritual matters as inspired as the Old Testament Scriptures. He wrote the Corinthians, "we also speak, not in words taught by human wisdom, but in words taught by the Spirit, combining spiritual thoughts with spiritual words" (1Cor. 2:13). To the Thessalonians he declared, "when you received from us the word of God's message, you accepted it not as the word of men, but for what it really is, the word of God …" (1Thess. 2:13). He warned the Corinthians, "If anyone thinks he is a prophet or spiritual, let him recognize that the things which I write to you are the Lord's commandment. But if anyone does not recognize this, he is not recognized" (1Cor. 14:37, 38). This insistence on claiming divine inspiration when he wrote concerning doctrinal and spiritual matters was only to remind the Christians that what he wrote in this regard he believed was truly from the Lord and that as an apostle of Christ he was therefore to be trusted and followed.

Peter's view of Paul's letters

Peter placed all of Paul's letters on a par with the Scriptures when he wrote,

> just as also our beloved brother Paul, according to the wisdom given him, wrote to you, as also in all his letters, speaking in them of these things, in which are some things hard to understand, which the untaught and unstable distort, as they do also the rest of the Scriptures, to their own destruction. (2Pet. 3:15, 16)

(When Paul wrote, "All Scripture is inspired by God …" [2Tim. 3:16] he was of course referring to the Old Testament Scriptures.)

"Stir up the fire!"

When Paul urged Timothy to stir up the gift of God which was in him through Paul's laying on of his hands (2 Tim 1:6 KJV), he must have had in mind the campfires around which he and Timothy had often relaxed after a long day's trek. Frequently they had watched the lively flames gradually burn down into embers, and then when stirred, suddenly flare up.

So too Timothy was urged to stir up his faith when he felt the fire of his preaching beginning to wane and his enthusiasm declining. In essence Paul was saying, "Let the fire be stirred; let the Spirit blow in! Let the Holy Ghost scatter all ashes of bitterness and despair! Stir up the fire! Stir up the fire!"

But Paul knew that too much poking at the coals and sifting of the ashes, too much introspection and self-analysis can easily put out the flames. Stir up the fire, yes, but then add the "firewood." Concentrate on God's power, His love and discipline.

The power of God

"God has not given us the spirit of fear, but of power" (2Tim. 1:7). Here Paul uses the Greek word *dunamis* from which comes the word *dynamite*. Repeatedly this word is found in Paul's writings: to the Thessalonians, "our gospel did not come to you in word only, but also in *power*" (1Thess. 1:5); to the Corinthians, "the kingdom of God does not consist in words, but in *power*" (1Cor. 4:20) and to the Romans, "I am not ashamed of the Gospel, for it is the *power* of God for salvation to everyone who believes, to the Jew first and also to the Greek" (Rom. 1:16). Paul prays that the Ephesians may know the greatness of this *power* (Eph. 1:19) and encourages the Colossians to be strengthened according to its might (Col. 1:11). It is this divine *dunamis* that kept Paul's ministry blazing; it fueled his faith and renewed his energy.

The love of God

Coupled with the power of God is His gift of love (*agape*), that unique kind of love, previously discussed,[15] which reaches out to help another with no desire to possess or enjoy. It is always based on a willingness for total sacrifice supremely exemplified at Calvary: "Greater love has no one than this, that one lay down his life for his friends" (Jn. 15:13).

---

[15]See Chapter 21, "A Highly Sensitive Issue" on p. 149.

Though John, the son of Zebedee, long has been known as the apostle of love, the title should also be given to Paul.[16] No one had a greater love for the Savior; and no one loved his converts more. Paul "loved his way into the hearts of men. His love begot love in others. People were devoted to Him because they were so sure of his devotion to them."[17] "Follow the way of love.... Do everything in love," Paul urged the Corinthians (1Cor. 14:1; 16:14 NIV).

All of Paul's epistles emphasize Christian *love*.

Owe nothing to anyone except to *love*. (Rom. 13:8)

If I speak with the tongue of men and of angels but do not have *love*, I have become a noisy gong or a clanging cymbal. (1Cor. 13:1)

... you are in our hearts to die together and to live together. (2Cor. 7:3)

I have you in my heart ... how I long for you all with the affection of Christ Jesus. (Phil. 1:7, 8)

... to abound in *love* one for another. (1Thess. 3:12; 4:9, 10; Phil. 1:9)

Be kind and *compassionate* to one another, forgiving each other, just as in Christ God forgave you. (Eph. 4:32)

... put on *love*, which is the perfect bond of unity. (Col. 3:14)

Among the fruit of the Spirit, the first mentioned is *love*. (Gal. 5:22)

Set an example for the believers in speech, in life, in *love*, in faith and in purity. (1Tim. 4:12 NIV)

... you, man of God ... pursue righteousness, godliness, faith, *love*, endurance and gentleness. (1Tim. 6:11)

For God did not give us a spirit of timidity, but a spirit of power, of *love* and of self-discipline. (2Tim. 1:7 NIV)

... pursue righteousness, faith, *love* and peace." (2Tim. 2:22)

[A church elder] must be hospitable, one who *loves* what is good.... (Tit. 1:8 NIV)

The primary theme of Paul's letter to Philemon too is *love*.

---

[16]See *The Character of Paul*, Charles Jefferson, p. 323.

[17]*Paul and His Epistles*, D. A. Hayes, p. 48.

Paul considered all Christians his brothers and sisters and felt himself both mother and father to those who he had won to Christ. "[W]e proved to be gentle among you," he reminds the Thessalonians, "as a nursing mother tenderly cares for her own children … (1Thess. 2:7) "exhorting and encouraging and imploring each one of you as a father would his own children …" (v. 11). "Having thus a fond affection for you, we were well-pleased to impart to you not only the gospel of God but also our own lives, because you had become very dear to us" (v. 8).

Paul's prayer for the Ephesians reveals not only his longing to share Christ's love, but also his view of the immensity of such love revealed at the Cross.

> I pray that out of his glorious riches he may strengthen you with power through his Spirit in your inner being, so that Christ may dwell in your hearts through faith. And I pray that you, being rooted and established in love, may have power, together with all the saints, to grasp how wide and long and high and deep is the love of Christ, and to know this love that surpasses knowledge—that you may be filled to the measure of all the fullness of God. (Eph. 3:16-19 NIV)

The discipline of God

Finally, Paul wrote of God's gift of discipline without which God's power and love cannot operate in the Christian's life. Such discipline is totally different from self-discipline which can degenerate into asceticism. Divine discipline is administered only from the heart of God: "whom the Lord loves He reproves, even as a father, the son in whom he delights" (Prov. 3:12). Refusing to accept such discipline leaves the Christian recalcitrant and totally ineffective for Christian service.

It was Paul's willingness to be chastened under the hand of God and to be willing to venture forth with Him to the edge by faith which enabled him at the end of his life to exclaim,

> I have fought the good fight, I have finished the course, I have kept the faith; in the future there is laid up for me the crown of righteousness, which the Lord, the righteous judge, will award to me on that day; and not only to me, but also to all who have loved His appearing. (2Tim. 4:7, 8)

Paul's death

Nothing is known of the details of Paul's death but that which is bequeathed in legend. It is said that he was removed from Rome's notorious Mamertine dungeon by being drawn up through its hole in the roof. In chains he was led along the

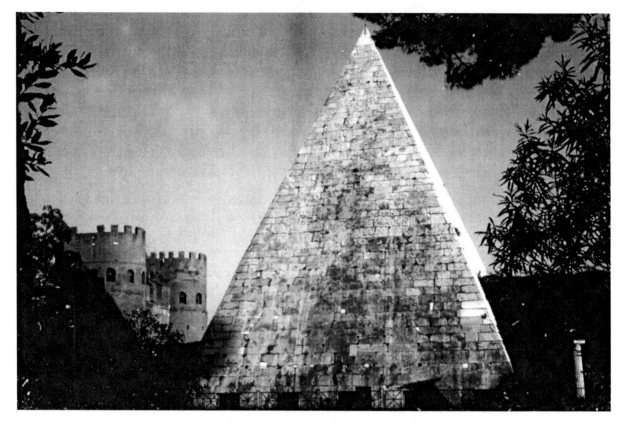

The pyramid of Caius Cestius.

Ostian Way for about three miles and then stripped and beaten and made to kneel before a brawny, naked[18] swordsman. After the executioner had taken careful aim, the sword flashed and Paul was beheaded.

If Paul had been led through the Ostian Gate on his way to his execution, he would have passed the pyramidal monument of Caius Cestius which still remains

---

[18]The custom for Roman executioners who decapitated prisoners was to strip down completely lest the blood of the victim spatter their garments.

According to one spurious tradition, Paul's head bounced three times and where it landed a fountain sprang up!

It is unknown where Paul's body and skull are buried. Some maintain the relics were placed in a Roman tomb and lovingly guarded by the church at Rome. Believing this, Emperor Constantine, in the third century, entombed the skeletal remains in a metal casket and built a church above it known today as St. Paul's Beyond the Walls. (See *In the Steps of St. Paul*, H. V. Mortan, p. 411.)

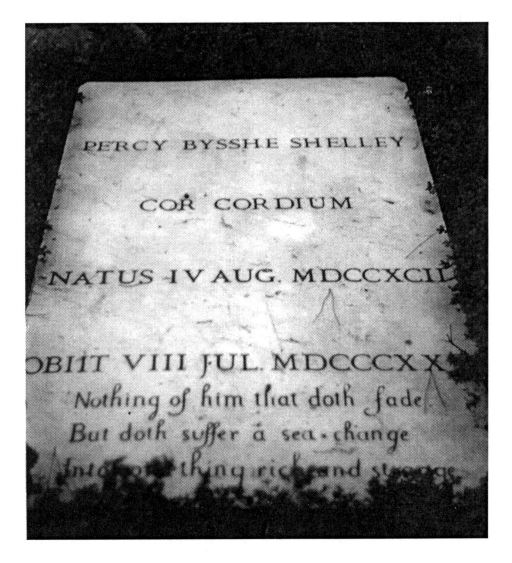

Percy Bysshe Shelley's gravestone.

not far from the gate. It overshadows the burial plots of Percy Bysshe Shelley and John Keats.

Shelley's provocative lines in his eulogy to Keats would provide a most fitting epitaph for the Great Apostle:

Peace, peace! he is not dead, he doth not sleep, ...
He has outsoar'd the shadow of our night;
Envy and calumny and hate and pain, ...
Can touch him not and torture not again; ...
He lives, he wakes—'tis Death is dead, not he; ...[19]

---

[19]*Adonais*, Percy Bysshe Shelley, selections from stanzas 39-41.

Paul in Review

Paul's stature

Of all history's renowned Christian leaders, reformers and theologians, none excel Paul.

[H]e dwarfs all men of his generation, and also all the men of the generations which immediately followed. The subapostolic fathers, Clement of Rome and Ignatius, Papias and Polycarp and Justin Martyr, all are pygmies compared to him. Clement of Alexandria, Irenaeus, Tertullian, and Cyprian were able and devoted men, but they do not belong to Paul's class. The farther away from him the taller he looms.[1]

He must never be consigned to any century; his message is much too timeless. He belongs to all the ages.

Paul's thirteen epistles

Paul's thirteen letters contain all the doctrines of the Christian faith and serve as the handbook of the Gospels; they provide their theological base. No one can know Christianity thoroughly without knowing the epistles of Paul; nor can anyone know Paul well without perusing his epistles. While Paul's character and personality are seen in part from what Luke records of him in his travels, it is Paul's letters which best reveal the breadth and depth of his thinking and the warmth and throb of his heart.

Paul never imagined that one day his writings would be read and studied all over the world, let alone that they would make up so much of the New Testament! Nor did he dream that what he wrote would be used as "sleuths" to investigate his inner nature in an attempt to discover the man he really was. It is well that Paul was unaware of this and felt free to write as he did, for had he known that his letters would be scrutinized and then carefully analyzed, he might never have written at all.

---

[1] *The Character of Paul*, Charles Jefferson, p. 374.

Paul converted outside or inside Damascus?

Paul's first encounter with Jesus outside the walls of Damascus was a reeling, horrific experience; it was anything but beatific. It left Paul (then known as Saul) and his men cowering in the sands and Paul totally blind. When Jesus cried "Saul, Saul, why are you persecuting Me?" (Ac. 9:4), Paul's question, "Who art Thou, Lord?" (v. 5), was only the bewildered response of a terrified man. When the answer came, "I am Jesus whom you are persecuting" (v. 5), Paul's use of the word *Lord* in "What shall I do, Lord?" (22:10) was in no way an acknowledgement of Jesus as his Lord, only an appellation to appease his assailant. It was not until three days later inside Damascus at the home of Judas on the street called "Straight" that the scales fell from Paul's eyes and he was converted.

Though Paul might forget the time, day, month and year of his new birth, he could never forget the place where it occurred. This was indelibly etched on his mind. So it is with all who are born of the Spirit; the place where they step from darkness into light will never be forgotten.

To claim that Paul was converted on the road to Damascus is to raise numerous perplexing questions. Why then did Paul refuse to eat or drink upon reaching the house of Judas and continued his fast for three days? Surely this is not the normal response for one just born into the family of God, nor is it the expected reaction of one completing a long journey in the heat of noonday. Since there is no evidence that Paul was physically or mentally disabled upon arriving in Damascus, his prolonged refusing to eat and drink suggests strongly that he was spiritually ill.

After his blazing encounter with Christ and being thrown to the ground and then discovering he had lost his sight, Paul could not help but know he was under the judgment of God. This frightening realization would have plunged him into deepest despair and could easily account for his loss of desire for food and drink.

If Paul was a believer when he was led into Damascus, why then did he not immediately call for the Christians and explain what had happened to him and assure them that he was now no longer their adversary, but had become their Christian brother? Why would he remain fasting in seclusion for three days and not inform the brethren of his dramatic conversion?

To say, as some do, that Paul was indwelt by the Holy Spirit outside Damascus and then, after Ananias laid his hands upon him, experienced a second baptism of the Spirit, raises the query as to the need for this second baptism. Surely the first indwelling of the Spirit was sufficient to give Paul his new birth and enable him to start growing in grace and knowledge of Christ.

But the hardest question of all to answer, for those who insist that Paul became a Christian *outside* Damascus, is why, in the experience and immediately following, is there no evidence of the fruit of the Spirit—no love, no joy, no inner peace (Gal. 5:22)? Gloom pervades Paul's darkened world, and gnawing guilt eats into his soul. It is only after his redemptive experienced and his awareness of the love of God in Christ, that the fruit of the Spirit begins to appear.

In light then of the above there can be no doubt that Paul was converted *inside* Damascus. Outside he only heard the voice of Jesus, but refused to open his heart; inside he heard the voice of his conscience and fell on his knees. It was here that the scales fell from his eyes and the great transformation took place; here it was that Christ entered in.

The edge-by-faith principle

The edge-by-faith principle was the axiom of Paul's life. Paul was "no armchair philosopher, no ivory tower scholar, but a man of almost incredible drive and courage living out in actual human dangers and agonies the implications of his unswerving faith."[2] Whatever he did he did with abandon. He was never one to stop until he reached the edge, and once there, never turned back. "I will not be mastered by anything" was his constant asseveration (1Cor. 6:12b). Beatings and imprisonment in Philippi and harassments in Thessalonica, Berea, Corinth and Ephesus all failed to dissuade him from proclaiming the Word. "I am under compulsion;" he exclaimed, "for woe is me if I do not preach the gospel" (1Cor. 9:16). He rejoiced in his tribulations and was confident they would result in his perseverance and the strengthening of his character and the building up of his hope (Rom. 5:3, 4). He was a man of indomitable faith!

Paul's visions

Paul is recorded as experiencing seven visions, but none of them evidence any emotional instability, violent seizures, catatonia or frenzied utterances. Definitely Paul was no wild-eyed fanatic swept in and out on tides of emotion.

---

[2] *Ring of Truth, A Translator's Testimony,* J. B. Phillips, p. 20.

1st—Damascan vision

Inside Damascus, while Paul was still blind, his first vision occurred. In it he saw Ananias coming and placing his hands upon him and declaring that he would receive his sight (Ac. 9:11, 12). Knowing that Ananias was one of the Jewish Christians whom he had come to apprehend, blind Paul would have realized Ananias could do him great harm. But Paul accepted by faith that he was a messenger of God and therefore could be trusted to place his hands upon him. The result: Paul was converted. His vision had not shattered his nerves; if anything, it had strengthened them.

2nd—Troas vision

After Paul in Troas had shared with his companions his night vision of the man calling him over to Macedonia, they were convinced it was the call of God, indeed so convinced they were willing to set sail with Paul to Macedonia the very next morning (Ac. 16:10). Had they felt Paul was a frenetic visionary who had experienced an aberration, they would never have accompanied him further, let alone into an unevangelized field where to preach Christ might well call forth severe persecution and even result in imprisonment and death.

3rd—Corinthian vision

When the Jews in Corinth violently renounced Paul's preaching, Jesus spoke to him in a vision and said, "Do not be afraid any longer, but go on speaking and do not be silent; for I am with you, and no man will attack you in order to harm you, for I have many people in this city" (Ac. 18:9, 10).[3] Convinced it was Christ who had spoken to him, Paul remained in Corinth for another eighteen months diligently teaching the Word (v. 11). Clearly his vision had in no way impaired his ability to teach.

4th and 5th—Jerusalem's visions

Twice in Jerusalem Paul saw the risen Christ: first in Jerusalem when he visited the temple after his conversion and was told to flee the city (Ac. 22:17, 18),[4] and a

---

[3] The *second* time Paul saw the risen Christ.

[4] The *first* time Paul saw the risen Christ.

second time, years later in Jerusalem's barracks when he was assured he was yet to see Rome (23:11).[5] Soon after both revelations Paul traveled on horseback to Caesarea, first accompanied by the brethren and later under military guard. Had Paul been emotionally disturbed by these two visions of the Savior, he could never have ridden a horse all the way to Caesarea, a distance of sixty-eight miles!

6th—Paradise vision

Paul's transport into Paradise where he "heard inexpressible words, which a man is not permitted to speak" (2Cor. 12:2-4), was, from what Paul wrote to the Corinthians, an awesome experience. But it did not leave him with a nervous breakdown, and he returned from his celestial journey perfectly sane and able to continue his vigorous ministry. Fourteen years later he wrote clearly of his arcane sojourn which indicates all the more it had not damaged his mind nor dulled his memory.

7th—Tempest vision

Paul's final vision occurred at sea in the midst of a hurricane when an angel appeared to him at night and assured him that he and all on board would not perish (Ac. 27:23, 24). Paul was not only able to convince his disbelieving pagan shipmates that he had indeed seen an angel and what the heavenly messenger had said was true, but more, he was able to persuade the crew to break bread with him after they had not eaten for fourteen days! Paul's angelic vision, startling as it was, did not unnerve him but rather left him poised and ready to face courageously in faith whatever lay before him. In the mariners' eyes he was perfectly rational and one in whom they could trust.

Paul's soundness of mind

Though Governor Felix in a moment of frustration declared Paul out of his mind (Ac. 26:24), this only raises questions as to the governor's own emotional stability. Paul was too astute and level-headed ever to be classed a lunatic. His letters attest to his high skill in handling delicate situations and solving quandaries. He was able to separate the "incidental from the essential, the temporal from the eter-

---

[5] The *third and final* time Paul saw the risen Christ.

nal."[6] Always he emphasized the importance of using one's intellect and counseled men, women and youth to be "sensible" (Tit. 2:2-8). "Set your *mind* on things above, and not on things that are on the earth" (Col. 3:2), he urged the Colossians; "be renewed in the spirit of your *mind* ..." (Eph. 4:23; Rom. 12:2), he counseled the Ephesians and the Romans; and let your *mind* dwell on whatever is true, honorable, right, pure, lovely and of good report, he instructed the Philippians (Phil. 4:8).

Significantly, it was Jesus who added the word *mind* (Mk. 12:30)[7] to the Jewish commandment, "you shall love the Lord your God with all your heart and with all your soul, and with all your might" (Deut. 6:4, 5). Paul would have welcomed the word *mind* in the famous commandment, for he viewed love through the *mind* as much as through the heart, and felt that love devoid of reason was woefully shallow.

Paul as an orator

Some denigrated Paul's preaching and claimed his speech was "contemptible" (2Cor. 10:10) and that he was anything but an orator. If an orator is one who only constructs formal speeches, observes rules of rhetoric and indulges in flowery language, then it is true Paul was not an orator. He openly admits this when he wrote the Corinthians that he came "not with superiority of speech ..." (1Cor. 2:1).

But if an orator is one who is set on fire with a great cause, then Paul was an orator of the first class. Though his message and his preaching "were not in persuasive words of wisdom," they were "in demonstration of the Spirit and of power ..." (1Cor. 2:4). His preaching might not have been polished, but it was powerful and it brought results and people were converted after listening to him. "[T]he weapons of our warfare," he declared, "are not of the flesh, but divinely powerful for the destruction of fortresses ... destroying speculations and every lofty thing raised against the knowledge of God ..." (2Cor. 10:4, 5).

Paul had an eloquence all his own, the eloquence of intense conviction and overwhelming enthusiasm and thoroughgoing consecration to his cause. His written words have stirred the hearts of millions, and have lost none of their power to

---

[6] *The Character of Paul*, Charles Jefferson, p. 77.

[7] In the story of the Good Samaritan, the lawyer included "mind" in the commandment (Lk. 10:27). Very possibly he knew that Jesus had added this.

move men through all the centuries and down to the present day.... He did not depend upon the form of his presentation of the truth, but he had absolute confidence in the power of the truth itself to commend it to all prepared people.[8]

"[I]f I am unskilled in speech," he declared, "yet I am not so in knowledge ..." (2Cor. 11:6). Paul knew whereof he spoke. His concern was not to gain a reputation for himself for eloquence but only to preach the unsearchable riches of Christ.

Sidetracking

Paul's letters were generally written impetuously to meet certain emergencies and to accomplish certain needs. He often wrote with such emotional fervor that he would begin with a thought only to leave it for another and another and another until finally he would come back to what he had originally intended to say.

Examples of this sidetracking are seen in Paul's letter to the Romans. In the first sentence he

> begins with his name and his titles in the ordinary form; but he does not stop there. He says that he is an apostle, separated unto the gospel of God. At that mention of the gospel he "goes off" to explain what it is. It was promised "afore through the prophets in the holy scriptures," and it is concerning his Son. At that mention of the Son he "goes off" to explain him, in the assertion of his true humanity and proven deity. Then he comes back to his apostleship as received through his Christ.[9]

Again sidetracking is seen in his letter to the Romans as Paul begins an enumeration with "First, I thank my God through Jesus Christ for you all, because your faith is being proclaimed throughout the whole world" (Rom. 1:8), but then forgets to add a second reason for being thankful.

And in the third chapter of the same letter Paul queries what advantage it is to be a Jew, and then answers, "Great in every respect. First of all, that they were entrusted with the oracles of God" (Rom. 3:2). Then Paul becomes involved in other topics, and not until the ninth chapter does he return to his listing of the advantages of being a Jew (Rom. 9:4, 5).

---

[8] *Paul and His Epistles*, D. A. Hayes, pp. 237, 238.

[9] Ibid., p. 86.

Breaking the rules of grammar

Paul's writings betrayed a constant carelessness as to the structure and grammar he used, and in no way can his compositions be classed as "polished." Often he coined words. For example, in his letter to the Ephesians he used three compound words which are translated "fellow heirs," "fellow members of the body" and "fellow partakers" (Eph. 3:6).[10] Such words do not occur in Greek and no classicist would have thought of coining them. But Paul's message was more important to him than following rules of speech or using perfect grammar.

Paul's statement, "I am less than the least of all God's people" (Eph. 3:8 NIV) is another example of verbal malformation.

> It is a comparative formed on a superlative—"I am *the leaster* of all the saints." It is the comparative of a superlative—"I am *the more least* of all the saints." It is a grammatical impossibility; it is a literal absurdity. If anyone is least, there can be no one more least than he. What is least can have nothing less than itself.[11]

But Paul, though he well knew the rules of Greek grammar, was so intent on stressing how unspeakably unworthy he felt himself in being entrusted with the gospel message that he purposely went beyond the bounds of legitimate rhetoric to make this abundantly clear.

Mixed metaphors

Mixed metaphors are also found in Paul's letters, as seen in his reminding the Corinthians that when their earthly bodies, compared to tents, were torn down, they would be replaced by an eternal house in heaven. He then wrote, "For indeed in this house we groan, longing to be clothed with our dwelling from heaven; inasmuch as we, having put it on, shall not be found naked" (2Cor. 5:2, 3). Being clothed with a house?

Again Paul's careless use of metaphors is evidenced in his letter to the Colossians where he exhorts them, "As you therefore have received Christ Jesus the Lord, so walk in Him, having been firmly rooted and now being built up in Him and established in your faith ..." (Col. 2:6, 7). Walk, rooted as a tree and built up as a house and firmly established?

---

[10]See Ibid., p. 87.
[11]Ibid., p. 88.

But with so much to say and too little time to say it, Paul paid little attention to how he said it. "His thoughts hurry each other, jostle each other, ride each other down sometimes. They do not march in orderly procession. They run and leap like rival contestants in Olympic games, like soldiers fighting their way through a narrow pass."[12] It is not to be wondered that at times there should be confusion as to what Paul was saying and that Peter would find some of what Paul wrote "hard to understand ..." (2Pet. 3:16).

Yet despite the profusion of his ideas and awkwardness of his compositions, it is impressive how clearly Paul's thought progresses.

> He never was ambitious to pose as a model of style. There were other things which seemed so much more important to him. There are beautiful things in Paul's writings, but they are spontaneously so, not made so by study. Paul's genius made him say great things. Sometimes the very elevation of his soul made him eloquent and elegant. He has written some of the greatest passages in the world's literature. He could have ranked high as a literary master if he had chosen to be one. He had a higher mission. His writing was incidental to his missionary career. It held a very subordinate place in his thought. His interest was in the matter of his message and not in the manner of its presentation. It was the substance of the gospel which absorbed him, and he was comparatively careless as to its form.[13]

If a Tarsian professor had been assigned to prepare one of Paul's lengthy epistles for publication, he would surely have softened down whole sentences and removed all bitter sarcasms and wrathful denunciations and all phrases not suited to polite society. Incomplete sentences would be finalized, and tedious repetitions of the same word eliminated along with all distressful boastings and grammatical errors. Yet though classically correct, the letter would be anything but Paul's and would have lost its characteristic features of impetuosity and bluntness as well as its passion and emotional power.[14]

Maternal metaphors

Though Paul was known for his boldness and aggressiveness and warlike tendencies, he was also known for his tenderness as a mother with a newborn babe.

---

[12]Ibid., p. 89.
[13]Ibid., pp. 89, 90.
[14]Paraphrased from *The Life and Work of Saint Paul*, Frederic W. Farrar, vol. 1, p. 577.

This is seen when Paul refers to himself (and sometimes his co-workers) in maternal metaphors.

> But we proved to be gentle among you, as a nursing mother tenderly cares for her own children. (1Thess. 2:7)

> And I, brethren, could not speak to you as to spiritual men, but as to men of flesh, as to babes in Christ. I gave you milk to drink, not solid food; for you were not yet able to receive it. Indeed, even now you were not yet able. (1Cor. 3:1, 2)

> My children, with whom I am in labor until Christ is formed in you.... (Gal. 4:19)

It is to be expected that Paul would refer to himself as a father in his working relationship with Timothy: "... he served with me in the furtherance of the Gospel like a child serving his father" (Phil. 2:2), but not expected for Paul to liken himself to a mother giving spiritual birth to his converts. Especially is this surprising in view of the fact that all women and those who became mothers were in Paul's day considered inferior to men and expected to be under their control. Though Epictetus, along with other Roman, Greek and Jewish writers, scorned the rôle of "mothers and wet-nurses," this was inconsequential to Paul. If assuming the rôle of a mother emphasized more clearly his overwhelming love for his children in the faith, then why not use the metaphor?

It is interesting to note that Paul depicting himself as a mother was not forgotten over the years and in the eleventh century Anselm of Canterbury actually went so far as to compose the following prayer to Paul:

> O St. Paul, where is he that was called the nurse of the faithful, caressing his sons? Who is that affectionate mother who declares everywhere that she is in labour for her sons? Sweet nurse, sweet mother, who are the sons you are in labour with, and nurse, but those whom by teaching the faith of Christ you bear and instruct? Or who is a Christian after your teaching who is not born into the faith and established in it by you? And if in that blessed faith we are born and nursed by other apostles also, it is most of all by you, for you have laboured and done more than them all in this; so if they are our mothers, you are our greatest mother.[15]

---

[15]The translation of Benedicta Ward in the *Prayers and Meditations of Saint Anselm*, p. 152. For further discussion on Paul's employment of maternal imagery, see Beverly Roberts Gaventa's *Inaugural Lecture* (Princeton Theological Seminary, Princeton, New Jersey), November 15, 1995.

Paul, were he to read this heretical prayer addressed to himself as a deity and called "Saint Paul" and "greatest mother," would be dumbfounded, not to mention sorely grieved. Immediately he would tear it up, and throw it in the fire and then do his best to see thereafter it was never offered up again. As he had done with the priests of Zeus at Lystra when they were about to sacrifice bulls to Barnabas and himself, he would exclaim, with the same vehemence, "I am not a man to be worshipped but only a servant of Christ to serve!"

Sampling of Paul's exhortations

Following are some of Paul's sparkling aphorisms and practical observations:

Do all things without grumbling or disputing. (Phil. 2:14)

[E]xamine everything carefully; hold fast to that which is good; abstain from every appearance of evil. (1Thess. 5:21, 22)

[T]he wages of sin is death, but the free gift of God is eternal life in Christ Jesus our Lord. (Rom. 6:23)

[H]e who sows sparingly shall also reap sparingly; and he who sows bountifully shall also reap bountifully. (2Cor. 9:6)

Do not be deceived, God is not mocked; for whatever a man sows, this he will also reap. (Gal. 6:7)

Be angry, and yet do not sin; do not let the sun go down on your anger, and do not give the devil an opportunity. (Eph. 4:26, 27)

Let your speech always be with grace, seasoned, as it were, with salt, so that you may know how you should respond to each person. (Col. 4:6)

See that no one repays another with evil for evil, but always seek after that which is good for one another and for all men. (1Thess. 5:15)

Pray without ceasing. (1Thess. 5:17)

Do not quench the Spirit. (1Thess. 5:19)

[I]f anyone will not work, neither let him eat. (2Thess. 3:10)

[D]o not grow weary of doing good. (2Thess. 3:13)

Let no one look down on your youthfulness.... (1Tim. 4:12)

[W]e have brought nothing into the world, so we cannot take anything out of it either. (1Tim. 6:7)

[T]he love of money is a root of all sorts of evil.... (1Tim. 6:10)

[A]void worldly and empty chatter, for it will lead to further ungodliness.... (2Tim. 2:16)

[D]o not merely look out for your own personal interests, but also for the interests of others. (Phil. 2:4)

Whatever you do, do your work heartily, as for the Lord rather than for men.... (Col. 3:23)

Let all you do be done in love. (1Cor. 16:14)

Paul's concept of sin

As a Pharisee Paul would have agreed wholeheartedly with the definition of sin found in the Westminster Shorter Catechism: "any want of conformity unto, or transgression of the Law of God."[16] Such a definition was identical with that of the rabbis. But as a Christian, Paul's view of sin radically changed.

> Sin now was not something a man did: it was something that took possession of him, something the man was, something that turned him into an open enemy of the God who loved him. It brought outward penalties: "whatsoever a man soweth, that shall he also reap." But far more appalling than these were its inward results. It tormented the conscience: "Oh wretched man that I am!" It brought the will into abject slavery: "the good that I would, I do not, but the evil which I would not, that I do." It destroyed fellowship with God: men were "alienated, without God in the world." It hardened the heart, and blinded the judgment, and warped the moral sense: "God gave them over to a reprobate mind." It destroyed life itself: "the wages of sin is death."[17]

While Paul was fully aware of the gravitational pull of sin, he was also aware of the superior magnetic power of the Cross. This power, he believed, is available to all believers. Man was not destined to sin; he sins of his own accord.

---

[16] *Westminster Confession of Faith*, Shorter Confession, Question 14.
[17] *A Man in Christ*, James S. Stewart, pp. 106, 107.

Paul's view of perdition

Paul accepted without questioning Christ's teaching regarding hell (Mt. 25:44, 46; Jn. 14:1, 2; 2Thess. 1:7-9), seeing it as an eternal, fiery abode prepared for Satan and his angels and for all unrepentant sinners. But finding the doctrine of perdition hard to reconcile with the doctrine of a loving and merciful Father, but nonetheless believing that the Judge of all the earth will do right, Paul wisely refrained from writing extensively on the subject.

To picture Paul as a fiery, shouting evangelist threatening eternal torment on all who refused to believe his gospel is to paint him completely out of character. Paul must rather be seen as he truly was, the herald of God's astounding good news that God loves the world and sent forth His Son as the atonement for sin that all who repent and believe in Him should not perish but have everlasting life.

Paul firmly believed that God desires all men to be saved and to come to the knowledge of the truth" (1Tim. 2:4; cf. 2Pet. 3:9). The voice of conscience is the voice of God within every man, therefore, man intuitively knows right from wrong and is without excuse for not believing in God. Natural revelation confirms the existence of God (Rom. 1:18-20), and, therefore, those who never heard the gospel will be justly judged according to the light that they had.

Paul's view of God the Father

Though Paul readily acknowledged the enigma of evil and suffering and with Jeremiah and Habakkuk must often have questioned why the wicked prosper and why God tolerates it (Jer. 12:1; Hab. 1:3), there is absolutely no evidence that Paul ever once questioned the love and justice of God. History he believed was unfolding the will of God and whatever transpired, whether it be victory or defeat, prosperity or poverty, pleasure or pain, was allowed for a good purpose. God "causes all things to work together for good to those who love God, to those who are called according to His purpose" (Rom. 8:28).

Paul knew the Lord as his Heavenly Father and was convinced of His holiness, absolute integrity and abiding love. For man to question this was to insult his Creator. "The thing molded will not say to the molder, 'Why did you make me like this,' will it?" (Rom. 9:20). Paul believed his Father's power would never be used except in love, and His loving purpose, because of His power, would never be frustrated.[18]

Paul's view of God the Son

Pre-eminently Paul's Christology is seen in his epistles to the Philippians and Colossians. In Philippians he declares, though Jesus existed in the form of God, He yet took the form of a bond-servant and was made in the likeness of men.

> And being found in appearance as a man, He humbled Himself by becoming obedient to the point of death, even death on a cross. Therefore God highly exalted Him, and bestowed on Him the name which is above every name, that at the name of Jesus every knee should bow, of those who are in heaven, and on earth, and under the earth, and that every tongue should confess that Jesus Christ is Lord, to the glory of God the Father (Phil. 2:6-11).

In Colossians Paul stresses the deity of Christ by whom "all things were created, both in the heavens and on earth, visible and invisible, whether thrones or dominions or rulers or authorities—all things have been created by Him and for Him" (Col. 1:16). "He is the head of the body, the church; ... the first-born from the dead; so that He Himself might come to have first place in everything" (v. 18).

Paul uses the phrase "in Christ" 176 times. "In Christ" denotes the absolute union between Christ and the Christian. Such unity promotes the love, joy and inner peace Jesus promised His disciples. To be in Christ is to enable the believer to live a consistent Christian life.

Paul's view of God the Holy Spirit

Paul never minimized the Third Person of the Trinity who is the One who brings sinners to Christ, imparts in them spiritual life and enables them to grow in grace and knowledge of the Savior. The Holy Spirit authenticates (seals) a person at his conversion (Eph. 1:13), imparts to him wisdom and revelation (1:17), gives him access to the Father (2:18) and supplies him with spiritual strength and power (3:16). The Christian is to keep the unity of the Spirit in the bond of peace (4:3), and is not to grieve the Holy Spirit (4:30). He is to remain filled with the Spirit (5:18) and to pray at all times in the Spirit (6:18).

---

[18]Paraphrased from *The Mind of Paul*, William Barclay, p. 33.

Paul's sufferings

Paul's physical sufferings were staggering and at one point so severe that he and his co-partners despaired of their very lives (2Cor. 1:8, 9). Paul's recalling of his afflictions in his last letter to the Corinthians, written approximately twelve years before his death, doubtless did not represent all of his hardships up to that time. Nor, of course, would they have included the sufferings which he may well have had to endure in the ensuing years and which may have been even more horrendous than anything he had experienced.

> Five times I received from the Jews thirty-nine lashes. Three times I was beaten with rods, once I was stoned, three times I was shipwrecked, a night and a day I have spent in the deep. I have been on frequent journeys, in dangers from rivers, dangers from robbers, dangers from my countrymen, dangers from the Gentiles, dangers in the city, dangers in the wilderness, dangers on the sea, dangers among false brethren; I have been in labor and hardship, through many sleepless nights, in hunger and thirst, often without food, in cold and exposure. Apart from such external things, there is the daily pressure upon me of concern for all the churches. (2Cor. 11:24-28)

Among the most brutal of Paul's known tortures was his stoning at Lystra. His attackers, after seeing him collapse unconscious under the heavy barrage of stones, immediately concluded he was dead. Not waiting to examine him to be certain, they jubilantly dragged his body out of the city and left it there for the dogs to devour. Paul never forgot the ghastly ordeal nor the faithfulness of his rescuers. At the end of his life he was still ruminating on the experience (2Tim. 3:11).

Paul, having been scourged one hundred and nine-five times by the Jews and three times beaten with heavy rods, would have left his body a mass of welts and keloid scars. But he made no attempt to conceal them. To him they were "the brand marks of Jesus" (Gal. 6:17 NIV), and, as His ambassador, he felt honored to bear them.

Fourteen attempts were made to murder Paul, and on twelve occasions he was forced to flee for his life. Yet never once did he flee from his missionary call. To finish his course was his constant resolve (Ac. 20:24).

Added to the physical tortures to which Paul was subjected was the heart-breaking knowledge that many of his long-time friends had forsaken him. Paul naturally expected, after his conversion, that he would be expelled from the heart of Israel, condemned by the Sanhedrin and harassed by fanatical Jews. But he must have clung to the proverb, "A friend loves at all times, and a brother is born for adversity" (Prov. 17:17), and counted on retaining many of his secular friends with whom he had had an amiable relationship. When he lost the majority of them, this would of course have grieved him deeply.

Paul's strength

A man reveals his strength by his mastery of circumstances and Paul was such a man.

Weak men are the slaves of things which happen. They are molded by their environment. A strong man makes use of his circumstances for his own advancement.... He cannot change the direction of the wind which is blowing in his face, but he can get out of it a stimulus which will help him toward his destination. He cannot change the current against which he is rowing, but can by contending with the current so increase his strength as to become able to reach his desired landing. He cannot escape his environment, but out of it he can draw nutriment for the nourishment of his growing soul.[19]

From the moment Paul is introduced in Scripture, surveying the brutal stoning of Stephen and surrounded by the clamorous, sanguinary mob, to the day when he knelt at his own execution waiting for the slash of the sword, he lived in a hostile and chaotic world. He was always battling the gale and struggling to forge ahead, never content to trod the easy road. Always he strove to achieve the seemingly impossible.

Paul by nature was impulsive and explosive and "his words sometimes flowed like molten lava ... and blazed like leaping tongues of flame."[20] He plunged into everything headlong, never content to do anything by halves. What he started he must finish. When he was attacked by his enemies and underwent excruciating suffering, he never allowed pain and the agony of it all to get the upper hand. "We are afflicted in every way," he once exclaimed, "but not crushed; perplexed, but not despairing; persecuted, but not forsaken; struck down, but not destroyed" (2Cor. 4:8).

Never was Paul afraid to speak out against any who would pervert the gospel, whether a Judaizer, Pharisee or Sadducee or the whole of the Sanhedrin, or

---

[19] *The Character of Paul*, Charles Edward Jefferson, p. 104.
[20] Ibid., p. 92.

whether the offenders were his dearest friends. Peter and Barnabas could never forget Paul's fiery rebukes against them when they refused to eat with the Gentiles at Antioch; nor could Mark forget Paul's bitter disappointment in him at Perga when he refused to go further and left Paul and Barnabas to carry on alone.

One can never rightly characterize Paul as a weak individual; he was no wimp. He exclaimed, "for Christ's sake, I delight in weaknesses, in insults, in hardships, in persecutions, in difficulties. For when I am weak, then I am strong" (2Cor. 12:10 NIV).

Not a Samson

Paul, however, must never be labeled another Samson; the two were totally different! Samson was spiritually weak; Paul spiritually strong. Samson laughed over others in pain; Paul cried over others in suffering. Samson was uncouth; Paul well-mannered. Samson relished conflict; Paul detested controversy. Paul was fully aware that Christian heroes emerge not in their own strength but in the strength of their Savior. Though their physical strength diminishes with age, their spiritual strength increases with the years (2Cor. 4:16).

Paul's pride

No one can study Paul and not be impressed with his innate pride. This is not to say he was haughty or in any way vain, but proud in the elevated sense of the word. "In the Greek sense of the word, he was an aristocrat, a member of a superior class, one of the country's best citizens. In the Roman sense, he was a patrician, a member of the nobility, separated from the plebeians."[21]

He was proud of the fact that he hailed from the royal tribe of Benjamin and bore the name Saul, Israel's first king (see Phil. 3:5), proud that he had been born a free Roman citizen in the celebrated city of Tarsus, famed for its university and culture. He was also proud that he had been nurtured in the strictest Jewish traditions and proud that he had been allowed to study in Jerusalem under Gamaliel, Israel's most eminent professor. Proud too was he that he was a Pharisee and could follow in the footsteps of his father.

But Saul's *amour-propre*, so evident in his early years, increased even more after becoming a Christian. Now, though he retained his status as a Pharisee, Jesus

---

[21]Ibid., p. 119.

bestowed upon him a far more significant title when he was set apart and marked as an apostle of Christ. This Paul proudly claimed all through his Christian life was divinely conferred upon him.

As the Stoics were proud of their ability to accept whatever came to them without flinching, so too Paul was proud he could affirm, "I have learned to be content in whatever circumstances I am" (Phil. 4:11). "I will not be mastered by anything (1Cor. 6:12b).

Paul never built on another man's foundation and he was proud of this as well as proud of remaining self-reliant and not dependent on others for his and his co-workers' livelihood. But it was at the end of his life from his dark Mamertine dungeon that his pride blazed the brightest when he wrote to his spiritual son, Timothy, and exclaimed, "I have fought the good fight, I have finished the course, I have kept the faith" (2Tim. 4:7).

Paul's concept of prayer

Paul was pre-eminently a man of prayer; praying was for him as natural as breathing. He believed that Christians must be in touch with God at all times, regardless of where they were and in what circumstances. "Be anxious for nothing," Paul counseled "but in everything by prayer and supplication with thanksgiving let your requests be made known to God" (Phil. 4:6).

Here Paul echoed Jesus' teaching not to be anxious or worried about anything (*anxiety* meaning "choke" and *worry* meaning "strangle") (see Mt. 6:25, 31, 34). Being *concerned* over a problem, however, is vastly different from being *anxious* or *worried* about it. *Concern* dares to tackle challenges which appear to have no solutions, tackles them in faith, faith that through God's power they *can* be solved if it is God's will. *Concern* is never pessimistic; it never gives up. It motivates all scientific and pioneering achievements. It is the *sine qua non* of the edge-by-faith principle and basic to the success of all Christian endeavors.

Paul believed that all requests of God must be made with the proviso, "if it be Thy will," and never should be made as a demand. Every prayer offered in the name of Jesus, Paul firmly believed, would be clearly answered with either "Yes," "No" or "Wait." Remain at the edge by faith for the answer, confident that God has heard the petition and will in His own way and in His own time answer it for the best of all concerned.

Weeping for others

Of the apostles, Peter and Paul are the only ones recorded as having wept. Peter wept over his own sins, but there is no record of him ever having wept over the sins of others. Paul on the other hand unashamedly confessed he wept over others, and this included their sins and weaknesses. No one was more concerned than Paul for his own race. "I am not lying," he exclaimed to the Romans,

> my conscience bearing me witness in the Holy Spirit, that I have great sorrow and unceasing grief in my heart. For I could wish that I myself were accursed, separated from Christ for the sake of my brethren, my kinsmen according to the flesh, who are Israelites.... (Rom. 9:1-4)

He grieved over those who allowed their fleshly appetites to be their god and who set their mind on earthly things. "I often told you," he wrote the Philippians, "and now tell you even weeping, that they are enemies of the cross of Christ, whose end is destruction ..." (Phil. 3:18, 19). For three years, night and day, while he was in Ephesus, he did not cease in admonishing each one with tears (Ac. 20:31), and in his last letter to the Corinthians he frankly admits that he shed copious tears as he wrote them his stern letter because of his special, deep love for them (2Cor. 2:4).

Paul's associates

Of all Paul's sixty-five friends and associates appearing in his letters, most proved loyal to him with the exception of Alexander and Hymenaeus the blasphemers, Alexander the coppersmith, Demas, Hermogenes, Philetus and Phygelus (1Tim. 1:19, 20; 2Tim. 1:15; 2:17; 4:10, 14).

Paul knew Timothy as his fellow-worker and "true child in the faith" and his "beloved son" (2Tim. 1:2). Titus also was regarded as his partner and fellow-worker and true son (Tit. 1:4; 2Cor. 8:23). Onesiphorus, after he was converted, continued to minister to Paul and often refreshed him and was not ashamed of his chains, and eagerly searched for him in Rome until he found him (2Tim. 1:16, 17). Aristarchus, Gaius, Secundus, Sopater, Timothy, Titus, Trophimus and Tychicus were so close to Paul and so trusted that they were the ones chosen to guard the large offering Paul brought to Jerusalem (Ac. 20:4; 2Cor. 8:23). Tychicus, whom Paul termed "our beloved brother and faithful servant and fellow bond-servant in the Lord" (Eph. 6:21; Col. 4:7), was so willing to serve Paul that he consented to carry Paul's two irreplaceable prison epistles from Rome, one to the Ephesians and the other to the Colossians requiring a round-trip journey of well over two thousand miles!

Aquila and Priscilla not only opened their home to Paul in Corinth and Ephesus and ministered to him in Rome, but also held him so close to their hearts that they were willing to risk their own necks for him (Rom. 16:3, 4). The relationship between the mother of Rufus and Paul was so endearing that Paul considered her his own mother (v. 13).

Luke, constantly with Paul during the last twelve years of his life, most probably was with him in Troas when he was arrested for preaching the gospel—a capital offense. Not forsaking him, however, though now a condemned prisoner, Luke is found with him back in Rome.

The Galatians went so far as to receive Paul as "an angel of God, as Christ Jesus Himself" (Gal. 4:14), and were so concerned over his illness, which seems to have affected his eyes, that they were willing to pluck out their own eyes and give them to him (v. 15)! And there were those among the Corinthians so devoted to Paul that they declared their allegiance to him above all others on earth (1Cor. 1:12).

Paul's letter to his devoted friend, Philemon, asking him to take back his runaway slave, Onesimus, and consider him as his brother in Christ, indicates how confident Paul was that Philemon would honor such a request.[22] Onesimus too, in agreeing to deliver Paul's letter to Philemon, indicates how much he trusted Paul. Doubtless, Onesimus was illiterate and unable to read Paul's letter, but he believed it contained no damaging statements about him. If it did he knew he could be branded on his forehead with the letter *F* standing for *fugitivus*, or even be tortured and put to death. But, though fully aware of this, Onesimus maintained his confidence in Paul and delivered his letter to Philemon.

Such were the friends surrounding Paul. A more devoted and loyal retinue would be hard to find.

Paul's view of himself

Convinced though Paul was of his divine call and, believing he was not in the least inferior to the most eminent of the apostles (2Cor. 11:5), he was equally aware of his unworthiness of that call. "I am the least of the apostles," he insisted to

---

[22]How Paul won Philemon to Christ is not known.

the Corinthians, "who am not fit to be called an apostle, because I persecuted the church of God" (1Cor. 15:9). Later he went so far as to write the Corinthians, "I am a nobody" (2Cor. 12:11).

Conscious of the strong downward pull of sin inherent in his and all humanity's fallen nature, as well as aware of the powerful upward pull of the Spirit, Paul clearly explained this dichotomy in his letters to the Galatians and Romans. "For the flesh sets its desire against the Spirit," he explained to the Galatians, "and the Spirit against the flesh; for these are in opposition to one another, so that you may not do the things that you please [wish]" (Gal. 5:17). And to the Romans he explained,

> I cannot understand my own actions. What I wish to do, I do not, and what I detest, I keep on doing. I know what is right, but I do not do it. I have not the strength to do it. I am acquainted with the Law, but the Law does not furnish me power. There is a conflict between my lower self and my higher self. My lower self often wins. I am held tight in a bondage which I cannot escape. Wretched man that I am, who shall deliver me out of the body of death?[23]

> I know that nothing good dwells in me, that is in my flesh … (Rom. 7:18)

Later he wrote to the Ephesians when he was first imprisoned in Rome that he was the very least of all saints (Eph. 3:8); and finally from his death cell declared to Timothy that he was the foremost of sinners (1Tim. 1:15).

> "[L]east of the apostles" (1Cor. 15:9);
> "a nobody" (2Cor. 12:11);
> "nothing good within me" (Rom. 7:18);
> "less than the least of all God's people" (Eph. 3:8 NIV);
> "foremost of all sinners" (1Tim. 1:15)

Such was Paul's concept of himself as he grew older.

But though Paul was well aware of his Adamic nature, he would never have allowed himself to exclaim as David did when brooding over his sins, "I am a worm, and not a man …" (Ps. 22:6). Paul was too aware of his affinity to his Father, too conscious of his sonship through Christ, ever to denounce himself as subhuman. He knew he was God's creation and through his new birth had become His son. Though sin could mar his witness and damage his walk with God, it could

---

[23]Rom. 7:15-24 paraphrased, *The Character of Paul*, Charles Edward Jefferson, p. 90.

never remove him from the family of God. Always his Father's great love for him would remain. Nothing could separate him from that love (Rom. 8:38, 39).

Paul's view of life

Paul was a born extrovert. He loved people and rarely wanted to be apart from them. Though he shied away from worldly, empty chatter and arguments (1 Tim. 6:20), he welcomed the opportunity of participating in discussions and always was ready to preach the Word.

Paul was not a perennial optimist, nor was he an inveterate pessimist. Paul was a Christian realist. He accepted life for what it was, sometimes fraught with pain and heartache, sometimes brimming with joy. He knew there was a time to weep and a time to laugh (Eccles. 3:4), and a time to wait at the edge by faith for his next marching orders from above. He also knew that a broken spirit dries up the bones but a joyful heart never fails as good medicine (Prov. 17:22).

To depict Paul as a lugubrious theologian, always with a frown and grappling with problems, is to represent him grossly and falsify his true character. Paul was anything but a cheerless theologian. His gospel was that of overwhelming good news: God loves the world, confirmed by the Cross; no burden so heavy that Jesus cannot lift; no sin so heinous that God cannot forgive; no limits on who can be offered free grace and no fear of death to those who are saved.

Paul and youth

Paul's popularity with youth cannot be disputed. Young people were instinctively drawn to him. Though callow Mark deserted him at Perga, it was not because he found Paul cantankerous and austere and without a sense of humor, but only because Mark was afraid of the dangers which might lie ahead.

Later he apologized to Paul and sought his forgiveness and asked to be allowed again to travel with him. Such a request would never have been made had not Mark been devoted to Paul and knew in turn Paul was devoted to him. Mark was keenly aware of how much Paul enjoyed being with young people and therefore he hoped Paul would take him back. But wisely Paul refused until years later when Mark had proven himself.

An excellent example of Paul's ability to hold the attention of youth is seen in the story of Eutychus sitting in his third-story window at Troas (Ac. 20:7-12). Paul's exciting preaching with apt illustrations and fascinating stories had held

Eutychus spellbound until midnight and probably would have held him much longer had not Morpheus (not Paul's preaching) caused him to fall asleep. Paul was anything but a dull speaker and always in his preaching sought to stress Cicero's three "*ins*": interest, instruct and inspire. First and foremost was *interest*. If Paul's hearers, particularly youth, were not kept interested in what he was saying, he knew he would have little hope of instructing let alone inspiring them.

Timothy is another example of a young man who never found Paul's preaching and company boring. He started traveling with Paul when he was not far out of his teens and continued his co-partnership for the remaining fifteen years of Paul's life. Though Timothy was not physically robust and often not well, he never deserted Paul and remained an impressive example of a Spirit-filled man with soldier-like qualities. "Fear nothing but fear itself,"[24] became Timothy's outlook on life as he followed the teaching and example of Paul.

Paul's view of death

The pagans met death with grim resignation. "Once a man dies there is no resurrection," pronounced Aeschylus; and Theocritus wrote, "There is hope for those who are alive, but those who have died are without hope."[25]

But death to Paul was not the termination of life, rather it was an instant transference from life on earth to Life Everlasting (See 2Cor. 5:8; Phil. 1:21; cf. Lk. 23:43). Though Paul spoke of the Christian dead as "those who have fallen asleep in Jesus" (1Thess. 4:13, 15; 1Cor. 15:6, 18, 20, 51) and used the same figure of speech Jesus had used when referring to the deaths of Jairus's daughter (Mk. 5:39) and Lazarus (Jn. 11:11), and which Luke employed when announcing Stephen's death (Ac. 7:60), this is not to say that Jesus, Paul, Luke or any of the early Christians believed that the dead sleep and know nothing until their bodies and souls are reunited at the Second Coming of Christ. Death for the Christian, they believed, was not a soporific experience (soul sleep) but a conscious and glorious entrance immediately into the presence of God.

---

[24]"Fear nothing but fear itself" was one of Franklin D. Roosevelt's most noted sayings. See 2Tim. 1:7.

[25]*The Letters to the Philippians, Colossians, and Thessalonians*, William Barclay, p. 235.

Death, therefore, in Paul's eyes was not a tragedy, but a triumph; not a loss but a gain. He believed it could never separate the Christian from the love of God. "Who shall separate us from the love of Christ?" he exclaimed.

> Shall trouble or hardship or persecution or famine or nakedness or danger or sword? ... in all these things we are more than conquerors through him who loved us. For I am convinced that neither death nor life, neither angels nor demons, neither the present nor the future, nor any powers, neither height nor depth, nor anything else in all creation, will be able to separate us from the love of God that is in Christ Jesus our Lord. (Rom. 8:35, 37-39 NIV)

Though Paul expressed to the Corinthians and the Philippians his longing to depart and be with Christ (2Cor. 5:8; Phil. 1:21-24), this did not mean he wanted his life on earth to end. It only meant that when his work was completed, he was eagerly anticipating being with the One he loved most.

Paul's view of Jesus' resurrection

The foundation of Paul's preaching was laid in his firm conviction that Jesus had come forth from the sealed tomb, not only spiritually, but corporeally, as man, very man, God, very God. The gospel which Paul preached was unique and must never be thought of as having been formulated from a complex of ideas derived from the past, whether from Eastern or Western pagan religions or from the monotheistic teachings of Judaism.

With Paul's world alive with insidious cults, some actually proclaiming their deities had been raised from the dead, such as the vegetation gods, Attis, Adonis and Osiris, whose withering in autumn and renewal in spring were equated with their deaths and resurrections, it was important for Paul to declare the uniqueness of Jesus' resurrection. This was to prevent anyone concluding that Jesus was just another god added to the pantheon.[26] Doubtless, it was with this in mind that Paul wrote the Corinthians the following:

> Now, brothers, I want to remind you of the gospel I preached to you, which you received and on which you have taken your stand. By this gospel you are saved, if

---

[26]Paul would certainly have pointed out in his teaching that nowhere in the cults of pagan religions were there gods who died voluntarily, as Jesus did, for the sake of mankind. Nor were there cults showing any interest in recording the times and places of the deaths and resurrections of their deities.

you hold firmly to the word I preached to you. Otherwise, you have believed in vain.

For what I received I passed on to you as of first importance: that Christ died for our sins according to the Scriptures, that he was buried, that he was raised on the third day according to the Scriptures, and appeared to Peter, and then to the Twelve.[27] After that, he appeared to more than five hundred of the brothers at the same time, most of whom are still living [twenty-five years after the event], though some have fallen asleep. Then he appeared to James, then to all the apostles, and last of all he appeared to me also.... (1Cor. 15:1-8 NIV)

The story of Jesus' death and resurrection, vastly different from the myths of legendary folklore, is indelibly written on the pages of history—history as it occurred in the reign of Emperor Tiberius just outside Jerusalem on a hill called Golgotha and subsequently at the nearby unused tomb of Joseph of Arimathea. Paul wholeheartedly embraced the story of Jesus' resurrection and vowed that he had been called of God—called from his mother's womb—to proclaim it to the world.[28] He held to his conviction unswervingly to the very end of his life.

At the final edge

Paul began his missionary career, at night at the edge of Damascus's wall. Thirty-four years later he completed his earthly pilgrimage, in the sunlight, at the edge of a Roman sword. He died as he lived, proclaiming Christ and His love. He died rejoicing; he had finished his course and kept the faith (2Tim. 4:7)!

FINIS

---

[27] See "Jesus' Resurrection Appearances" on p. 292, regarding Jesus appearing to the Twelve.
[28] Gal. 1:15.

Appendix I

The Sabbath and the New Testament

Then the LORD said to Moses, "Say to the Israelites, 'You must observe my Sabbaths. This will be a sign between me and you for the generations to come, so you may know that I am the LORD, who makes you holy.

"'Observe the Sabbath, because it is holy to you. Anyone who desecrates it must be put to death; whoever does any work on that day must be cut off from his people. For six days, work is to be done, but the seventh day is a Sabbath of rest, holy to the LORD. Whoever does any work on the Sabbath day must be put to death. The Israelites are to observe the Sabbath, celebrating it for the generations to come as a lasting covenant. It will be a sign between me and the Israelites forever, for in six days the LORD made the heavens and the earth, and on the seventh day he abstained from work and rested.'" (Ex. 31:12-17 NIV; see also Deut. 5:15; Ezek. 20:12)

Below are the New Testament references for the remaining nine commandments:

First: No Gods before Me (Mt. 4:10).
Second: No idols (Rom. 1:23; 1Cor. 6:9; 10:7, 14; 1Jn. 5:21).
Third: No profanity (Rom. 12:14).
Fifth: No disrespect to parents (Eph. 6:2; Col. 3:20).
Sixth: No murder (Rom. 1:29; 1Jn. 3:15).
Seventh: No adultery (Mt. 5:27, 28; 1Thess. 4:3-5).
Eighth: No stealing (1Cor. 6:10; Eph. 4:28).
Ninth: No false witness (Eph. 4:15, 25; Col. 3:9).
Tenth: No coveting (Rom. 7:7).

On the Sabbath a Jew was allowed to walk only two thousand cubits (about 3,500 feet) from the place in which he lived. However, if he placed food at this point, then that place would be considered part of his abode and he would be allowed to walk another 3,500 feet.[1]

---

[1] *The Day Christ Died*, Jim Bishop, p. 39.

The Sabbath commandment forbade any work to be done on the Sabbath.

But there were those who were not content to leave that a principle. They asked the question, "What is work?" They then laid down thirty-nine different kinds of activity, which they called "fathers" of work. Not content with that, they tried to define every possible kind of sub-section of these thirty-nine different kinds of work.... One kind of work is carrying a burden; therefore the carrying of burdens on the Sabbath was prohibited.... It was forbidden to wear any kind of brooch or clasp on the Sabbath or even to carry a pin stuck in the coat, for that would be to carry a burden. It was gravely debated whether it was right to wear false hair or false teeth on the Sabbath; that might be said to be carrying a burden. It was debated whether a man was carrying a burden if he lifted up his child on the Sabbath. It was conceded that he might do that but, if the child had in his hand a stone, that was carrying a burden. Shoes studded with nails might not be worn on the Sabbath for that would be to carry a burden.[2]

The scribes and Pharisees who studied Moses' law, for example, tacked on many additions to its 613 regulations. The rabbi Eliezer the Great specified how often a common laborer ass driver, camel driver, or sailor should have sex with his wife. Pharisees added scores of emendations on Sabbath behavior alone. A man could ride a donkey without breaking the Sabbath rules, but if he carried a switch to speed up the animal he would be guilty of laying a burden on it. A woman could not look in the mirror on the Sabbath lest she see a grey hair and be tempted to pluck it out. You could swallow vinegar but not gargle it.[3]

Lengthened rules were prescribed as to the kinds of knots which might legally be tied on the Sabbath. The camel-driver's knot and the sailor's knot were unlawful, and it was equally illegal to tie or to loose them. A knot which could be untied with one hand might be undone.... A pitcher at a spring might be tied to the body-sash, but not with a cord.... To kindle or extinguish a fire on the Sabbath was a great desecration of the day, nor was even sickness allowed to violate Rabbinical rules. It was forbidden to give an emetic on the Sabbath—to set a broken bone, or put back a dislocated joint, though some Rabbis, more liberal, held that whatever endangered life made the Sabbath law void, "for the commands were given to Israel only that they might live by them."[4]

---

[2] *Ambassador for Christ*, William Barclay, p. 18.

[3] *What's So Amazing About Grace?* Philip Yancey, p. 198.

[4] *Life and Words of Christ*, Cunningham Geikie, p. 450.

Appendix II

Messianic Prophecies

From the tribe of Judah: "The scepter shall not depart from Judah, Nor a ruler's staff from between his feet, Until Shiloh comes, And to him shall be the obedience of the peoples." (Gen. 49:10)

Born in Bethlehem: "But as for you, Bethlehem Ephrathah, Too little to be among the clans of Judah, From you One will go forth for Me to be ruler in Israel. His goings forth are from long ago, From the days of eternity." (Mic. 5:2)

Born of a virgin: "Therefore the Lord Himself will give you a sign: Behold, a virgin will be with child and bear a son, and she will call His name Immanuel." (Isa. 7:14)

Return from Egypt: "When Israel was a youth I loved him, And out of Egypt I called My son." (Hos. 11:1)

Declared the Son of God: "I will surely tell of the decree of the Lord: He said to Me, 'Thou art My Son. Today I have begotten Thee.'" (Ps. 2:7)

Rejected by His own people, the Jews: "He was despised and forsaken of men, A man of sorrows, and acquainted with grief; And like one from whom men hide their face, He was despised, and we did not esteem Him." (Isa. 53:3)

Triumphal entry into Jerusalem, riding a colt: "Rejoice greatly, O daughter of Zion! Shout in triumph, O daughter of Jerusalem! Behold, your king is coming to you; He is just and endowed with salvation, Humble, and mounted on a donkey, Even on a colt, the foal of a donkey." (Zech. 9:9)

Betrayed by a friend: "Even my close friend, in whom I trusted, Who ate my bread, Has lifted up his heel against me." (Ps. 41:9)

Sold for thirty pieces of silver: "And I said to them, 'If it is good in your sight, give me my wages; but if not, never mind!' So they weighed out thirty shekels of silver as my wages." (Zech. 11:12)

Spat upon: "I gave My back to those who strike Me, and My cheeks to those who pluck out the beard; I did not cover My face from humiliation and spitting." (Isa. 50:6)

Crucified with malefactors: "Because He poured out Himself to death, and was numbered with the transgressors; Yet He Himself bore the sin of many, And interceded for the transgressors." (Isa. 53:12)

Given vinegar and gall: "They also gave me gall for my food, And for my thirst they gave me vinegar to drink." (Ps. 69:21)

Soldiers gambled for His coat: "I can count all my bones. They look, they stare at me; They divide my garments among them, And for my clothing they cast lots." (Ps. 22:17, 18)

No broken bones: "He keeps all his bones; Not one of them is broken." (Ps. 34:20)

Buried with the rich: "His grave was assigned with wicked men, Yet He was with a rich man in His death, Because He had done no violence, Nor was there any deceit in His mouth." (Isa. 53:9)

To be resurrected: "For thou wilt not abandon my soul to Sheol; Neither wilt Thou allow Thy Holy One to undergo decay." (Ps. 16:10)

Appendix III

Jesus' Resurrection Appearances

To Paul

Paul saw the risen Christ only THREE recorded times: *first* in Jerusalem (Ac. 22:17, 18, 21), *second* in Corinth (18:9, 10), and *third* in Jerusalem (23:11). Paul's statement in 1Cor. 15:8 that Jesus appeared to him refers only to these three occurrences. Though Ananias stated that Jesus had appeared to Paul on the road leading to Damascus (Ac. 9:17), and Barnabas declared that Paul "had seen the Lord on the road" (9:3, 4), these appearances refer only to the brilliant light which blinded Paul and to the voice of Jesus which he heard. Paul never claimed to have seen the risen Christ on the way to Damascus, only that he heard Him speak to him.

To others

1. Mary Magdalene, in Jerusalem (Sunday) (Mk. 16:9-11; Jn. 20:11-18).
2. Mary Magdalene and the other Mary, in Jerusalem (Sunday) (Mt. 18:1, 9, 10).
3. Peter, in Jerusalem (Sunday) (Lk. 24:34; 1Cor. 15:5).
4. Emmaus disciples, on the road to Emmaus (Sunday) (Lk. 24:13-35).
5. Ten disciples, in Jerusalem (Sunday) (Lk. 24:36-43; Jn. 20:19-25). Note: Luke states eleven disciples were present, but John records ten since Thomas was not among them (Jn. 20:24). Since Luke was not there and John was, John's account must be accepted as the correct one.
6. Eleven disciples, in Jerusalem (a week later) (Jn. 20:26-31).
7. Twelve disciples, probably in vicinity of Jerusalem (Matthew replaced Judas) (1Cor. 15:5).
8. Seven disciples, in Galilee (Jn. 21:1-25).
9. 500 at one time, probably in vicinity of Jerusalem (1Cor. 15:6).
10. James (half brother of Jesus), probably in vicinity of Jerusalem (1Cor. 15:7).
11. Eleven disciples, in Galilee (Mt. 28:16-20).
12. Eleven disciples, over a period of forty days after the resurrection (Ac. 1:3-12).
13. Eleven disciples, in the vicinity of Bethany (Lk. 24:50, 51).

Appendix IV

Chronology of the Life of Paul

Estimated miles traveled on land and sea: 15,950

A.D.

30 or 31	Beginning public life: about thirty years of age
30–33	Events leading to the death of Stephen
33	Journey to Damascus and conversion
33	Retirement to Arabia
35–43	First visit to Jerusalem: rejected; first time to see the risen Christ; escapes to Tarsus; following estimated ten years unknown
37	Caligula succeeds Tiberius
41	Claudius succeeds Caligula
43	Barnabas brings Saul to Antioch, Syria
44	Prophecy of Agabus
45	Famine in Jerusalem
45–46	Second visit to Jerusalem: famine
46–47	Returns to Antioch, Syria: commissioned a missionary
47	FIRST MISSIONARY JOURNEY, 1,450 miles; Barnabas, Saul (Paul), and Mark
47	In Cyprus: "Saul" becomes "Paul"
47	In Perga: Mark deserts
47	In Antioch, Pisidia
48	In Iconium
48	In Lystra
48–49	In Derbe
49	Returns to Syrian Antioch via Lystra, Pisidian Antioch and Perga Attalia
49–50	Third visit to Jerusalem: before the council
50	SECOND MISSIONARY JOURNEY, 2,800 miles; Paul and Silas
50	In Lystra: Timothy joins Paul
50	In Troas: first visit; Luke joins Paul
50	In Philippi: first visit
51	In Thessalonica

51	In Berea
51	In Athens
52	In Corinth: writes 1 and 2 Thessalonians; second time to see the risen Christ
53	Arrival of Gallio
53	Fourth visit to Jerusalem: cool reception
53	Returns to Antioch, Syria
53	THIRD MISSIONARY JOURNEY, 3,900 miles
54	Nero succeeds Claudius
55	In Ephesus: writes 1 Corinthians; possibly imprisoned in Ephesus: suspected of murdering Silanus and his brother
56	Returns to Troas: second visit
56	In Macedonia: writes 2 Corinthians
57	Returns to Corinth: writes Romans and probably Galatians
57	Returns to Philippi: second visit
57	Returns to Troas: third visit; Eutychus falls
57	Fifth visit to Jerusalem: before the Sanhedrin; third and last time to see the risen Christ
59	Imprisoned in Caesarea, 2 years
60	VOYAGE TO ROME, 2,000 miles
61	House arrest in Rome: writes Ephesians, Philippians, Colossians and Philemon
61	Acquitted
62–66	LATER TRAVELS, 5,800 miles; writes 1 Timothy and Titus
64	Possibly imprisoned in Rome: suspected of burning Rome
64	Released
67	Arrested for preaching the Gospel, a capital offense
67	Imprisoned in Rome's Mamertine dungeon: writes 2 Timothy
69	Martyred

The history and dates of Paul's Roman trials and subsequent travels and martyrdom are conjectural.

Appendix V

Probable Dates and Chronology of New Testament Writings

BOOK	DATE (A.D.)
Mark[1]	49
Matthew	50–60
Luke	60
John	85
Acts	60–62
James	47–48
1 Thessalonians	51
2 Thessalonians	51
1 Corinthians	55
2 Corinthians	56
Galatians	56–57
Romans	57
Ephesians	60
Colossians	60
Philemon	60
Philippians	62
1 Timothy	65
Titus	65
1 Peter	65
2 Timothy	67
2 Peter	67
Hebrews	68
Jude	75
1 John	90–95
2 John	90–95
3 John	90–95
Revelation	95

[1] Some scholars date Mark A.D. 67–68.

About the Author

Educated through high school in his native city, Schenectady, New York, Stuart H. Merriam, in 1942 felt called into the Christian ministry and began his tertiary education in North Carolina so as to familiarize himself with the challenges and heartbreaks of segregation. He chose Davidson College in the town of Davidson.

Having recently become a Christian, he was zealous to proclaim the gospel and crossed over "the tracks" and started a mission among the underprivileged African Americans. It was this close contact with African Americans that infused in him his great love for the dark-skinned race, a love which has never left him, and which later was to revolutionize his life.

Not feeling right to use his pre-ministerial status to exempt him from military service, he soon left college and enlisted in the U.S. Army where he served for three years, which included fifteen months overseas and in combat under Gen. George Patton.

Following the war he continued his education at the University of Biarritz, France, and Union College, Schenectady, then entered Princeton Theological Seminary in Princeton, New Jersey. He transferred in his final year to Knox Divinity College, University of Toronto, Canada, from which he graduated. Subsequently he studied at the University of Edinburgh, Scotland, and was awarded his doctorate from New College.

After pastoring two churches (First Presbyterian in Portsmouth, Virginia, and Broadway Presbyterian in New York City), he embarked on a round-the-world tour of Christian missions and the biblical world. Traveling extensively in the footsteps of Paul and photographing as he went, he became thoroughly conversant with the byways and beachheads of Paul's ministry and the topography of his world.

It was while visiting missionaries in the Territory of New Guinea (now known as Papua New Guinea) that he accepted the call of the nationals to remain and be their missionary. Out of this momentous decision the Highland Christian Mission was born—an international, evangelical and interdenominational outreach—which for thirty eight years has evangelized and educated thousands, and continues in its ministry today.

In 1965 Dr. Merriam married Miss Carol Robinson, his former New York executive secretary. Together they established four primary schools and the first provincial high school in the remote Okapa district of the Eastern Highlands province. On April 23, 2001, Carol suffered a massive stroke which instantly rendered her comatose. Day and night Dr. Merriam helped in caring for her, until finally, on November 6, 2001, she breathed her last. She proved throughout her married life a superb and devoted helpmate and left behind an unexcelled record of sacrificial service for her Lord.

Bibliography

Abbott, Lyman. *The Life and Letters of Paul the Apostle*. London: James Clark & Company.

Achtemeier, Paul J. *Harper's Bible Dictionary*. New York: Harper & Rowe Publishers.

Agnew, Milton S. *The Holy Spirit: Friend and Counselor*. Kansas City, Missouri: Beacon Press.

Alexander, Pat. *Encyclopedia of the Bible*. A Lion Book, Sydney.

Asch, Sholem. *The Apostle*. New York: G. P. Putnam's Sons.

Barclay, William. *A New Testament Word Book*. New York: Harper & Brothers.

———. *Ambassador for Christ: The Life and Teachings of Paul*. Edinburgh: The Church of Scotland Youth Committee.

———. *Letters to the Seven Churches*. New York: Abingdon Press.

———. *The Acts of the Apostles*. Philadelphia: The Westminster Press.

———. *The Gospel of Mark*. Philadelphia: The Westminster Press.

———. *The Letters to the Corinthians*. Philadelphia: The Westminster Press.

———. *The Letters to the Galatians and Ephesians*. Philadelphia: The Westminster Press.

———. *The Letter to the Hebrews*. Philadelphia: The Westminster Press.

———. *The Letters to the Philippians, Colossians and Thessalonians*. Philadelphia: The Westminster Press.

———. *The Letter to the Romans*. Philadelphia: The Westminster Press.

———. *The Letters to Timothy, Titus and Philemon*. Philadelphia: The Westminster Press.

———. *The Master's Men*. New York: Harper & Brothers.

———. *The Mind of Saint Paul*. New York: Harper & Brothers.

———. *The Revelation of John*. Vols. 1 and 2. Philadelphia: The Westminster Press.

Beet, J. Agar. *St. Paul's Epistle to the Romans*. London: Hodder and Stoughton.

Beitzel, Barry J. *The Moody Atlas of Bible Lands*. Chicago: The Moody Press.

Beker, J. Christiaan. *Paul the Apostle: The Triumph of God in Life and Thought*. Philadelphia: Fortress Press.

Bishop, Jim. *The Day Christ Died*. New York: Harper & Brothers.

Blackwood, Andrew W. *The Protestant Pulpit*. New York: Abingdon-Cokesbury Press.

Bouquet, A. C. *Everyday Life in New Testament Times*. New York: Charles Scribner's Sons.

Bowie, Walter R. *Finding God Through St. Paul.* Nashville: The Upper Room.

Brumback, Carl. *"What Meaneth This?" A Pentecostal Answer to a Pentecostal Question.* Springfield, Missouri: The Gospel Publishing House.

Bruce, F. F. *Paul: Apostle of the Heart Set Free.* Grand Rapids, Michigan: William B. Eerdmans Publishing Company.

Budgen, Victor. *The Charismatics and the Word of God.* Hertfordshire, England: Evangelical Press.

Burdick, Donald W. *Tongues: To Speak Or Not to Speak.* Chicago: Moody Press.

Carey, S. Pearce. *William Carey.* London: Hodden & Stoughton.

Cone, Orello. *Paul, the Man, the Missionary, and the Teacher.* New York: Macmillan & Co.

Conybeare, W. J. and Howson, J. S. *Life and Epistles of Saint Paul.* Vols. 1 and 2. London: Longmans, Green & Co.

Cornell, George W. *They Knew Jesus.* New York: William Morrow & Co.

Cutten, George B. *Speaking with Tongues: Historically and Psychologically Considered.* New Haven: Yale University Press.

Davis, John D. *Dictionary of the Bible.* 4th ed. Grand Rapids, Michigan: Baker House.

De Haan, Richard. *The Charismatic Controversy.* Grand Rapids, Michigan: Radio Bible Class.

Dods, Marcus. *The First Epistle to the Corinthians (Expositor's Bible).* New York: Armstrong.

Edersheim, Alfred. *The Life and Times of Jesus the Messiah.* McLean: MacDonald Publishing Co.

Encyclopædia Britannica, Vol. 17, 1964, Chicago, Illinois: William Benton.

Ensley, Francis Gerald. *Paul's Letters to Local Churches.* New York: Women's Division of Christian Service, Board of Missions of the Methodist Church.

Epp, Theodore. *The Other Comforter.* Lincoln, Nebraska: Back to the Bible Publication.

Erdman, Charles W. *The Epistle of Paul to the Philippians.* Philadelphia: The Westminster Press.

Farrar, Frederic W. *Message of the Books.* London: Macmillan.

————. *The Life and Work of Saint Paul.* Vols. 1 and 2. Paris and New York: Cassell, Petter, Galpin & Co.

Gaventa, Beverly Roberts. *Inaugural Address*, 15 November 1995, Princeton Theological Seminary, New Jersey.

Geikie, Cunningham. *Life and Words of Christ.* New York: D. Appleton.

Godet, Frederic. *Commentary on St. Paul's Epistle to the Romans.* Edinburgh: T. & T. Clark.

————. *Introduction to the New Testament.* Edinburgh: T. & T. Clark.

Goodspeed, Edgar J. *Paul.* Philadelphia: The John C. Winston Co.

Gore, Charles. *A Practical Exposition of the Epistle to the Romans.* New York: Charles Scribner's Sons.

Graham, Billy. *The Holy Spirit.* New York: Warner Bros., Inc.

Greig, Clarence. *Great Civilizations: Rome.* Loughborough, England: Ladybird Books.

Guthrie, Donald. *The Pauline Epistles: New Testament Introduction.* Illinois: InterVarsity Press.

Halley, Henry H. *Halley's Bible Handbook.* Grand Rapids: Zondervan Publishing House.

Hayes, D. A. *Paul and His Epistles.* New York, Cincinnati: The Methodist Book Concern.

———. *The Gift of Tongues.* New York: Eaton and Mains.

Henry, Matthew. *New Testament Commentary.* New York: Fleming H. Revell.

Hoekema, Anthony. *What About Tongue-Speaking?* Grand Rapids: Eerdmans.

Horrel, David. *An Introduction to the Study of Paul.* London: Continuum.

House, H. Wayne. *Chronological and Background Charts of the New Testament.* Grand Rapids: Zondervan.

Ironside, H. A. *The Mission of the Holy Spirit and Praying in the Holy Spirit.* New York: Loizeaux Brothers, Inc.

Jefferson, Charles Edward. *The Character of Paul.* New York: Macmillan & Co.

Johnson, Christopher N. *St. Paul and His Mission to the Roman Empire.* London: A. & C. Black.

Jones, Maurice. *Saint Paul the Orator.* London: Hodder & Stoughton.

Keller, Werner. *The Bible As History.* New York: William Morrow and Co.

Lewin, Thomas. *The Life and Epistles of St. Paul.* 5th ed. 1890,London: George Bell & Sons.

Lightfoot, J. B. *St. Paul's Epistles to the Colossians and to Philemon.* London: Macmillan & Co.

Macartney, Clarence Edward. *The Woman of Tekoah.* Nashville: Abingdon Press.

Machen, Gresham J. *The Origin of Paul's Religion.* Grand Rapids, Michigan: William B. Eerdmans Publishing Company.

Matheson, George. *The Representative Men of the New Testament*, Volume III. London: Hodder and Stoughton.

Matheson, George. *Spiritual Development of Saint Paul.* London: Wm. Blackwood & Sons.

Matthews, Basil. *Paul the Dauntless: The Course of a Great Adventure.* London: Fleming H. Revell Co.

Mayhue, Richard L. *Divine Healing Today.* Chicago: Moody Press.

McBirnie, William Steuart. *The Search for the Early Church.* Illinois: Living Books, Tyndale House Publishers, Inc.

———. *The Search for the Twelve Apostles.* Illinois: Living Books, Tyndale House Publishers, Inc.

McGiffert, Arthur C. *The Apostle Age.* New York: Charles Scribner's Sons.

McSpadden, J. Walker. *How They Blazed the Way.* New York: Dodds, Mead & Co. Inc.

Moe, Olaf. *The Apostle Paul: His Life and Work.* Grand Rapids: Baker Book House.

Morgan, G. Campbell. *The Great Physician.* London: Marshall, Morgan & Scott, Ltd.

Morton, H. V. *In the Steps of the Master.* New York: Dodd, Mead & Co., Inc.

———. *In the Steps of St. Paul.* London: Rich & Cowan Ltd.

Moss, Robert V., Jr. *The Life of Paul.* Pennsylvania: Christian Education Press.

Mueller, F. J. *They Knew Christ.* Milwaukee: The Bruce Publishing Co.

Myer, F. B. *Paul.* London: Marshall, Morgan & Scott.

Phillips, J. B. *Ring of Truth: A Translator's Testimony.* London: Hodder & Stoughton.

Polhill, John B. *Paul and His Epistles.* Broadman & Holman publishers, Nashville, TN.

Pollock, John. *The Apostle: A Life of Paul.* USA, Canada, England: Victor Books, A Division of Scripture Press Publications, Inc.

Ramsay, W. M. *Saint Paul the Traveler and Roman Citizen.* London: Hodder & Stoughton.

Reader's Digest Association, Inc. *Jesus and His Times.* Pleasantville, New York.

Robertson, A. T. *Paul's Joy in Christ.* London: Fleming H. Revell Co.

Rolston, Holmes. *Faces About the Christ.* Richmond: John Knox Press.

———. *Personalities Around Paul.* Richmond: John Knox Press.

———. *The Social Message of the Apostle Paul.* Richmond: John Knox Press.

Ryrie, Charles Caldwell. *Ryrie Study Bible Expanded Edition. New International Version.* Chicago: Moody Press.

Sanday, W. and Headlam, A. C. *Critical and Exegetical Commentary on the Epistle to the Romans* (International Critical Commentary). Edinburgh: T. & T. Clark.

Sanders, J. Oswald. *Paul the Leader.* Colorado Springs: Navpress.

Schaff, Philip. *History of the Christian Church.* New York: Charles Scribner's Sons.

Smeaton, George. *The Doctrine of the Holy Spirit.* London: The Banner of Truth Trust.

Smith, David. *The Life and Letters of St. Paul.* London: Hodder & Stoughton.

Smyth, J. Paterson. *The Story of Saint Paul's Life and Letters,* New York: James Pott & Co.

Stalker, James. *Life of Saint Paul.* London: Fleming H. Revell Co.

Stanley, Dean. *Scripture Portraits*. London: Alexander Strohan.

Stevens, George B. *The Pauline Theology: A Study of the Origin and Correlation of the Doctrinal Teachings of the Apostle Paul*. New York: Charles Scribner's Sons.

Stevenson, Herbert F. *A Galaxy of Saints: Lesser Known Bible Men and Women*. New Jersey: Fleming H. Revell Co.

Stewart, James S. *A Man in Christ: The Vital Elements of St. Paul's Religion*. New York: Harper & Brothers.

Swindoll, Charles, R. *Paul: A Man of Grace and Grit*. W. Publishing Group.

Taylor, William M. *Paul the Missionary*. New York: Sampson Low, Marston, Searle & Rivington.

Unger, Merrill F. *Archeology in the New Testament*. Grand Rapids: Zondervan Publishing House.

———. *New Testament Teaching on Tongues*. Michigan: Kregel Publications.

———. *Unger's Bible Dictionary*. Chicago: Moody Press.

Ward, Benedicta. *The Prayers and Meditations of Saint Anselm*. London: Penguin Books.

Whiteley, D. E. H. *The Theology of St. Paul*. Pennsylvania: Fortress Press.

Whyte, Alexander. *The Apostle Paul*. London: Oliphant Anderson & Ferrier.

Wiersbe, Warren W. *Be Free*. Wheaton: Victor Books.

Yancey, Philip. *What's So Amazing About Grace?* Grand Rapid: Zondervan Publishing House.

Zodhiates, Spiros. *Tongues!?* Chattanooga: AMG Publishers.

———. *Tongues and Their Interpretation*. Chattanooga: AMG Publishers.

Index

Printed in the United States
104708LV00004B/11-18/A